WORDSWORTH
A Philosophical Approach

WORDSWORTH

A Philosophical Approach

———

BY

MELVIN RADER

———

... With an eye made quiet by the power
Of harmony, and the deep power of joy,
We see into the life of things.
Tintern Abbey

OXFORD
AT THE CLARENDON PRESS

Oxford University Press, Ely House, London W. 1

GLASGOW   NEW YORK   TORONTO   MELBOURNE   WELLINGTON
CAPE TOWN   SALISBURY   IBADAN   NAIROBI   LUSAKA   ADDIS ABABA
BOMBAY   CALCUTTA   MADRAS   KARACHI   LAHORE   DACCA
KUALA LUMPUR   HONG KONG   TOKYO

FIRST PUBLISHED 1967
REPRINTED LITHOGRAPHICALLY (WITH CORRECTIONS) 1968

PRINTED IN GREAT BRITAIN

FOR
MY DAUGHTERS
MIRIAM AND BARBARA

ACKNOWLEDGEMENTS

M y initial exploration of Wordsworth's thought was under the expert guidance of the late Frederick Morgan Padelford of the University of Washington. Bertram Jessup of the University of Oregon has read the entire manuscript and has made a number of excellent criticisms. Donald R. Ellegood, Director of the University of Washington Press, has kindly granted permission to reproduce the substance of my monograph, *Presiding Ideas in Wordsworth's Poetry* (University of Washington Publications in Language and Literature, Vol. 8, No. 2, November 1931).

CONTENTS

PREFACE

No one has defined more revealingly the character of Wordsworth's philosophical verse than the poet himself:

Aristotle, I have been told, has said that poetry is the most philosophic of all writing: it is so: its object is truth, not individual and local, but general, and operative; not standing upon external testimony, but carried alive into the heart by passion; truth which is its own testimony, which gives competence and confidence to the tribunal to which it appeals, and receives them from the same tribunal. Poetry is the image of man and nature.[1]

'Truth', not dry and abstract, but 'carried alive into the heart by passion', is the object of his greatest poetry. To convey this kind of truth, 'imagery is as important as thought, and sound as important as either, when sensuous and intellectual elements are fused in a compelling harmony'.[2] This is the kind of philosophical truth—the impact of fact upon sensibility and imagination—that the poet tried to communicate.

Critics have differed in their estimate of his success in this endeavour. Coleridge declared: 'Wordsworth possessed more of the genius of a great philosophical poet than any man I ever knew, or, as I believe, has existed in England since Milton.'[3] Matthew Arnold, in the next generation, expressed a different point of view. Wordsworth's poetry, he insisted, 'is the reality', his philosophy, as a formal or scientific system, 'is the illusion'. But he did not deny that Wordsworth combined 'profound truth of subject with profound truth of execution', and that his poetry constitutes a powerful 'criticism of life'.[4] A recent author, F. W. Bateson, goes farther than Arnold in dismissing

[1] Preface to the *Lyrical Ballads* (1800).
[2] Helen Darbishire, *The Poet Wordsworth* (Oxford: Clarendon Press, 1950), p. 66.
[3] Coleridge, *Table Talk*, ed. T. Ashe (London: Bell, 1884), p. 171 (21 July 1832).
[4] Matthew Arnold, 'Wordsworth', *Essays in Criticism*, Second Series (London: Macmillan, 1888).

Wordsworth as a philosophical poet. 'Critics and biographers', he declares, 'have paid too much attention in the past to Words-worth's ideas.' These ideas, he argues, have only a 'marginal relevance' to an elucidation of the poetry. 'Wordsworth was not primarily a thinker but a feeler', he concludes. 'The determining events of his career and the sources of all that is essential in his poetry were the personal tragedies, the anguished decisions, the half-conscious half-animal terrors and ecstasies, and *not* the dis-coveries of the intellect.'[1]

Bateson, it seems to me, implies too sharp a dualism of head and heart. Wordsworth may have been 'primarily a feeler', but his feelings were deeply interfused with thought. He believed that 'poetry is the breath and finer spirit of all knowledge', and he informed his poems with 'meditations passionate from deep Recesses in man's heart'.[2] His capacity to blend profound thought and deep feeling was, as Pater declared, his greatest achievement.[3]

We can agree with Bateson that Wordsworth was a man of feeling, and with Arnold that he sometimes descended to bad moralizing and worse preaching. We may disagree with Cole-ridge's judgement that he was the greatest philosophical poet since Milton. But to dismiss his ideas as irrelevant is surely perverse. Many able critics have emphasized the philosophical affinities of his poetry, and even such an accomplished philoso-pher as Whitehead has found Wordsworth's insights important for their own sake. At the very least, his doctrines have played a major role in the development of romanticism, and must not be neglected by the historian of ideas.

There is an urgent need to dispel some of the conflicts now rife among students of Wordsworth's thought. Not only do the scholars disagree, but the chasms which separate their inter-pretations are broad and deep. A. C. Bradley, in 1909, defined the extreme position of one wing of criticism:

The statement that Wordsworth and Hegel, or Byron and Schopen-hauer, express one substance in different forms would be a misleading

---

[1] F. W. Bateson, *Wordsworth*, second edition (London: Longmans, Green, 1956), pp. 39–40.

[2] Preface to the *Lyrical Ballads* (1800) and *Prelude*, I. 231–2. References to *The Prelude* are to the 1850 version unless otherwise noted.

[3] Walter Pater, 'Wordsworth', *Appreciations* (London: Macmillan, 1889).

exaggeration, but not a paradox. But who could dream of saying such a thing of Wordsworth and Byron on the one side and of our native philosophers on the other? . . . When we pass from the poetry . . . of Wordsworth's age to Locke or Hume or any of our most purely native philosophers . . . we find ourselves in the presence . . . of a view of the world incongruous with the substance of the poetry.[1]

Another trend is represented by the poet's biographers, Émile Legouis and George McLean Harper, who maintain that Wordsworth is intellectually 'a son of Rousseau'. Arthur Beatty, who takes issue with both Bradley and these biographers, finds that the mature Wordsworth revolted 'against Rousseau and Godwin' and hearkened instead 'to Hartley, Locke, and the general tradition of English philosophy'.[2] Confronted by the diverse opinions of these and more recent scholars,[3] the reader of Wordsworth is plunged into bewilderment, which only a rigorous study of the evidence can resolve.

As I interpret Wordsworth, he was a bold and romantic thinker, gathering ideas from many sources and adapting them freely to his own purposes. His direct experience of life was by far the most important source of his ideas; next to this was the living presence of Coleridge; finally there was the influence of books, and among these he roamed far and wide. To think of him as mainly harking back to *the Lockian or any other tradition* seems to me to obscure the freshness of his vision. As Peter Burra has said, 'Poetry is never the slave of philosophy',[4] and Wordsworth was far too great a poet to be enslaved to any philosophical movement.

I shall focus almost exclusively upon the poetry of 1797–1807. In this decade Wordsworth composed his greatest works, not only *The Prelude* (1805 version) but the best passages in *The Excursion* and, with few exceptions, the finest of his shorter poems. This is the period when his ideas were most vigorous and profound. I shall try to interpret these ideas as faithfully as possible, setting aside my personal convictions.

---

[1] A. C. Bradley, *English Poetry and German Philosophy in the Age of Wordsworth* (Manchester: Sherrat, 1909), pp. 8, 10.

[2] Arthur Beatty, *William Wordsworth: His Doctrine and Art in Their Historical Relations*, third edition (Madison: University of Wisconsin Press, 1960), p. 19.

[3] Cf. James V. Logan, *Wordsworthian Criticism* (Columbus: Ohio State University Press, 1961), ch. 6.

[4] Peter Burra, *Wordsworth* (New York: Macmillan, 1936), p. 60.

I disagree with critics who deny that Wordsworth is expressing his own beliefs. The following statement by Monroe Beardsley seems to me unconvincing: 'It is not Wordsworth, in the poem, but a speaker who may or may not be similar to him, musing near Tintern Abbey; it is entirely irrelevant to the understanding of the poem—though relevant to a causal explanation of its having been written—that Wordsworth himself visited the spot.'[1] Admitting that it may be a fallacy to attribute the ideas expressed in a work to its author, I believe that Wordsworth, more than most poets, is expressing his *own* convictions, and that the bulk of his poetry is more or less autobiographical. There is too much internal coherence in the total body of the poetry to suppose that each separate poem expresses the ideas of a purely fictional speaker. It is this body of coherent ideas that I shall now try to lay bare.

[1] Monroe Beardsley, *Aesthetics* (New York: Harcourt, Brace, 1958), pp. 240-1.

I. WORDSWORTH AND COLERIDGE

1. 'Twins Almost in Genius and in Mind!'

A N indispensable key to the interpretation of Wordsworth's ideas is the influence of Coleridge. How great that influence was is suggested by the remarks of Wordsworth after his friend's death. A neighbour recorded this conversation:

It was Sunday evening after the death occurred that my brother and I walked over to the Mount, where we found the Poet alone. One of the first things we heard from him was the death of one who had been, he said, his friend for more than thirty years. He then continued to speak of him; called him the most *wonderful* man he had ever known—wonderful for the originality of his mind, and the power he possessed of throwing off in profusion grand central truths from which might be evolved the most comprehensive systems. . . . Though a considerable period had elapsed during which they had not seen much of each other. Coleridge and he had been, uninterruptedly, in as close intimacy as man could be with man.[1]

So close were the bonds of thought and feeling between the two friends during this intimacy that each was bound profoundly to affect the other. Wordsworth was not exaggerating when he declared that Coleridge and 'my beloved sister are the two beings to whom my intellect is most indebted'.[2]

A number of passages in Wordsworth's poetry refer to their friendship. Writing in 1804, when Coleridge was seeking better health in the warm climate of Malta, Wordsworth was convinced that neither illness nor great distance could separate friends so united in 'mind' and 'genius':

---

[1] 'Recollections of Reverend R. P. Graves', *The Prose Works of William Wordsworth*, ed. A. B. Grosart (London: Moxon, 1876), iii, p. 469. Hereafter referred to as *Prose Works*.
[2] *The Letters of William and Dorothy Wordsworth: The Later Years*, ed. Ernest de Selincourt (Oxford: Clarendon Press, 1939), ii, p. 625. (To W. R. Hamilton, 25 June 1832.) Hereafter referred to as *Letters: The Later Years*.

> I, too, have been a Wanderer; but, alas!
> How different is the fate of different men
> Though Twins almost in genius and in mind!
> Unknown unto each other, yea, and breathing
> As if in different elements, we were framed
> To bend at last to the same discipline,
> Predestin'd, if two Beings ever were,
> To seek the same delights, and have one health,
> One happiness.[1]

Wordsworth's love was so great that, in recalling the years before the friends had met, he could scarcely conceive that Coleridge had ever been absent:

> O Friend! we had not seen thee at that time,
> And yet a power is on me, and a strong
> Confusion, and I seem to plant thee there. . . .
> . . . Thou art with us, with us in the past,
> The present, with us in the times to come.
> There is no grief, no sorrow, no despair,
> No languor, no dejection, no dismay,
> No absence scarcely can there be, for those
> Who love as we do.[2]

After the quarrel of 1810 the friendship was much less intense, but until the very end of his life Wordsworth preserved his admiration for

> The rapt One, of the godlike forehead,
> The heaven-eyed creature.[3]

A number of factors combined to magnify the influence of Coleridge. One of these was his marvellous conversational power. Dorothy Wordsworth exclaimed: 'Coleridge is a wonderful creature, pouring out such treasures of thought and knowledge, almost, we may say, without premeditation, and in language so eloquent.'[4] Wordsworth likewise regarded Coleridge as the greatest talker that he had ever met:

---

[1] *Prelude* (1805), VI. 261–9.

[2] *Prelude*, VI. 237–47.

[3] *Extempore Effusion upon the Death of James Hogg. Wordsworth's Poetical Works*, ed. E. de Selincourt and H. Darbishire (Oxford: Clarendon Press, 1940–9), iv. 276. Hereafter referred to as *Poetical Works*.

[4] *The Letters of William and Dorothy Wordsworth: The Middle Years*, ed. E. de Selincourt (Oxford: Clarendon Press, 1937), i, p. 199. (To Lady Beaumont, 20 Apr. 1808.) Hereafter referred to as *Letters: The Middle Years*.

I have known many that might be called very *clever* men, and a good many of real and vigorous *abilities*, but few of genius; and only one whom I should call 'wonderful.' That one was Coleridge. At any hour of the day or night he would talk by the hour, if there chanced to be *any* sympathetic listener, and talk better than the best page of his writings; for a pen half paralysed his genius. A child would sit quietly at his feet and wonder, till the torrent had passed.[1]

Similar impressions have been recorded by Lamb, Hazlitt, and many others.

Coleridge's conversations were enriched by his marvellous memory. A college friend, writing of evenings spent in Coleridge's quarters at Cambridge, thus described the amazing performances that he witnessed:

What evenings have I spent in these rooms! What little suppers, or *sizings*, as they were called, have I enjoyed; when Aeschylus, and Plato, and Thucydides were pushed aside . . . to discuss the pamphlets of the day. Ever and anon, a pamphlet issued from the pen of Burke. There was no need of having the book before us. Coleridge had read it in the morning, and in the evening he would repeat whole pages verbatim. Frend's trial was then in progress. Pamphlets swarmed from the press. Coleridge had read them all; and in the evening, with our negus, we had them *viva voce* gloriously.[2]

Since Wordsworth also had an astonishing memory, he did not easily forget what he learned by listening to such discourse.

Commensurate with Coleridge's power of recollection was his erudition. 'I am, and ever have been, a great reader—', he remarked, 'and have read almost everything—a library-cormorant.'[3] This is scarcely an exaggeration, since few men have ever read so voraciously.

---

[1] Aubrey De Vere, 'Recollections of Wordsworth', *Prose Works*, ed. Grosart, iii, p. 492. See also Richard W. Armour and Raymond F. Howes, *Coleridge the Talker* (Cornell University Press, 1940).

[2] C. V. LeGrice, *Gentlemen's Magazine*, Dec. 1834, p. 606; quoted by John Livingston Lowes, *The Road to Xanadu* (Boston: Houghton, Mifflin, 1930), p. 43. The 'trial' referred to is that of William Frend, a republican and free-thinker, who was tried in 1793 before the Vice-Chancellor and Heads of Colleges at Cambridge and banished from the University. The undergraduates, Coleridge among them, were vociferous in his favour.

[3] *The Collected Letters of Samuel Taylor Coleridge*, ed. Earl Leslie Griggs (Oxford: Clarendon Press, 1956–9), i, p. 260. (To John Thelwall, 19 Nov. 1796.) Hereafter referred to as *Collected Letters*.

He believed that one should bring vast erudition to bear upon the writing of poetry. With amusing bravado, he presented this recipe:

I should not think of devoting less than twenty years to an epic poem. Ten years to collect my materials, and warm my mind with universal science. I should be a tolerable mathematician. I would thoroughly understand Mechanics, Hydrostatics, Optics and Astronomy; Botany, Metallurgy, Fossilism; Chemistry; Geology, Anatomy, Medicine; then the mind of man in all Travels, Voyages and Histories. So would I spend ten years; the next five in the composition of the poem, and the five last in the correction of it.[1]

That the above prescription was not entirely facetious is proved by the way in which Coleridge prepared for his projected *Hymns to the Elements* and the great learning that actually went into the texture of *The Rime of the Ancient Mariner*.[2]

Imagine his recipe for writing a philosophical poem like *The Recluse*! As originally conceived,· this was to be very grand in scope. Wordsworth described the projected work as 'a poem in which I contrive to convey most of the knowledge of which I am possessed. My object is to give pictures of Nature, Man, and Society. Indeed I know not any thing which will not come within the scope of my plan.'[3] *The Prelude* was to be an introduction to, and *The Excursion* was to be a part of, this vast work. Coleridge regarded the project with intense enthusiasm, believing that Wordsworth was destined to write 'the *first* and *only* true Philosophical poem in existence'.[4]

Wordsworth, in turn, relied heavily upon his friend for guidance and advice. This fact is evident from the letters that he wrote after Coleridge left the Lake Country early in 1804 to seek better health in Malta. While in London, *en route*, the latter apparently wrote to Wordsworth promising to send him some notes on *The Recluse*. On 6 March 1804 Wordsworth

---

[1] Joseph Cottle, *Early Recollections* (London: Houlston, 1837), i, p. 192. (Letter of Coleridge to Cottle.)

[2] Cf. Lowes, *The Road to Xanadu* (Boston: Houghton, Mifflin, 1930), pp. 32–37 and *passim*.

[3] *The Early Letters of William and Dorothy Wordsworth*, ed. E. de Selincourt (Oxford: Clarendon Press, 1939), p. 188. Hereafter referred to as *Early Letters*.

[4] *Collected Letters*, iv, p. 574.

wrote in reply: 'I am very anxious to have your notes for *The Recluse*. I cannot say how much importance I attach to this; if it should please God that I survive you, I should reproach myself forever in writing the work if I had neglected to procure this help.'[1] Three weeks later, just before Coleridge sailed, Wordsworth wrote even more insistently: 'I cannot help saying that I would gladly have given three-fourths of my possessions for your letter on *The Recluse*. . . . I cannot say what a load it would be to me, should I survive you and you die without this memorial left behind. Do, for heaven's sake, put this out of the reach of accident immediately.'[2] On 1 August 1806, when Coleridge was about ready to return to England, Wordsworth wrote to George Beaumont: 'Within this last month I have returned to *The Recluse*, and have written 700 additional lines. Should Coleridge return, so that I might have some conversation with him on the subject, I should go on swimmingly.'[3] These letters indicate how much Wordsworth valued his friend's criticism.

The influence of Coleridge was all the greater in consequence of the unsettled state of Wordsworth's convictions. When he first met Coleridge, he was just emerging from a stage of extreme intellectual demoralization. This was his 'soul's last and lowest ebb', when his faith in Godwin's theories had crumbled and he had given 'up moral questions in despair'.[4] The crisis occurred in 1795, but the poet's bewilderment gave way slowly, and recovery was not complete until the summer of 1797 or thereafter. In this most impressionable period of his life Coleridge extended aid:

> Ah! then it was
> That Thou, most precious Friend! about this time
> First known to me, didst lend a living help
> To regulate my Soul.[5]

In their endless talk the expansive mind of Coleridge must have invigorated his comrade's entire intellectual being. The friendship rapidly matured into close intimacy, and the genius of both poets burst into full bloom.

---

[1] *Early Letters*, p. 368.
[3] *Letters: The Middle Years*, i, p. 51.
[5] *Prelude* (1805), X. 905–8.

[2] Ibid., pp. 379–80.
[4] Cf. *Prelude*, XI. 194–305.

2. *The Cast of Coleridge's Philosophy*

When one tries to explore Coleridge's ideas during this period of intimacy, one discovers an almost impenetrable thicket of philosophical allusions; but at least the complex and eclectic character of his thought may be discerned.

Among British writers none excited his enthusiasm more than the psychologist David Hartley (1705–57), author of the famous book, *Observations on Man* (1749), and the principal founder of the Associationist school. In 1796 Coleridge named his eldest child 'David Hartley', expressing the hope that if he grew to maturity 'his head will be convinced of, and his heart saturated with, the truths so ably supported by that great master of *Christian* philosophy'.[1] This is one of many indications of Coleridge's devotion to Hartley.

The latter's 'Christian philosophy' exhibited that 'holy alliance' between religion and science of which Locke and Newton are among the greatest exemplars. Despite his piety, Hartley made all mental processes rest on vibrations in the brain which follow mechanical laws—psychological associations being attended by physiological linkages—but he was not sure whether the relation between the mental and physical events ought to be regarded as causal. In general, he sought to trace every mental state back through chains of 'necessity' to simple, discrete components in the form of sensations or ideas. The whole of the mental life, he believed, is explicable by the combination and recombination of these elementary states in conformity with the necessary laws of association. These laws explain not only the mechanism of our mental life but the growth of all our moral and religious traits. The trick, if one wants to rear a child aright, is to surround him with the right stimuli, and then he will form associations leading inevitably to correct ideas in morality and religion. Thus 'science' can be devoted to the glory of God and the salvation of man. The details of Hartley's system we need not now consider.

The question of the influence of Hartley on Wordsworth takes us to the heart of our problem. No one has stated this influence in stronger terms than Arthur Beatty in his widely quoted book, *William Wordsworth: His Doctrine and Art in*

---

[1] *Collected Letters*, i, p. 236. (To Thomas Poole, 24 Sept. 1796.)

their Historical Relations. Let us carefully examine the evidence advanced by Beatty that this influence was mediated through Coleridge.

Beatty refers us to Coleridge's reminiscences in the *Biographia Literaria.* There we find that Coleridge does indeed discuss at some length his early devotion to Hartley, but that his allegiance appears never to have been exclusive. He thus speaks of the influence of the mystics on him during his most Hartleian period: 'The writings of these mystics acted in no slight degree to prevent my mind from being imprisoned within the outline of any single dogmatic system. They contributed to keep alive the *heart* in the *head*; gave me an indistinct, yet stirring and working presentiment that all the products of the mere *reflective* faculty partook of Death.'[1] In discussing the period before his discovery of Kant, Coleridge goes on to say: 'After I had successively studied in the schools of Locke, Berkeley, Leibnitz, and Hartley, and could find in neither of them an abiding place for my reason, I began to ask myself, is a system of philosophy, as different from mere history and historic classification, possible?'[2] He then relates his discovery of Jacob Boehme and Immanuel Kant. We know that the serious study of Kant was begun early in 1801 and that some familiarity with Boehme preceded.[3] We must, therefore, date his dissatisfaction with Locke, Berkeley, and Hartley as prior to 1801. The impression that we derive from the *Biographia Literaria* is that Coleridge's enthusiasm for Hartley was not of long duration and was combined with quite different allegiances.

The next item of evidence is the testimony of Joseph Cottle, the original publisher of the *Lyrical Ballads.* He tells us that Coleridge, in 1795, 'generally contrived, either by direct amalgamation, or digression, to notice, in the warmest encomiastic language, Bishop Berkeley, David Hartley, or Mr. Bowles. . . . He urged the purchase of three works, indispensable to all who

---

[1] *Biographia Literaria*, ed. J. Shawcross (Oxford: Clarendon Press, 1907), i, p. 98. (That Coleridge before writing *The Ancient Mariner* was familiar with Plotinus, Porphyry, Iamblichus, Proclus, Julian, Hermes Trismegistus, and Marsilio Ficino—all neo-Platonic mystics—is indicated by Lowes, op. cit., pp. 229–38.)

[2] Ibid., p. 93.

[3] Ibid., p. xli, and the notations from Boehme in *The Notebooks of Samuel Taylor Coleridge*, ed. Kathleen Coburn (New York: Pantheon Books, 1957), i. Hereafter referred to as *Notebooks*.

wished to excel in sound reasoning, or a correct taste; namely: Simpson's Euclid; Hartley on Man; and Bowles's Poems.' Yet in the very next paragraph occurs this addition: 'In process of time, however, *when reflection had rendered his mind more mature*, he appeared to renounce the fanciful and brain-bewildering system of Berkeley; whilst he sparingly extolled Hartley; and was almost silent respecting Mr. Bowles. I noticed a marked change in his commendation of Mr. Bowles *from the time he paid that man of genius a visit.*'[1] The words that I have italicized indicate when Coleridge's change of mind took place. Since we know that the visit to Bowles occurred in September 1797, the alteration seems to have occurred about this time.[2] Also Cottle's great admiration for the *Lyrical Ballads* would indicate that, in his judgement, Coleridge was 'more mature' by the time this joint production was completed. The implication is that Coleridge's coolness towards Berkeley and Hartley must have developed during the *early* period of his acquaintance with Wordsworth.

In *Religious Musings*, a poem written by Coleridge in 1795, we find this tribute to Hartley's theory of brain-vibrations:

> and he of mortal kind
> Wisest, he first who marked the ideal tribes
> Down the fine fibres from the sentient brain
> Roll subtly-surging.

In a footnote to a passage on the transformation of the love of self and the world into the love of God, Coleridge states: 'See this *demonstrated* by Hartley, vol. 1, p. 114, and vol. 2, p. 329.' The poem as a whole has a Hartleian flavour.

The evidence in this instance would be impressive if we were considering a more consistent and less eclectic thinker, and if the poem had been written later. Since Coleridge's beliefs underwent a change in 1797–8, these early opinions will not greatly affect our study.

Another item of evidence must be discounted for the same reason. This is the letter already quoted in which Coleridge reported that he had christened his first-born after 'that great

---

[1] Joseph Cottle, op. cit., p. 21. The 'Mr. Bowles' here mentioned is William Lisle Bowles, the poet.

[2] Cf. ibid., p. 234, and *Collected Letters*, i, p. 344 fn.

master of *Christian* philosophy', David Hartley. Once more we learn of Coleridge's state of mind *prior* to 1797. To evaluate this evidence, we must also remember that he was a zealous Unitarian and that Hartley was also. The second volume of Hartley is an exposition of the writer's theology, and even the first volume is deeply tinged with theological doctrines. When we find Coleridge devoted to the 'great master of *Christian* philosophy', we cannot be sure that it was primarily the psychology and materialistic metaphysics, as distinct from the Unitarian theology, that led him to christen his son with the name of Hartley.[1]

Perhaps some indication of Coleridge's interest in Hartleian psychology is furnished by Lamb, in a letter written to Coleridge, 5 February 1797. Suggesting subjects for a long poem, Lamb recommends this: 'Or a Five Days' Dream, which shall illustrate, in sensible imagery, Hartley's five Motives to Conduct:—1. Sensation; 2. Imagination; 3. Ambition; 4. Sympathy; 5. Theopathy.'[2] He then proposes appropriate details for the development of each part. But the suggestion is that of *Lamb*, not Coleridge, and we do not know how it was received by the latter. The response may have been apathetic, for the poem was never written.

More positive information is supplied by Clement Carlyon, a companion who tramped with Coleridge in Germany (1799). Mentioning some doggerel that Coleridge extemporized as they walked through 'forests of beech', Carlyon goes on to say:

But if his muse was dull, the genius of metaphysics was in full activity, and he endeavoured to enlighten the minds of his companions by a long discussion, among other things, in favour of an opinion . . . that, throughout nature, pleasurable sensations greatly predominate over painful. He said, that it must be so, for as the tendency of pain is to disorganize, the disorganization of the whole living system must ensue if the balance lay on its side. Exquisite pleasure becomes pain; does exquisite pain, he asked, ever become pleasure? There was another point which he could not settle so entirely to his satisfaction, and that was the nature or essential quality of happiness. He seemed

---

[1] For evidence that Coleridge was deeply impressed by Hartley's theology, see H. N. Fairchild, 'Hartley, Pistorius and Coleridge', *Publications of the Modern Language Association*, vol. 62 (1947), pp. 1016–21.

[2] *The Works of Charles and Mary Lamb*, ed. E. V. Lucas (London: Methuen, 1905), vi, p. 92.

to think that it might be defined 'as consciousness of an excess of pleasurable sensations, direct or reflex'.[1]

Even if one supposes that the opinions thus expressed by Coleridge must have come from Hartley, this report can prove no more than acceptance of Hartley's hedonism and optimism.

After combing the book for any further evidence of Coleridge's indebtedness to Hartley, one can discover this single item:

It will readily be believed, from the well-known circumstance of his having christened one of his sons Hartley and another Berkeley, that he took opportunities of analysing and illustrating the philosophical tenets of these great men. They were in fact the frequent subjects of his conversation, not only during our Alpine tour, but in our evening walks on the ramparts of Göttingen, which, from the fine rows of trees that adorn them, claim the honour, not merely of being the walls, but the woods of Academus.[2]

One must supplement this statement with other remarks of Carlyon. Coleridge 'was capable of being as much in character with Fielding or Smollett', he declares, 'as with Spinoza or Berkeley, or those holier and wiser men with whom he eventually coincided in his religious creed'. Coleridge 'used frequently' to make the doctrines of Spinoza 'the subject of our conversation, and took pains to explain them to us'; and 'Bruno was a great favourite with Coleridge; he often spoke of him energetically, and always, apparently, with the wish to give a favourable interpretation of his metaphysics'.[3] Thus the evidence presented by Carlyon discloses the catholicity of Coleridge's philosophical tastes rather than exclusive infatuation with Hartley.

According to Beatty, 'Hazlitt's account of his visit to the joint authors of the *Lyrical Ballads* in the very year of the publication of the volume shows that benevolence and association, two fundamentals in the system of Hartley, were fully accepted by Coleridge'.[4] The only portion of the relevant essay, 'My

---

[1] Clement Carlyon, *Early Years and Late Reflections* (London: Whittaker, 1856), i, pp. 33–34.
[2] Ibid., p. 90.
[3] Ibid., pp. 119, 193, 195 fn. In his reference to Bruno, Carlyon seems to be referring to a later period in Coleridge's life than his sojourn in Germany.
[4] Beatty, *William Wordsworth*, op. cit., p. 101.

First Acquaintance with Poets', that might seem to refer to the doctrine of benevolence occurs in the last paragraph but one:

A fisherman gave Coleridge an account of a boy that had been drowned the day before, and that they had tried to save him at the risk of their own lives. He [the fisherman] said 'he did not know how it was that they had ventured, but, sir, we have a *nature* towards one another'. This expression, Coleridge remarked to me, was a fine illustration of that theory of disinterestedness which I (in common with Butler)[1] had adopted.

The 'theory of disinterestedness' (which Beatty seems to have identified with Hartley's concept of benevolence) is explained in a previous statement: 'I told Coleridge I had written a few remarks, and was sometimes foolish enough to believe that I had made a discovery on the same subject (the *Natural Disinterestedness of the Human Mind*)—and I tried to explain my view to Coleridge, who listened with great willingness, but I did not succeed in making myself understood.' Thus the theory being discussed is that of Hazlitt, not that of Coleridge, and it is said to resemble Butler's theory of disinterestedness. Butler was a very different sort of philosopher from Hartley.

A careful reading of the penultimate paragraph of Hazlitt's essay will also reveal that the mention of 'the association of ideas' emanated *from Hazlitt*, and that Coleridge agreed that *mere* association of ideas, without taking account of structural similarities, is inadequate as an explanatory principle. I leave the perspicuous reader to find anything else in the essay that will lend support to the belief that Coleridge was then devoted to Hartley.

In a letter to William Godwin, 4 June 1803, Coleridge proposed to prefix to a new edition of Abraham Tucker's *Light of Nature Pursued* an essay 'containing the whole substance of the first Volume of Hartley, entirely defecated from all the corpuscular hypotheses'.[2] A statement of this sort would be more conclusive if Coleridge did not have a mania for planning works which he never undertook and probably never seriously

---

[1] The reference is to Bishop Joseph Butler, the philosopher. For a review of Hazlitt's theory of benevolence in relation to Butler and Hartley, see Herschel Baker, *William Hazlitt* (Harvard University Press, 1962), pp. 142–52. Hazlitt was already critical of Hartley when he first visited Coleridge and Wordsworth in 1798.

[2] *Collected Letters*, ii, p. 949

considered. Humorously, he addressed these words to himself, apropos of his innumerable schemes for writing: 'My dear fellow! never be ashamed of scheming—you can't think of living less than 4000 years, and that would nearly suffice for your present schemes.'[1]

In the same letter to Godwin, Coleridge tells of another work he plans to write, entitled *Organum Vere Organum, or an Instrument of Practical Reasoning in the Business of Real Life.* Summarizing the chapters, he mentions a number of philosophers, such as Aristotle, Plato, Bacon, and Descartes, to each of whom he intends to devote a chapter, but there is no chapter on Hartley. The plan of the work, he declares, 'has not been the labour of one year or of two, but the result of many years' meditations, and of very various Reading'.[2] It is this much-meditated plan, rather than the project of expounding Hartley, that appears to indicate the main drift of Coleridge's philosophical interests.

It is also noteworthy that the new edition of Tucker was to be prepared by Hazlitt who, in 1803, was far from being a whole-hearted disciple of Hartley. Hazlitt's abridgement of Tucker finally appeared in 1807, but without Coleridge's introductory essay.

That Coleridge had ceased to accept Hartleianism before the date of this publication is indicated by a passage from Thomas De Quincey: 'It is well known to most literary people that Coleridge was, in early life, so passionate an admirer of the Hartleian philosophy, that Hartley was the sole baptismal name which he gave his eldest child. . . . But at present [August 1807] all this was a *forgotten* thing.'[3] The implication is that the desertion of Hartley was *considerably* prior to 1807.

I have examined Beatty's evidence bit by bit, omitting nothing, in order to leave no doubt about an important matter. We may conclude with perfect safety that Coleridge, in his typically eclectic fashion, adhered to Hartley in 1795–7; that there is nothing in the evidence so far considered that would show him whole-heartedly committed to Hartley after 1797;

---

[1] *Anima Poetae* (Boston: Houghton, Mifflin, 1895), p. 89. (Written in 1804.)
[2] *Collected Letters*, ii, pp. 947–8.
[3] De Quincey, *Works*, ed. David Masson (Edinburgh: Black, 1862), ii, p. 56. My italics.

and that the indications are that he was breaking away from his former master and embracing philosophers of a quite different complexion in 1798–1803.

The date of Coleridge's disillusionment with Hartleian psychology can be determined with a good deal of precision. Early in 1801 he passed through a crisis that wrought a sharp change in his convictions. The consequences of a serious illness are thus described in a letter of 3 February 1801 to Humphry Davy: 'I have been *thinking* vigorously during my Illness—so that I cannot say that my long, long wakeful nights have been all lost to me. The subject of my meditations has been the Relations of Thoughts to Things, in the language of Hume, of Ideas to Impressions.'[1] This was the beginning of a period of intense intellectual activity. During this same month of February he wrote four long letters to his patron, Josiah Wedgwood, expressing his dissatisfaction with Locke and British empiricism but a lingering admiration for Hartley. Less than a month thereafter (16 March 1801) he composed a letter to his friend Thomas Poole reporting that, as a result of 'the most intense Study', he had 'overthrown the doctrine of Association, as taught by Hartley, and with it all the irreligious metaphysics of modern Infidels—especially the doctrine of Necessity'.[2] In rejecting associationism and necessitarianism Coleridge was expressing his aversion to the entire philosophical tradition to which Hartley owed allegiance. In a letter of 22 July he announced: 'I am burning Locke, Hume, and Hobbes . . . —they stink worse than Feather or Assafetida.'[3] It was about this time that the teaching of Kant took hold of him with 'giant hands'.[4] Although he retained considerable admiration for Hartley, it may have been the more 'Christian' aspects of the latter's thought that primarily impressed him. Perhaps this explains how it was still possible for Coleridge, as late as 1811, to refer to Hartley as a 'great metaphysician'.[5]

Coleridge's philosophical interests expanded rapidly during the next several years, throughout which he remained in fairly close contact with Wordsworth until his departure for Malta,

---

[1] *Collected Letters*, ii, pp. 671–2.   [2] Ibid., p. 706.
[3] Ibid., p. 746. (To Robert Southey.)   [4] *Biographia Literaria*, i, p. 99.
[5] John Payne Collier, *Seven Lectures on Shakespeare and Milton by the Late S. T. Coleridge* (London: Chapman & Hall, 1856), pp. xxix–xxxi. (20 Oct. 1811.)

2 April 1804. The evidence bearing upon this development is too
vast to include in this chapter. It will suffice to quote the following indication of his intellectual allegiances in 1805:

> Let me not confound the discriminating character and genius of
> a nation with the conflux of its individuals in cities and reviews. Let
> England be Sir Philip Sidney, Shakespeare, Milton, Bacon, Harrington,
> Swift, Wordsworth; and never let the names of Darwin, Johnson,
> Hume, *fur* it over. If these, too, must be England let them be another
> England; or, rather, let the first be old England, the spiritual, Platonic
> old England; and the second, with Locke at the head of the philo-
> sophers and Pope [at the head] of the poets, together with the long
> list of Priestleys, Paleys, Hayleys, Darwins, Mr. Pitts, Dundasses,
> &c., &c., be the representatives of commercial Great Britain. These
> have [indeed] their merits, but are as alien to me as the Mandarin
> philosophers and poets of China. Even so Leibnitz, Lessing, Voss,
> Kant, shall be *Germany* to me, let whatever coxcombs rise up, and
> *shrill* it away in the grasshopper vale of reviews. And so shall Dante,
> Ariosto, Giordano Bruno, be my Italy; Cervantes my Spain; and O!
> that I could find a France for my love. But spite of Pascal, Madame
> Guyon, and Molière, France is my Babylon, the mother of whoredoms
> in morality, philosophy and taste.[1]

Coleridge is allied to mystics like Madame Guyon, neo-
Platonists like Giordano Bruno, opponents of sensationism like
Leibnitz, defenders of Christian faith like Pascal, advocates of
the mind's power to shape all experience, such as Kant, and
representatives of the spiritual, Platonic old England, such as
Richard Hooker, Jeremy Taylor, and the Cambridge Platonists.
Wordsworth is specifically linked with this 'England' that
Coleridge so much admired. The France of Voltaire, Rousseau,
Diderot, Condorcet, Holbach, and Condillac, representatives of
the empirical or deistic outlook, was his Babylon. The Britain
of Locke, Hume, Priestley, Paley, and Erasmus Darwin, all
of whom were deeply imbedded in the empirical tradition, was
the land of 'commercialism' alien to Coleridge's sympathies.

3. *The Rejection of Necessitarianism*

Let us now turn to our primary concern—the manner in
which Coleridge influenced Wordsworth. Fortunately we can

---

[1] *Anima Poetae*, pp. 127–8. Joseph Priestley and Erasmus Darwin, referred to in
this quotation, were sympathetic to Hartley.

define the nature of this influence with some precision. We have direct testimony, for instance, that Wordsworth abandoned necessitarianism as a result of Coleridge's persuasion.

The doctrine of necessity, which denies free will to man, had been embraced by Coleridge while under the sway of William Godwin and David Hartley. 'I am a complete Necessitarian', Coleridge wrote to Southey (11 December 1794), 'and understand the subject as well almost as Hartley himself—but I go farther than Hartley and believe the corporeality of *thought*— namely, that it is motion.'[1] But he soon manifested a repugnance towards materialism and necessitarianism. This aversion is indicated by his plan for a series of 'Hymns' which he had in preparation during 1796–7. In the first record of his intention, dated December 1795 or January 1796, he decried 'the Godwinian System of Pride', which made man 'an outcast of blind Nature ruled by a fatal Necessity'.[2] Years later he wrote the following comment on his poem, *The Destiny of Nations*, composed in 1796: 'Within twelve months after the writing of this poem my bold Optimism, and Necessitarianism . . . down to which, step by step, I had *unbelieved*, gave way to the day-break of a more genial and less shallow system.'[3] Thus, despite his enthusiasm for Hartley, Coleridge soon abandoned the necessitarian creed.

In Wordsworth the attachment to the doctrine of necessity was deeper and more enduring. 'Throw aside your books of chemistry', he is said to have advised a student, 'and read Godwin on Necessity.'[4] Even after his rejection of Godwinism, his interest in Hartley and Spinoza sustained his necessitarian convictions. In his Preface to the *Lyrical Ballads* (1800) he spoke of the effect of the association of ideas in establishing firm habits of mind: 'By obeying blindly and mechanically the impulses of those habits' the poet is bound to 'describe objects, and utter sentiments, of such a nature, and in such connection with each other, that the understanding of the reader must necessarily be in some degree enlightened, and his affections strengthened and

---

[1] *Collected Letters*, i, p. 137.

[2] *Notebooks*, i, entry 174. (? Dec. 1795–Jan. 1796.)

[3] *The Poetical Works of Samuel Taylor Coleridge*, ed. James Dykes Campbell (London: Macmillan, 1938), p. 586.

[4] 'The Spirit of the Age', *Collected Works of William Hazlitt*, ed. A. R. Waller and Arnold Glover (London: Dent, 1902–4), iv, p. 201.

purified.' Quite a number of early passages in the poetical works reflect such necessitarian and perfectibilist doctrines.

Wordsworth's subsequent abandonment of necessitarianism appears to have been primarily the result of Coleridge's influence. In the letter written to Poole on 16 March 1801 Coleridge declared: 'If I do not greatly delude myself, I have not only extricated the notions of Time, and Space; but have overthrown the doctrine of Association, as taught by Hartley, and with it all the irreligious metaphysics of modern Infidels—especially, the doctrine of Necessity.'[1] The reference to 'the notions of Time and Space' strongly suggests the influence of Kant; for in the first part of the *Critique of Pure Reason* Kant seeks to demonstrate the ideality of space and time, which are thus 'extricated' from the materialism of 'modern infidels'.[2] The later argument of Kant is designed to overthrow the doctrine of moral necessity and defend the concepts of 'God, Freedom, and Immortality' as doctrines of 'Practical Reason'.

In a subsequent letter to Poole, 15 January 1804, Coleridge refers again to his 'escape from the pernicious doctrine of Necessity', and finding 'a better clue' to help others to do likewise. Since Coleridge was much preoccupied with Kant during the interval between the two letters, it appears to be a safe inference that the 'better clue' was Kant's doctrine of the ideality of the phenomenal world and the reality of freedom in the noumenal order.

From the letter to Poole it is clear that he converted Wordsworth to his new way of looking at things:

I love and honour you, Poole! for many things—scarcely for any thing more than that, trusting firmly in the Rectitude and simplicity of your own Heart, and listening with faith to it's revealing Voice, you never suffered either my Subtlety or my Eloquence to proselyte you to the pernicious Doctrine of Necessity. All praise to the Great Being who has graciously enabled me to find my way out of that labyrinth-Den of Sophistry, and, I would fain believe, to bring with me a better clue than has hitherto been known, to enable others to do the same. I have convinced Southey—and Wordsworth, and W, you know, was even to Extravagance a Necessitarian. Southey never believed, and abhorred the Doctrine, yet thought the arguments for it

---

[1] *Collected Letters*, ii, p. 706.
[2] That Coleridge at about this time was reading Kant on space is indicated by *Notebooks*, i, entry 887.

unanswerable by human Reason. I have convinced both of them of the sophistry of the arguments, and wherein the Sophism consists—viz. that all have hitherto, both the Necessitarians and their Antagonists, confounded two essentially different Things under one name—and in consequence of *this* Mistake the Victory has been always hollow in favour of the Necessitarians.[1]

The final sentence in this quotation requires some interpretation. I think it means that both the necessitarians and their antagonists had failed to make Kant's distinction between the *phenomenal* will determined according to natural causes and the *noumenal* will as morally free. Once this distinction is made the victory of the necessitarians, according to Coleridge, is seen to be 'hollow'.

Since his letter indicated that Wordsworth had abandoned necessitarianism by January 1804, the latter had changed his mind at least a year before the completion of the 1805 version of *The Prelude*. Judging from his frequent emphasis upon the *active* role of the human faculties, I think that Wordsworth already had strong tendencies to believe in free will, and that Coleridge's argument reinforced his native bent. As we shall discover in later chapters, the idea of freedom was made basic in Wordsworth's subsequent poetry. All of nature—the 'human Mind', the 'little Meadow flower', the grand 'Forest tree', the 'Soul of all the worlds'—was thought to be free, active, alive, palpitating with 'its own divine vitality'.[2]

4. The Criticism of Associationism

Coleridge's rejection of necessitarianism was incidental to his escape from the Associational psychology of the eighteenth century. In the writings of Hartley and other associationists, he had found a plausible explanation of mental states, but his mind was not permanently satisfied with such theories.

Postponing until Chapter IV the detailed exposition of Hartley's psychology, I shall point to a few of the salient concepts against which Coleridge reacted. The notion of the association of ideas, of course, was by no means original with Hartley.

[1] *Collected Letters*, ii, p. 1037.
[2] *Excursion*, IX. 1–19, *Poetical Works*, v. 5; and the sonnet '*A Poet!*—He hath put his heart to school,' ibid. iii. 52.

Aristotle had similarly described the nature of association and used it to explain memory. Hobbes noted that spatial or temporal coexistence in previous experience, as, for example, when two things are seen together, is the basis of the idea of the one recalling the other. Locke introduced the phrase 'the association of ideas', emphasizing repetition ('custom') as a cause of the linking together of ideas or images. Berkeley likewise spoke of 'an habitual and customary connection' by which one idea is the occasion for another. Hume compared the association of ideas to the law of gravitation in physics: 'Here', he declared, 'is a kind of attraction which in the mental world will be found to have as extraordinary effects as in the natural, and to show itself in as many and as various forms.'[1] The principle of the association of ideas had been greatly developed by these predecessors of Hartley, but he wrote a whole psychology around it and thus 'founded' a school of 'associationism'.

If we leave aside the theory of physical 'vibrations', Hartley's doctrine is as follows. Sensations by being repeated leave vestiges or images of themselves which are *simple ideas* of sensation. Any sensations, *A*, *B*, *C*, by occurring contiguously with one another, get such a power over the corresponding ideas, *a*, *b*, *c*, that any one, as for example, *A*, can excite *b*, *c*, the ideas of the rest. The Aristotelian principles of association —that is, likeness and difference, cause and effect, and contiguity in space and time—were thus reduced by Hartley in one stroke to the single principle of contiguity, either simultaneous or successive. If experiences happen together often enough, for instance the sight of a fire burning in a fireplace and the enjoyment of a friendly chat, then the recurrence in actuality or thought of the one (the fire) will recall the idea of the other (the friendly conversation). Associations thus formed run into clusters, and out of simple sensations and ideas, by a gradual process of accretion, complex ideas are formed. The strength of these associations depends on the vividness of the feelings or ideas associated and the frequency with which any association is repeated. By these laws of association, Hartley sought to explain all of our more complex mental states.

In his *Observations on Man* we find the principle of association stated so broadly and applied so ubiquitously as to cover the

[1] *A Treatise of Human Nature* (1739), Bk. I, Pt. I, sect. 4.

entire field of human experience and activity. We also find a characteristic tendency towards psychological atomism: sensations are bits of perceived data, ideas are bits of meanings—each bit is as separate and impenetrable as a Newtonian physical atom. Even in complex combinations, the ideas are like beads, strung on the thread of association. The implication is that the way to understand anything is to break it down into its parts. Since a complex thought is the summation of very small units, we can understand its nature and origin by tracing it back to its constituents.

Coleridge was not the man to cling exclusively or permanently to any such psychology. His whole temperament was opposed to the analytical approach that sought to trace ideas back to original sensations and to resolve wholes into the mere sums of their constituent parts. In an early letter to Poole (16 October 1797) he wrote thus of his childhood:

. . . From my early reading of Faery Tales, and Genii &c &c—my mind had been habituated *to the Vast*—and I never regarded *my senses* in any way as the criteria of my belief. I regulated all my creeds by my conceptions, not by my *sight*—even at that age. . . . Those who have been led to the same truths step by step through the constant testimony of their senses, seem to me to want a sense which I possess. They contemplate nothing but *parts*—and all *parts* are necessarily little—and the Universe to them is but a mass of *little things*.[1]

In his aversion to 'little things' Coleridge shunned the division of experience into tiny units, such as single moments and sensations:

How opposite to nature and the fact to talk of the 'one moment' of Hume, of our whole being an aggregate of successive single sensations! Who ever felt a single sensation? Is not every one at the same moment conscious that there coexists a thousand others, a darker shade, or less light, even as when I fix my attention on a white house, or a gray, bare hill, or rather long ridge that runs out of sight each way.·. . . And what is a moment? Succession with interspace? Absurdity! It is evidently only the *licht-punct* in the indivisible undivided duration.[2]

Coleridge in this passage was anticipating more recent philosophy and psychology, such as Bergson's insistence upon the continuity of duration, and the *Gestalt* psychologists' emphasis

[1] *Collected Letters*, i, p. 354.
[2] *Anima Poetae*, pp. 86–87. (Written in 1804.)

upon the structure of the entire field of which associated objects are integral parts.

With this anti-atomistic approach Coleridge denied that it is possible to find the beginning of a unitary thing in terms of its constituents. In a note written in December 1801 we find him planning to write a refutation of the doctrine that origins may be discovered by analysis: 'N.B. to make a detailed comparison in the manner of Jerome Taylor between the searching for the first Cause of a Thing and the seeking the fountains of the Nile —so many streams, each with their junction &—&—at last, it all comes to a name.'[1] Coleridge is fond of this image of the river whose currents run together indistinguishably, or whose fountains are undiscoverable—he repeats it on a number of occasions.[2] In a similar passage he declares that we cannot trace our acts, volitions, and ideas back to their original sources:

For the same impossibility exists as to the first acts and movements of our own will—the farthest distance our recollection can follow the traces, never leads us to the first footmark—the lowest depth that the light of our Consciousness can visit even with a doubtful glimmering, is still at an unknown distance from the ground: and so, indeed, must it be with all Truths, and all modes of Being that can neither be counted, coloured, or delineated. Before and After, when applied to such Subjects, are but allegories, which the Sense or Imagination supplies to the Understanding.[3]

Mental states and processes are not to be exhaustively analysed into elementary constituents, for several reasons. First, complex wholes often result, not from the mere additive summation of their parts, but from creative fusion. A synthesis is more than a sum of its parts, a musical chord is more than the individual sounds, a boy's love is more than the kiss, the sweet words, and the warm silences. Especially is this true of imaginative creations; for imagination, according to Coleridge, is 'the power by which one image or feeling is made to modify many others, and by a sort of fusion to force many into one'.[4] Second,

---

[1] *Notebooks*, i, entry 1056 (Nov. 1801–Jan. 1802). By 'Jerome Taylor' Coleridge must have meant Jeremy Taylor.

[2] For example, see *Inquiring Spirit*, ed. Kathleen Coburn (New York: Pantheon Books, 1951), pp. 279–80, and *Biographia Literaria*, i, pp. 76–77.

[3] *Aids to Reflection* (London: Bell, 1913), pp. 43–44.

[4] 'Shakespeare as a Poet Generally', in *Criticism: the Major Texts*, ed. Walter Jackson Bate (New York: Harcourt, Brace, 1952), p. 388.

the thoughts and feelings are possessed by a mind that exists prior to sensation; the love is not any love, it is *the boy's* love, part and parcel of his being, expressive of his essence. 'What is a Thought', asks Coleridge, 'but another word for "I thinking"?'[1] Hence 'the mind' is 'part organ, part constituent, of all knowledge'.[2] Coleridge remarked how often perception is dependent on the preceding state of consciousness:

. . . What small and remote resemblances, what mere hints of likeness from some real external object, especially if the shape be aided by colour, will suffice to make a vivid thought consubstantiate with the real object, and derive from it an outward perceptibility. Even when we are broad awake, if we are in anxious expectation, how often will not the most confused sounds of nature be heard by us as articulate sounds? For instance, the babbling of a brook will appear for a moment the voice of a friend, for whom we are waiting. . . .[3]

Hence thought does not originate in sense; it arises within the mind under stimulus. To find its origin, in the radical sense, would be to discover the beginning of one's mind.

> Dark fluxion, all unfixable by thought,
> A phantom dim of past and future wrought.[4]

Third, the mind or self, including its more unfathomable contents, cannot be traced back to its origins because its roots are too deep and obscure in the unconscious. Coleridge, the visionary poet, was aware of the unconscious depths of the human mind. He insisted upon 'a full sharp distinction of Mind from Consciousness—the Consciousness being the narrow *Neck* of the Bottle'.[5]

Hence he believed that the deep subliminal self, the essential ego, must not be identified with the 'ideas' of the Lockian and Hartleian psychology. Opposing Hartley's tendency to regard emotion as secondary and derivative from association, he identified the ego with the more obscure and emotional phases of mental life:

By deep feeling we make our *ideas dim*, and this is what we mean by

---

[1] *Inquiring Spirit*, p. 30.
[2] *The Complete Works of Samuel Taylor Coleridge*, ed. W. G. T. Shedd (New York: Harper, 1853), v, p. 267.
[3] *Inquiring Spirit*, p. 53. (*The Friend*, 1809–10.)
[4] Coleridge's poem, *Self-Knowledge* (1832).
[5] *Inquiring Spirit*, p. 31.

our life, ourselves. I think of the wall. It is before me a distinct image. Here I necessarily think of the *idea* and the thinking *I* as two distinct and opposite things. Now let me think of *myself*, of the thinking being. The idea becomes dim, whatever it be—so dim that I know not what it is; but the feeling is deep and steady, and this I call *I*—identifying the percipient and the perceived.[1]

Coleridge here used 'idea', in the broad meaning of Locke and Hartley, as including images (in this case, the image of the wall). It was 'idea' and 'thought' in this inclusive sense that he regarded as a mere excrescence on the ego. 'In the moral being', he declared, 'lies the source of the intellectual.'[2]

Association seemed to him rather an emotional than an intellectual process. What links ideas or images together is the emotional stream that runs through them: 'I hold that association depends in a much greater degree on the recurrence of resembling states of Feeling, than on Trains of Idea . . . and if this be true, Hartley's system totters. . . . I almost think, that Ideas *never* recall Ideas, as far as they are Ideas—any more than Leaves in a forest create each other's motion. The Breeze it is that runs through them—it is the Soul, the state of Feeling.'[3] This emotional current accounts for 'the streamy nature of association which thinking curbs and rudders'.[4] The 'function' of 'acts of thought and attention', he believed, 'is to control, determine and modify the phantasmal chaos of association'.[5]

In contrast, Hartley declared: 'I have endeavoured to shew . . . that all reasoning, as well as affection, is the mere result of association.'[6] In thus subordinating both emotion and reason to the association of ideas, he was, according to Coleridge, guilty of a double error. First, he mistook the process by which association comes about. What determines the association of ideas is not the temporal or spatial contiguity of the original sensations (as Hartley wrongly supposed) so much as a pervasive emotional current which connects and joins together the thoughts or images. Second, the thinking process, which 'curbs and rudders' the stream of associations, was wrongly interpreted by Hartley as the mere by-product of association. Writing to Poole

---

[1] *Anima Poetae*, pp. 12–13. (Jan. 1801.)   [2] *Inquiring Spirit*, p. 29.
[3] *Collected Letters*, ii, p. 961. (To Robert Southey, 7 Aug. 1803.)
[4] *Anima Poetae*, p. 46.   [5] *Biographia Literaria*, i, p. 81.
[6] David Hartley, *Observations on Man*, sixth edition (London: Thomas Tegg and Son, 1834), First Book, prop. xcix. (First edition, 1749.)

(23 March 1801) Coleridge denied that the mind is 'a lazy Looker-on on an external world', remarking that 'any system built on the passiveness of the mind must be false, as a system'.[1] That he regarded Hartley's psychology as just such a system is made clear by many passages in the *Biographia Literaria*. From this kind of theory, he alleged, it 'results inevitably, that the will, the reason, and the judgement, and the understanding, instead of being the determining causes of association, must needs be represented as its *creatures*, and among its mechanical *effects*'.[2] These two criticisms constitute his most profound objections to Hartley's system.

Wordsworth must have learned a great deal about the associational psychology from his friend, at first in enthusiastic praise, but soon in disparagement. In a letter which berates Hartley (16 March 1801) Coleridge mentions a manuscript in which he criticizes Hobbes, Locke, and Hume. 'I am *confident*', he says, 'that I can prove that the Reputation of these three men has been wholly unmerited, and I have in what I have already written traced the whole history of the causes that effected this reputation *entirely to Wordsworth's satisfaction*.'[3] Similarly, in an early version of his poem *Dejection* (contained in a letter to Sotheby, 19 July 1802), Coleridge addressed to Wordsworth his conviction that the mind, contrary to Locke and Hartley, is far from being 'a lazy Looker-on on an external world':

> O Wordsworth! we receive but what we give,
> And in our Life alone does Nature live:
> Our's is her Wedding-garment, our's her Shroud!
> And would we aught behold of higher Worth
> Than that inanimate cold World *allow'd*
> To the poor loveless ever-anxious Crowd,
> Ah! from the Soul itself must issue forth
> A Light, a Glory, a fair luminous cloud
>   Enveloping the Earth!
> And from the Soul itself must there be sent
> A sweet and pow'rful Voice, of it's own Birth,
> Of all sweet Sounds the Life and Element![4]

[1] *Collected Letters*, ii, p. 709.   [2] *Biographia Literaria*, i, p. 76.
[3] *Collected Letters*, ii, p. 707. Latter italics mine.
[4] Ibid. ii, p. 817.

This poem, written in a mood of dejection, expresses the two thoughts, first, that in our life alone does nature live, and second, that from the soul must issue forth a light that envelops and transforms natural appearances. In a subsequent letter to Sotheby (10 September 1802) Coleridge retracts the first thought while re-expressing the second: 'Nature has her proper interest; and he will know what it is, who believes and feels, that every Thing has a Life of it's own, and that we are all *one Life*. A Poet's Heart and Intellect should be *combined, intimately* combined and *unified*, with the great appearances in Nature—and not merely held in solution and loose mixture with them. . . .'[1]

That Wordsworth agreed with this particular remark of Coleridge is evident from many passages in his poetry, as, for example, his statement that the poet should preserve

> A balance, an ennobling interchange
> Of action from without and from within;
> The excellence, pure function, and best power
> Both of the object seen, and eye that sees.[2]

Imagination can build up 'greatest things From least suggestions',[3] and even in sensory experience we 'half create' as well as 'perceive'.[4] In words that recall his friend's poem, *Dejection*, Wordsworth declared

> The mind is lord and master—outward sense
> The obedient servant of her will.[5]

That this conviction was not a transient one is indicated by lines that Wordsworth wrote as late as 1845:

> Minds that have nothing to confer
> Find little to perceive.[6]

But he never shared Coleridge's belief, as stated in *Dejection*, that nature, when unredeemed by imagination, is an 'inanimate cold world'. For Wordsworth the outer world pulsates with life and beauty.

Otherwise Coleridge and Wordsworth must have reached substantial agreement in converse with each other, not entirely

---

[1] *Collected Letters*, ii, p. 864.   [2] *Prelude*, XIII. 375–8.
[3] Ibid. XIV. 101–2.   [4] *Tintern Abbey*, 106–7.
[5] *Prelude*, XII. 222–3.
[6] 'Yes! thou art fair,' *Poetical Works*, ii. 35.

rejecting associationism, but modifying and subordinating it. This coincidence in their beliefs is indicated by the following address of Wordsworth to his friend (in which he borrows from the latter the image of the river that cannot be traced to its sources):

> Who knows the individual hour in which
> His habits were first sown, even as a seed?
> Who that shall point as with a wand and say
> 'This portion of the river of my mind
> Came from yon fountain?' Thou, my Friend! art one
> More deeply read in thy own thoughts; to thee
> Science appears but what in truth she is,
> Not as our glory and our absolute boast,
> But as a succedaneum, and a prop
> To our infirmity. No officious slave
> Art thou of that false secondary power
> By which we multiply distinctions, then
> Deem that our puny boundaries are things
> That we perceive, and not that we have made.
> To thee, unblinded by these formal arts,
> The unity of all hath been revealed,
> And thou wilt doubt, with me less aptly skilled
> Than many are to range the faculties
> In scale and order, class the cabinet
> Of their sensations, and in voluble phrase
> Run through the history and birth of each
> As of a single independent thing.
> Hard task, vain hope, to analyse the mind,
> If each most obvious and particular thought,
> Not in a mystical and idle sense,
> But in the words of Reason deeply weighed,
> Hath no beginning.[1]

Wordsworth thus shared Coleridge's belief that it is vain to search for the beginning of a thing, especially of a thought, and that the analysis of complexes into their components, which are regarded as ultimate and exhaustive of the whole, is a blind and servile procedure. The 'puny boundaries' of analytical reason ('that false secondary power') are not things that we perceive, but things that we have made falsely and artificially. In reality, there are no such distinct and elementary components. If there

---

[1] *Prelude*, II. 206–32.

ever were such parts, they have been merged and lost in the
unity of the whole, just as the various streams in a river inter-
mingle.

Especially significant in the quotation is Wordsworth's emphasis upon the unity of consciousness. A particular thought
has no beginning, because it is rooted in the mind, an integer
to itself, which is implicated in each mental process. To find the
beginning would be to find the origin of the mind itself, but
this can never be done since the sources of the human psyche
can be traced back indefinitely, or are not sufficiently distinct
to be traced. In this very fundamental conception of the unity
of the mind, the two poets agree. Coleridge must either have
confirmed his friend's independent point of view or else must
have converted him. In any event, we have this tribute to
Coleridge's wisdom, which clearly impressed Wordsworth.

5. *Idealism and Transcendentalism*

The development of Coleridge's thought during the early
period of his friendship with Wordsworth (1797–1805) had a
dual aspect: negatively, it was a movement away from necessitarianism and associationism; positively, it was a movement
towards philosophical idealism and transcendentalism. So far we
have traced the negative movement—it is now time to turn to
the positive.

By 'idealism' I mean the theory that ultimate reality is mental
or spiritual. Related to idealism is the doctrine of transcendentalism. This is the theory of knowledge that emphasizes
the intuitive or *a priori* above the empirical. For instance, Plato's
forms, Descartes's innate ideas, and Kant's *a priori* ideas and
categories, are all 'transcendental' in the sense that they pre-
dicate or imply non-experiential factors in knowledge.

Even during the period of his greatest devotion to Hartley,
Coleridge appears to have rejected a purely sensationistic and
empirical account of the origin of our ideas. In a poem admired
by Wordsworth, *The Destiny of Nations* (1796), Coleridge spoke
of the inner voice that directed Joan of Arc:

> She went forth alone
> Urged by the indwelling angel-guide, that oft
> With dim inexplicable sympathies

Disquieting the heart, shapes out Man's course
To the predoomed adventure.

In the same poem, Coleridge indicated that the body's report
of external things must be interpreted symbolically:

All that meets the bodily sense I deem
Symbolic, one mighty alphabet
To infant minds; and we in this low world
Placed with our backs to bright reality,
That we might learn with young untroubled ken
The substance from the shadow.

This adaptation of Plato's parable of the cave suggests a different attitude towards the senses from that conveyed by Hartley's
empiricism.

A Memorandum Notebook, written by Coleridge between
the spring of 1795 and the spring or summer of 1798, contains
several notations of an idealistic or transcendentalist drift. Following a quotation from the neo-Platonic mystic Jacob Boehme,
the following entry (written in September or October 1796)
appears:

. . . Certainly, there are strange things in the other World, and so
there are in all the immediate Preparations to it; and a little *Glimpse*
of Heaven, a minute's conversing with an angel, any ray of God, any
communication from the Spirit of Comfort which God gives to his
servants in strange and unknown manners, are infinitely far from
Illusions; and they shall then be understood by us, when we feel them,
and when our new and strange needs shall be refreshed by such
unusual Visitations.[1]

Thus when Coleridge first became a close friend of Wordsworth he believed that certain mental states should be explained
partially at least by transcendental factors.

In the ensuing months his idealism became explicit. He was
quick to renounce Hartley's theory of physical vibrations and
to seek an alternative interpretation in Berkeley's metaphysics.
As early as December 1796 he announced in a letter to Thelwall 'I am a Berkeleian', and he repeated these words in a letter
to Southey (July 1797) written during his first intimacy with
Wordsworth.[2] When Hazlitt visited the Lake poets in January

---

[1] *Notebooks*, i, entry 186.
[2] *Collected Letters*, i, pp. 278, 335. See also Lawrence Hanson, *The Life of
Samuel Taylor Coleridge: The Early Years* (New York: Russell & Russell, 1962),
pp. 298–300.

1798 Coleridge spoke of Berkeley with great enthusiasm. Declared Hazlitt: 'I had heard a great deal of his powers of conversation, and was not disappointed. In fact, I never met with anything at all like them, either before or since. I could easily credit the accounts which were circulated of his holding forth to a large party of ladies and gentlemen, an evening or two before, on the Berkeleian Theory, when he made the whole material universe look like a transparency of fine words. . . .'[1] According to Hazlitt's narrative, Coleridge also referred to Berkeley's *Essay on Vision* 'as a masterpiece of analytical reasoning', and was angry at Samuel Johnson for kicking a stone in an attempt to confute Berkeley's idealism. Finally, in May 1798, Coleridge paid the ultimate compliment to the object of his devotion by bestowing upon his second son the baptismal name of 'Berkeley', just as he had earlier given the name 'Hartley' to his eldest child.

Coleridge's philosophical interests, however, were too overflowing to be contained within any one philosophical system. During the very period of his enthusiasm for Berkeley he was also 'sunk in Spinoza'.[2] More significant in the long run than the influence of either Spinoza or Berkeley was that of Kant, Plato, and the neo-Platonic mystics and divines. Southey wrote in 1808 of Coleridge's philosophical development: 'Hartley was ousted by Berkeley, Berkeley by Spinoza, and Spinoza by Plato.'[3] If we add the name 'Kant' to Southey's list, we have a fair indication of Coleridge's deepest affiliations during the period of his close association with Wordsworth. But Southey's remark is misleading if it suggests that Coleridge's commitment to these philosophers was, at any time, exclusive, or that he entirely discarded one philosophical system before he embraced another.

During the deep and protracted studies of 1801–3 Coleridge formulated the main tenets of his mature philosophical creed, although the first detailed exposition did not appear until the publication of *The Friend* in 1809–10. The phrasing of his ideas was predominantly influenced by Kant, whose work he first deeply probed in the spring of 1801. Nevertheless, he declared

---

[1] 'My First Acquaintance with Poets', *Collected Works of William Hazlitt*, op. cit. xii, pp. 266–7.

[2] *Collected Letters*, i, p. 534. (To Robert Southey, 30 Sept. 1799.)

[3] Letter to William Taylor, 11 July 1808, quoted in Hanson, op. cit., p. 295.

over and over again that the main tenets of his philosophy had
been foreshadowed in his earlier reading of Plato, the neo-
Platonists, and the English divines of the seventeenth century.
Writing in 1804 he said: 'In the preface of my metaphysical
works, I should say, "Once for all, read Kant, Fichte, etc., and
then you will trace, or, if you are on the hunt, track me." Why,
then, not acknowledge your obligations step by step? Because
I could not do so in a multitude of glaring resemblances without
a lie, for they had been mine, formed and full-formed, before
I ever heard of these writers.'[1] Whether or not Coleridge was
understating the influence of the German philosophers, his
transcendentalist convictions were formulated early enough to
have greatly influenced *The Prelude*, *The Excursion*, and such
important poems as the *Ode to Duty* and the *Ode on the Intimations of Immortality*.

The basic notion of Coleridge's transcendentalism is that
man is equipped with a faculty of 'pure Reason, which dictates
unconditionally',[2] and which 'affirms truths which no sense could
perceive, nor experiment verify, nor experience confirm'.[3] He
distinguished between understanding as the faculty which deals
analytically and discursively with the data of sensation, and
Reason as the organ of insight into spiritual realities. Understanding is 'a faculty of thinking and forming judgments on the
notices furnished by sense'. It has a legitimate field of employ-
ment in measurement, analysis, classification, and prudential
calculation, but it errs if it encroaches on the higher domain of
Reason. Not absolute but relative, it is 'possessed in very different degrees by different persons'. It varies in its scope and
reliability as experience itself varies; and in emphasizing the
differences between things it tends to be divisive. Reason, as the
faculty of intuition and synthesis, is 'the knowledge of the laws
of the whole considered as one'. It is absolute and universal,
being 'the same in all men' and 'not susceptible of degree'. Its
core and essence is man's moral being, as expressed in free will,
faith, and conscience.[4] In the name of Reason, Coleridge objected
to a utilitarian and hedonistic morality, because it is not based

[1] *Anima Poetae*, op. cit., pp. 89–90.
[2] *Collected Letters*, iii, p. 146. (To George Beaumont, c. 14 Dec. 1808.)
[3] *Aids to Reflection*, op. cit., aphorism viii.
[4] Cf. *The Friend*, in *Works*, ed. Shedd, ii, especially pp. 142–6, 164, 175–6.

upon that 'part of our nature which in all men may and ought to be the same,—in the conscience and the common sense'.[1]

Wordsworth—as I shall indicate at greater length in Chapter V—similarly distinguished between 'the grand and simple Reason'[2] and 'that false secondary power By which we multiply distinctions'.[3] Like Coleridge, he announced that men have 'One sense for moral judgments, as one eye For the sun's light'.[4] This phrasing is strikingly similar to Coleridge's later remark in *Aids to Reflection*: 'Reason indeed is much nearer to SENSE than to Understanding; for Reason . . . is a direct aspect of Truth, an inward Beholding, having a similar relation to the Intelligible or spiritual, as SENSE has to the material or phenomenal.'[5] In *The Convention of Cintra*, a political tract written in 1808, Wordsworth spoke of the 'dictates of paramount and infallible conscience'. Surely infallible dictates do not derive solely from the incomplete and fallible evidence of experience. In the last lines of *The Prelude*, Wordsworth addressed Coleridge directly:

> what we have loved
> Others will love, and we will teach them how;
> Instruct them how the mind of man becomes
> A thousand times more beautiful than the earth
> On which he dwells, above this frame of things. . . .
> In beauty exalted, as it is itself
> Of quality and fabric more divine.[6]

Thus Wordsworth proposed to join hands with Coleridge in promoting the point of view that both of them accepted. The outlook thus expressed must have rested upon a transcendental foundation. If the human mind is a thousand times more beautiful than the earth, if man's spiritual faculties are immeasurably more divine than the external world, presumably there must be some internal, supersensuous factors in knowledge.

Fortunately we are not left to this conjecture, since Wordsworth definitely announced that he was indebted to Coleridge for his conception of 'duty' and 'Reason'. The important passage in which this reference occurs[7] needs to be very carefully scrutinized, for it mentions also Wordsworth's change of opinion

---

[1] Cf. *The Friend*, in *Works*, ed. Shedd, ii, p. 286.   [2] *Prelude* (1805), XI. 123–4.
[3] *Prelude*, II. 216–17.   [4] Ibid. VIII. 671–2.
[5] *Aids to Reflection*, op. cit., p. 148.   [6] *Prelude*, XIV. 446–54.
[7] Quoted below, pp. 36–37.

in regard to pantheism. This alteration was subsequent to a similar reversal in the convictions of Coleridge. It is well known that the latter passed through a stage of incipient pantheism, as recorded in such early poems as *Religious Musings* and *The Eolian Harp*, and that this pantheistic tendency was later reinforced by a study of Spinoza. As Coleridge reflected more deeply, he felt that pantheism could not be reconciled with the reality of the individual human person. 'For a very long time . . .', he later explained, 'I could not reconcile personality with infinity; and my head was with Spinoza, though my whole heart remained with Paul and John.'[1] He believed that Spinoza's pantheistic monism implied the negation of all the determinations that go to make the individual, and that hence its basic premisses were mistaken. 'Did philosophy start with an *it is*', he commented, 'instead of an *I am*, Spinoza would be altogether true.'[2] The reality of the 'I' was undeniable, and hence pantheism had to be rejected.

When he finally abandoned his pantheistic faith he immediately tried to convert Wordsworth, but at first with no success. On 26 October 1803 he recorded in his notebook 'a most unpleasant dispute with Wordsworth and Hazlitt'. It appears that Coleridge used the argument from design in an attempt to convince Hazlitt and Wordsworth that nature, instead of being itself divine, is the handiwork of a transcendent God:

I spoke, I fear, too contemptuously; but they spoke so irreverently, so malignantly of the Divine Wisdom that it overset me. Hazlitt, how easily raised to rage and hatred self-projected! . . . But *thou*, dearest Wordsworth—and what if Ray, Derham, Paley have carried the observation of the aptitude of things too far, too habitually into pedantry? O how much worse pedantries! how few so harmless, with so much efficient good! Dear William, pardon pedantry in others, and avoid it in yourself, instead of scoffing and reviling at pedantry in good men and a good cause. . . . But, surely, always to look at the superficies of objects for the purpose of taking delight in their beauty, and sympathy with their real or imagined life, is as deleterious to the health and manhood of intellect as always to be peering and unravelling contrivance may be to the simplicity of the affection and the grandeur

---

[1] *Biographia Literaria*, i, p. 134.

[2] *Diary, Reminiscenses and Correspondence of Henry Crabb Robinson*, ed. Thomas Sadler (London: Macmillan, 1869), i, p. 400. Coleridge's emphasis upon 'I am' is like that of a modern existentialist.

and unity of the imagination. O dearest William! would Ray or Derham have spoken of God as you spoke of Nature?[1]

Coleridge is objecting to the view which he later denounced as 'the vague, misty, rather than mystic, confusion of God with the world, and the accompanying nature-worship, . . . the trait in Wordsworth's poetic works which I most dislike as unhealthful, and denounce as contagious'.[2] The opposition of Wordsworth to the argument from design was based on his profound belief in 'the one interior life' in which 'all beings live with god, themselves Are god'.[3] Obviously Coleridge was shocked by Wordsworth's scornful dismissal of the argument from design and by his readiness to speak of 'Nature' even more reverently than the deists spoke of God.

In the course of time, however, Coleridge did bring about a fundamental change in his friend's convictions. Although Wordsworth, like Coleridge himself, still believed in a 'mighty unity', he modified his earlier pantheistic ideas as a result of this influence:

> With such a theme,
> Coleridge! with this my argument, of thee
> Shall I be silent? O most loving Soul!
> Placed on this earth to love and understand,
> And from thy presence shed the light of love,
> Shall I be mute ere thou be spoken of?
> Thy gentle Spirit to my heart of hearts
> Did also find its way; and thus the life
> Of all things and the mighty unity
> In all which we behold, and feel, and are,
> Admitted more habitually a mild
> Interposition, and closelier gathering thoughts
> Of man and his concerns, such as become
> A human Creature, be he who he may!
> Poet, or destined for a humbler name;
> And so the deep enthusiastic joy,
> The rapture of the Hallelujah sent

[1] *Anima Poetae*, p. 29. John Ray's *Wisdom of God in the Creation* (1701), William Derham's *Physico-Theology* (1713), and William Paley's *Natural Theology* (1802) were standard expositions of 'the argument from design'.

[2] Thomas Allsop, *Letters, Conversations and Recollections of S. T. Coleridge*, third edition (London: Farrah, 1864), pp. 57–58. (Letter of 8 Aug. 1820.)

[3] *The Prelude*, ed. by Ernest de Selincourt, first edition (Oxford: Clarendon Press, 1926), p. 512.

From all that breathes and is, was chasten'd, stemm'd
And balanced by a Reason which indeed
Is reason; duty and pathetic truth;
And God and Man divided, as they ought,
Between them the great system of the world
Where Man is sphered, and which God animates.[1]

This is one of the most important passages among those confined to the 1805 version of *The Prelude*. It shows that Wordsworth not only recognized his indebtedness to Coleridge for
his interpretation of reason, duty, and truth, but that he passed
through two stages, pantheism and immanent theism.

The recognition that Wordsworth did change his mind is
prerequisite to a sound interpretation of his thought. An attempt
to force all of his poetry into a doctrinally consistent whole is
simply an effort at mutilation. The valid approach, which recognizes the rich variety of his thought and the unfolding nature of
his development, discloses a man in place of an effigy. Once we
have recognized the diversity of Wordsworth's poetry, we can
more readily correlate his growth with the changing philosophy
of Coleridge.

Both men may have overestimated the similarities between
their philosophical beliefs. Certainly there was a marked difference in temperament and this was reflected in a difference in
outlook. Coleridge was more visionary and romantic, Wordsworth more naturalistic and tough-minded. In course of time
they became aware of their differences and drifted apart. But it
would be a mistake to discount the evidence that I have reviewed
in this chapter.

We have examined the major ideas of Coleridge, with two
notable exceptions—his political and aesthetic theories. I have
chosen not to include political doctrines within the scope of the
present book, but I shall briefly discuss the aesthetic theories
of Coleridge and Wordsworth in subsequent chapters. So far in
our survey we have seen that Coleridge abandoned necessitarianism, revised associationism and subordinated it to an
intuitional psychology, embraced ideas of an idealistic and
transcendentalist import, and changed from pantheism to immanent theism. Wordsworth attained, with Coleridge's assist-
ance, to like convictions. Explicit statements to this effect and

[1] *Prelude* (1805), XIII. 246–68.

similarities between their views leave scarcely any room for doubt. These similarities should not be exaggerated. There were profound differences in temperament and stubborn differences in belief. If, as Wordsworth declared, they were 'twins almost' in mind and genius, they were far from identical; yet their community of heart and intellect, during the period of their greatest creativity, remains one of the undying wonders of literary history.

II. BOOKS

1. *The British Empiricists*

I N this chapter I shall try to play the role of a literary Sherlock Holmes, tracking down the sources of Wordsworth's ideas in the books that he must have known. So uncommunicative was he in regard to his philosophical reading that there are few direct clues, but enough can be discovered to throw considerable light on his intellectual affiliations.

Although less of a bibliophile than Coleridge, he was a great lover of books. He frequently borrowed from public libraries, and he also bought many volumes for his private collection. During his years at Cambridge University he did not lead a particularly studious life, but he did run through a good many works. Of his first residence at Cambridge he remarked:

> Not that I slighted books,—that were to lack
> All sense,—but other passions in me ruled.[1]

Concerning the later years at Cambridge he wrote:

> many books
> Were skimmed, devoured, or studiously perused,
> But with no settled plan.[2]

During his friendship with Coleridge he must have heard about many authors and been stimulated to examine a considerable number of their works. 'Our talk ran most upon books,' wrote Coleridge, 'and we were perpetually desiring each other to look at *this*, and to listen at *that*. . . .'[3] Writing in 1802 Wordsworth included books among the sources of his intellectual strength:

> Books, leisure, perfect freedom, and the talk
> Man holds with week-day man in the hourly walk
> Of the mind's business: these are the degrees
> By which true Sway doth mount; this is the stalk
> True Power doth grow on; and her rights are these.[4]

[1] *Prelude*, III. 367–8.
[2] Ibid. VI. 23–25.
[3] *Biographia Literaria*, i, p. 127.
[4] 'I grieved for Buonaparté', *Poetical Works*, iii. 110.

Such are some of the indications that books made a deep impression on his mind.[1]

What books did he take to heart? One answer is supplied by Arthur Beatty:

> Wordsworth was a reactionary in the fullest sense of the term, both in art and in his general theory of morals and conduct, and his reaction was toward those earlier authors and philosophers whose teachings and practice had been distorted by later practitioners. . . . In the sphere of art he revolts against poetic diction and harks back to Milton and Shakespeare and Chaucer; in doctrine he revolts against Rousseau and Godwin and appeals to Hartley, Locke, and the general tradition of English philosophy.[2]

This interpretation of Wordsworth as 'a poet of reaction'—an unromantic figure in a romantic generation—has made a deep impression on scholars. I shall begin this chapter by examining the relevant evidence as it pertains to philosophical influences.

Perhaps some indication of the poet's philosophical sympathies may be gleaned by consulting the list of books sold at an auction by the executors of his estate. The books listed totalled nearly three thousand volumes, including many on philosophy or religion.[3] The only major works by English empiricists were Sir Francis Bacon's *Two Books of the Proficience and Advancement of Learning*, and George Berkeley's *Alciphron*. In contrast, there was a considerable number of books on Platonism. Either Wordsworth never possessed the works of the empiricists, or he was not sufficiently attached to them to keep them until his death, or the books were withheld from the sale. At any rate, it is surprising that no philosophical work of Hobbes, Hume, Hartley, Godwin, or Priestley appeared in the catalogue. Included were two of Locke's minor works—*A Letter to the Right Reverend Lord Bishop of Worcester* (i.e. to Stillingfleet) and *Mr. Locke's Reply to the Right Reverend The Lord Bishop of Worcester's Answer to his Letter*. But these works are of more significance as contributions to the deistic controversy than as repositories of Locke's own philosophy. If, as Beatty maintains, the British Empirical tradition was the almost exclusive source

---

[1] See also *The Early Letters of William and Dorothy Wordsworth*, i, pp. 198, 228, and *Collected Letters of Samuel Taylor Coleridge*, i, pp. 490–1.

[2] Beatty, *William Wordsworth*, op. cit., p. 19.

[3] See 'Catalogue of the Rydal Mount Library', *Transactions of the Wordsworth Society*, No. 6 (Edinburgh, 1884), pp. 199–257.

of Wordsworth's philosophical affinities, it seems a bit surprising that it was not more adequately represented in the Catalogue of the Rydal Mount library.

We do know, however, that the Empirical tradition was strongly entrenched at Cambridge, and that Wordsworth must have been introduced to it during his student days. Some insight into the books that he might have read is afforded by Christopher Wordsworth, the poet's grand-nephew, in his study of Cambridge education. His list of 'Books on Moral Philosophy and Metaphysics' recommended or in use at the University indicates a scattered reading, the names of intuitionists and Platonists appearing beside those of empiricists.[1] But the Empirical tradition was predominant, and two books were especially favoured: 'Sir Isaac Newton had published his *Principia* in 1687, and John Locke his *Essay* in 1689:—which two works were to mould the mind of Cambridge for the coming century.'[2] In an excellent study of the poet's education, Ben Ross Schneider has emphasized the same two classics.[3]

The most influential philosophical works produced by Cambridge men during the eighteenth century were Paley's *Moral Philosophy* and Hartley's *Observations on Man*, both in the Lockian tradition. Since Paley's book was required reading for University examinations, Wordsworth must have perused it. Writing *c.* 1800, Hazlitt remarks that Wordsworth 'approves' of Paley's works;[4] on the other hand, an entry in Coleridge's notebook (quoted above, pp. 35–36) indicates that Wordsworth disliked Paley's argument from design.

Some indication of the poet's *general* reaction to English philosophy is to be found in a letter of 6 October 1844, in which he speaks of the philosophy of Kant, Fichte, and Schelling as 'dreary work'. 'However,' he adds, 'they have much of Plato in them, and for this I respect them; the English, with their devotion to Aristotle, have but half the truth; a sound Philosophy must contain both Plato and Aristotle.'[5] Wordsworth evidently was thinking not so much of these individual philosophers as

---

[1] *Scholae Academicae* (Cambridge University Press, 1877, reprinted 1910), pp. 121–2.   [2] Ibid., p. 2.
[3] *Wordsworth's Cambridge Education* (Cambridge University Press, 1957).
[4] *The Collected Works of William Hazlitt*, op. cit., iv, p. 277.
[5] Markham L. Peacock, Jr., *The Critical Opinions of William Wordsworth* (Baltimore: Johns Hopkins Press, 1950), p. 76.

the traditions that they symbolize. He must have been familiar
with the interpretation of Coleridge who, on several occasions,
maintained that Plato and Aristotle divide philosophy between
them, every man being either a Platonist or an Aristotelian,
or haply some combination of both. Plato, according to Coleridge, represents the more intuitive and idealistic strain, with
its transcendentalist doctrine of Ideas, and its attempt to reconcile reason and religion; whereas Aristotle is the father of
scientific empiricism, which is the intellectual source of materialism, associationist psychology, utilitarian ethics, and religious
scepticism.[1]

In criticizing the one-sidedness of British philosophy Wordsworth was obviously not referring to Coleridge's favourites
among British thinkers—the Divines and Platonists of the
seventeenth century, such as John Donne, Richard Baxter,
Ralph Cudworth, and Henry More—but rather to the main
tradition of British empiricism as represented by such philosophers as Locke and Hume and Hartley. He thought that this
'Aristotelian' tradition left out that 'half the truth' represented
by the Platonic tradition and, derivatively, by German transcendentalism. His remark suggests a view of the world which
seems to me the heart and core of his thought—that the truth
is not to be found in either inner vision or outward experience
alone, but in 'an ennobling interchange Of action from within
and from without'.[2]

We can quickly pass over some of the British philosophers.
Wordsworth, for example, referred to Bacon in eulogistic
terms,[3] but I can add nothing to Professor Potts's discussion
of Bacon's influence on the poet.[4] Coleridge's open hostility to
Hume seems to have been shared by Wordsworth. Discussing
the idea that there are 'no fixed principles in human nature' for
poetry to rest upon, Wordsworth appended the footnote: 'This
opinion seems actually to have been held by Adam Smith, the

[1] *The Philosophical Lectures of Samuel Taylor Coleridge*, ed. Kathleen Coburn
(New York: Philosophical Library, 1949), pp. 52–55; *Table Talk*, ed. T. Ashe
(London: Bell, 1884), pp. 99–100; and *Unpublished Letters of Samuel Taylor
Coleridge*, ed. Earl Leslie Griggs (Yale University Press, 1933), ii, pp. 264–5.

[2] *Prelude*, XIII. 375–6.

[3] See Peacock, *The Critical Opinions of William Wordsworth*, op. cit., pp. 179–80.

[4] Cf. Abbie Findlay Potts, *Wordsworth's Prelude* (Cornell University Press,
1953), pp. 372–9.

worst critic, *David Hume not excepted*, that Scotland, a soil to which this sort of weed seems natural, has produced.'[1] It is just possible, despite this disparaging reference to Hume, that the poet admired his philosophical writings, but since nobody has presented evidence to this effect, it will be unnecessary to consider the matter. I shall not discuss the question of Wordsworth's relation to Godwin, because others have done so fully, and critics agree that the positive influence of Godwin's *Political Justice* on the *Lyrical Ballads* and the later poetry was slight. It will suffice to quote from an essay which Wordsworth wrote in 1799 or thereabouts: 'I consider such books as Mr Godwyn's [*sic*], Mr Paley's and those of the whole tribe of authors of that class as impotent to all their intended good purposes. . . . All this is the consequence of an undue value set upon that faculty which we call reason. . . . These bald and naked reasonings are impotent over our habits, they cannot form them. . . . They contain no picture of human life, they *describe* nothing.'[2] However intense may have been Wordsworth's initial enthusiasm for *Political Justice*, he retained very little sympathy for Godwin or system-makers of his ilk. Let us now turn to writers that had a more lasting influence.

2. *Newton, Locke, and Berkeley*

The poet's reference to the statue of Newton is famous:

> . . . with his prism and silent face,
> The marble index of a mind for ever
> Voyaging through strange seas of Thought, alone.[3]

Even before he went to Cambridge, Wordsworth had conceived a romantic veneration for the name of Newton, and this emotion continued unabated throughout his life. He looked upon Newton's 'discoveries' as 'the grandest ever known',[4] but one suspects that it was less the scientist than the religious 'philosopher' that impressed him.

The Newtonian influence was inescapable, since it was not

[1] 'Essay, Supplementary to The Preface' (1815), fn. My italics.

[2] A fragment of this unpublished essay is contained in Dorothy Wordsworth's Goslar Notebook written at Dove Cottage, Grasmere. Quoted by Ben Ross Schneider, *Wordsworth's Cambridge Education*, op. cit., p. 233.

[3] *Prelude*, III. 61–63.

[4] James Patrick Muirhead, 'A Day with Wordsworth', *Blackwood's Magazine*, vol. 221 (June 1927), p. 741. (Remark of Wordsworth, 31 Aug. 1841.)

only regnant at Cambridge but part of the more general climate of opinion. By 1789 eighteen editions of the *Principia* and forty popularizations of the Newtonian theories had been published in England. Wordsworth's interest in physics and 'natural philosophy' was well represented in his library, and in this respect he was following the pattern of his age.

At first glance it appears unlikely that he could have been much influenced by Newton, since the connotations of the Newtonian theory seem uncongenial to romantic poetry. According to the prevalent interpretation Newton had furnished scientific proof that the universe is a perpetual-motion machine constructed by a kind of Divine Mechanic. (I have already pointed out that Wordsworth had a profound aversion for this Deistic notion.) In the external world, as it has come from the hands of the Creator, there are no sounds, no colours, no warmth, no odours, nothing but 'solid, massy, hard, impenetrable, movable particles' governed by uniform mathematical laws. All the vivid qualities of nature are merely our subjective reactions to the bustling of invisible atoms. Just as the tickle that a person feels when a feather grazes his hand is not in the feather but in his *reaction* to the feather, so all the beauty and the vividness of nature are not in the atoms but merely in the mind's reaction to the atoms. Writing of the implications of this theory, the philosopher E. A. Burtt has said:

. . . It was of the greatest consequence for succeeding thought that now the great Newton's authority was squarely behind that view of the cosmos which saw in man a puny, irrelevant spectator (so far as a being wholly imprisoned in a dark room can be called such) of the vast mathematical system whose regular motions according to mechanical principles constituted the world of nature. . . . The world that people had thought themselves living in—a world rich with color and sound, redolent with fragrance, filled with gladness, love and beauty, speaking everywhere of purposive harmony and creative ideals—was crowded now into minute corners in the brains of scattered organic beings. The really important world outside was a world, hard, cold, colorless, silent and dead; a world of quantity, a world of mathematically computable motions in mechanical regularity. The world of qualities as immediately perceived by man became just a curious and quite minor effect of that infinite machine, beyond.[1]

[1] E. A. Burtt, *The Metaphysical Foundations of Modern Physical Science* (New York: Harcourt, Brace, 1927), pp. 236–7.

If I read Wordsworth aright, his poetry was a passionate protest against this neutralization of nature. Newton and Locke,
when interpreted in this way, set the terms of Wordsworth's
problem, but could not supply the answer.

But this interpretation of Newton is misleading. Whatever
be the strict implications of his scientific theories, he did not
really believe in an 'inanimate cold world' without values or
qualities. As a religious man, he was convinced that the whole
natural universe is animated by an indwelling God. In the *Opticks* (Query 28) he maintained

that there is a Being incorporeal, living, intelligent, omnipresent, who
in infinite Space, as it were in his Sensory, sees the things themselves
intimately, and thoroughly perceives them, and comprehends them
wholly by their immediate presence to himself: Of which things the
Images only carried through the Organs of Sense into our little
Sensoriums, are there seen and beheld by that which in us perceives
and thinks. And though every true Step made in this Philosophy brings
us not immediately to the Knowledge of the first Cause, yet it brings
us nearer to it, and on that account is to be highly valued.

There is a similar passage at the end of the *Principia* in which
Newton speaks of 'ethereal spirits' and 'active principles' in
nature acting as agents of God in maintaining the natural order:
'If it were not for these Principles, the Bodies of the Earth,
Planets, Comets, Sun and all things in them, would grow cold
and freeze, and become inactive Masses; and all Putrefaction,
Generation, Vegetation and Life would cease, and the Planets
and Comets would not remain in their Orbs.'[1] In these passages
Newton is close to More, Cudworth, and the other Cambridge
Platonists, whom he admired.

His conception of subtle spirits and active principles in nature
seems to be echoed in a passage from *The Excursion* (written
in 1799 or before) in which Wordsworth affirms that 'To every
Form of being is assigned . . . An *active* Principle'.[2] In the same
passage 'the Soul of all the worlds' reminds one of Newton's
'Being incorporeal . . . in infinite Space'. Also reminiscent of
Newton is the language of *Tintern Abbey*:

[1] Newton, *Opticks*, reprint of fourth edition (London: Bell, 1931), p. 286.
These notions, which link Newton to the Cambridge Platonists, should be distinguished from his scientific theories.
[2] *Excursion*, IX. 1–3. (The opening lines of Book IX are to be found in a manuscript dating from 1798–9.)

A motion and a spirit, that impels
All thinking things, all objects of all thought,
And rolls through all things.

But Wordsworth could have derived these ideas from a number
of sources, such as Bruno and Spinoza.

Among the later British empiricists, George Berkeley maintained that the vivid qualitative features of the natural world are
genuinely real—much more real than Newton's atoms. One of
the Berkelian doctrines that inspired Coleridge and that may
have impressed Wordsworth was the notion that we '*see* God'
in the same way that we 'see a man'; that is to say, by means
of sense data (misleadingly called 'ideas' in Berkeley's terminology):

. . . It is plain that we do not see a man—if by *man* is meant that
which lives, moves, perceives, and thinks as we do—but only such
a certain collocation of ideas as directs us to think there is a distinct
principle of thought and motion, like to ourselves, accompanying and
represented by it. And after the same manner we see God: all the
difference is that, whereas some one finite and narrow assemblage of
ideas denotes a particular human mind, whithersoever we direct our
view, we do at all times see manifest tokens of the Divinity: everything we see, hear, feel, or otherwise perceive by Sense; being a sign
or effect of the power of God; as in our perception of those very
motions which are produced by men.[1]

This conception of sense data as 'the divine visual language'
was elaborated in Berkeley's *Alciphron*, a copy of which Wordsworth owned. The same conception was rendered into poetry
by Coleridge during the period of his closest intimacy with
Wordsworth:

For I was reared
In the great city, pent 'mid cloisters dim,
And saw naught lovely but the sky and stars.
But *thou*, my babe! shalt wander like a breeze
By lakes and sandy shores, beneath the crags
Of ancient mountain, and beneath the clouds,
Which image in their bulk both lakes and shores
And mountain crags; so shalt thou see and hear
The lovely shapes and sounds intelligible
Of that eternal language, which thy God

[1] Berkeley, *Principles of Human Knowledge*, § 148.

Utters, who from eternity doth teach
Himself in all, and all things in himself.[1]

In these quotations from Berkeley and Coleridge the sense of sacredness, which had traditionally been associated with the supernatural, has become attached to Nature itself.

The essence of the Wordsworthian revolution is precisely this transfer of the 'numinous' from the remote heavenly sphere to

> . . . the very world, which is the world
> Of all of us—the place where, in the end,
> We find our happiness, or not at all![2]

We can illustrate this revolution by typical quotations from Wordsworth's poetry:

> Listen! the mighty Being is awake,
> And doth with his eternal motion make
> A sound like thunder—everlastingly.[3]

> . . . Nature's self, which is the breath of God.[4]

> For feeling has to him imparted power
> That through the growing faculties of sense
> Doth like an agent of the one great Mind
> Create, creator and receiver both,
> Working but in alliance with the works
> Which it beholds.[5]

> . . . th' eternal spirit, he that has
> His life in unimaginable things
> And he who painting what he is in all
> The visible imagery of all the world.[6]

In combining a sensationist theory of knowledge with an immanent theism Berkeley may have contributed substantially to Wordsworth's religion of Nature. Whether the poet ever carefully studied Berkeley's works at first hand is immaterial, since Coleridge must have conveyed their import to him in conversations.

---

[1] *Frost at Midnight* (February 1798).
[2] *Prelude*, XI. 142–4.
[3] 'It is a beauteous evening,' *Poetical Works*, iii. 17.
[4] *Prelude* (1805), V. 221.   [5] *Prelude*, II. 255–60.
[6] *The Prelude*, ed. Ernest de Selincourt and Helen Darbishire, revised edition (Oxford University Press, 1959), p. 636.

His familiarity with, and favourable reaction to, the writings of Locke are implied by his remark in conversation: 'The influence of Locke's Essay was not due to its own merits, which are considerable; but to external circumstances. It came forth at a happy opportunity, and coincided with the prevalent opinions of the time. . . . The best of Locke's works, it seems to me, is that in which he attempts the least—his *Conduct of the Understanding*.'[1] In *The Vale of Esthwaite* (1787) and *An Evening Walk* (1788–9) Wordsworth uses Locke's famous metaphor of the *tabula rasa*, or mental tablet, on which sensation writes impressions. But in the later poetry this metaphor, implying the passivity of the human mind, no longer fits the strong and active role of our mental faculties as Wordsworth conceives them. The influence of other ideas of Locke, as distinguishable from those of Hartley, is hard to trace. Perhaps the most we can say is that Locke's 'historical plain method' contributed to the realistic strain in Wordsworth's poetry—its frequent matter-of-factness, its strong emphasis upon observation, its preoccupation with 'the laws of thought' and 'our intellectual constitution', its unadorned diction and avoidance of myths and classical allusions. As Basil Willey has pointed out:

[Locke's] doctrine which derived all our knowledge from sensation was capable of serving Wordsworth, who imbibed it through Hartley, as a philosophic sanction for his own deep-rooted instincts, and furnished him with at least a foundation for his conscious poetic theory. Wordsworth was working in the spirit and tradition of Locke when he rejected gaudy and inane phraseology and devoted his powers to the task of making verse 'deal boldly with substantial things.' And in a sense, moreover, Locke's 'new way of knowing by ideas,' his insistence that all that we can contemplate is mind-stuff, contained the implication (though Locke would not have welcomed it) that 'mind is incorrigibly poetical.'[2] . . . But, of course, much more than this was required before there could arise a theory of the imagination adequate to the dignity of poetry, and much had to be added to Locke's sensationalism before it could be pressed into the service of the creative power. Above all, there was required the conviction that the 'in-

[1] *Prose Works*, ed. Grosart, iii, pp. 461–2. Locke's *Conduct of the Understanding* is a restatement, with some additions, of the more famous *Essay Concerning the Human Understanding*.

[2] George Santayana, *Some Turns of Thought in Modern Philosophy* (Cambridge University Press, 1933), p. 22.

animate cold world' of the mechanical philosophy was not the whole reality, that there was a closer bond between the mind and nature than the old dualism could conceive, and that 'Truth' was not given to the naked Reason, but was constituted, in moments of impassioned vigilance, by the whole soul of man

> Working but in alliance with the works
> Which it beholds.[1]

3. *Hartley and Associational Psychology*

The question of the influence of David Hartley is crucial to our study. Arthur Beatty, as we have noted, maintains that Hartley's *Observations on Man* is the main source of Wordsworth's doctrines throughout his poetical maturity; but the evidence to this effect, apart from the poet's own works, is slight. We are told by Beatty that Godwin had been influenced by Hartley and that Wordsworth was for a time a disciple of Godwin. Quite true—but Wordsworth's attachment to Godwin was short-lived. We are informed that Hazlitt, while under the spell of Hartley, visited Wordsworth and Coleridge in the summer of 1798 and engaged in philosophical discussions. But this evidence merely indicates that Wordsworth knew something about Hartley—a point that no one will dispute. Again we are told that Coleridge was a devotee of Hartley during his intimacy with Wordsworth. But the evidence that I have reviewed in Chapter I indicates that Coleridge, even in his most Hartleian period, was an eclectic thinker; that his influence was soon turned away from Locke and Hartley and directed towards transcendentalism; and that Wordsworth appears to have been swept along in the same current.

There is good reason to suppose that Wordsworth must have learned about Hartley during his years at the University. Schneider, in his study of the poet's Cambridge education, comments on Hartley:

I cannot prove that he was commonly read by undergraduates of Wordsworth's day. Nevertheless, John Jebb, who exerted a powerful influence on the liberal-minded population of Cambridge, was a devout disciple of Hartley, and Hartley is mentioned in the *Cambridge*

---

[1] Basil Willey, *The Seventeenth Century Background* (London: Chatto & Windus, 1949), pp. 294–5. (The final quotation is from *Prelude*, II. 259–60.)

University Calendar for 1802 as a subject of college lectures and of disputations for the B.A. degree. It is therefore likely that most of the undergraduates knew of his existence and probably of his famous theory of association.[1]

The poet's grand-nephew, Christopher Wordsworth, in tracing the studies of Cambridge men, also remarks:

Towards the end of the last century, Hartley was considered a great light among philosophical minds at Cambridge. He was a contemporary of Hume and a fellow-follower of Locke. His system (which was based on physiology) gathered up the floating materialism current at Cambridge, and was for a time adopted by Coleridge while he was still at the University, as well as by Priestley and other Necessitarians and Unitarians.[2]

But nowhere in this work does the author mention any connexion between Hartley and his grand-uncle.

Wordsworth himself refers to Hartley in a letter to Richard Sharp written 27 September 1808. The poet is discussing the limited protection provided by the Copyright Law:

The law, as it now stands, merely consults the interest of the useful drudges in Literature, or of flimsy and shallow writers, whose works are upon a level with the taste and knowledge of the age; while men of real power, who go before their age, are deprived of all hope of their families being benefited by their exertions. Take, for instance, in Philosophy, Hartley's book upon Man, how many years did it sleep in almost entire oblivion! What sale had Collins' Poems during his lifetime, or during the fourteen years after his death, and how great has been the sale since? The product of it, if secured to his family, would have been an independence to them.[3]

This quotation cannot be accurately understood apart from its context. To illustrate his contention that a copyright runs for too short a time (twenty-eight years) Wordsworth needed to cite worthy writers who had been unappreciated during their lifetime, who were neglected for some time after their death, whose books finally came into public favour, and whose families remained in distress. Obviously not many such examples would occur to his mind. Can we attach any large significance to

    [1] *Wordsworth's Cambridge Education*, op. cit., p. 109 fn.
    [2] *Scholae Academicae*, op. cit., p. 123.
    [3] *Letters: The Middle Years*, ed. E. de Selincourt. (To Richard Sharp, 27 Oct. 1808.)

the mention of Hartley, who happened to be an appropriate example? Collins is also mentioned, but his influence upon Wordsworth does not appear to have been great.

If Hartley did furnish the lasting foundation for Wordsworth's outlook upon life, it is strange that the poet did not mention him on any other occasion of which we have record. There is no other mention of Hartley in Wordsworth's *Letters* or *Prose Works*. Henry Crabb Robinson, who knew both Coleridge and Wordsworth intimately from 1810 throughout most of the subsequent years, refers to Hartley only once in his *Diary and Reminiscences*; and this single reference states that Coleridge, in 1810, was opposed to both Locke and Hartley.[1] The omission is significant, because Robinson faithfully recorded Wordsworth's ideas upon a considerable number of subjects, and almost certainly would have known the poet's main allegiance. Even more significant is the negative evidence in Coleridge's *Biographia Literaria* (published 1817). Chapters V and VI contain a denunciation of Hartley and associationism. A half-dozen of the subsequent chapters are devoted to Coleridge's most complete criticism of Wordsworth. What would be more natural, if Wordsworth were at that time a devout Hartleian, than to mention this as one of his faults? In view of the previous attack upon Hartley it is very probable that Coleridge would have done so.

Another writer who must have known about Wordsworth's philosophical affinities was John Wilson ('Christopher North'), one of the important critics of the period. When he was only seventeen years old, Wilson wrote Wordsworth an admiring letter to which the poet warmly responded. Seven years later he again wrote about Wordsworth's poetry, this time in a letter to a magazine, *The Friend*, signing himself 'Mathetes'. This second letter stimulated Wordsworth to answer with one of his important prose utterances, *Reply to Mathetes* (1808–10). From 1809 onwards Wilson lived at Elleray, an estate on the banks of Windermere, and became a close friend and companion of the Wordsworth household. Finally, he contributed an article to *Blackwood's Edinburgh Magazine* (December 1818) in which

[1] *Blake, Coleridge, Wordsworth, Lamb, etc., being Selections from the Remains of Henry Crabb Robinson*, ed. Edith J. Morley (Manchester University Press, 1922), p. 36.

he characterized Wordsworth's creed as a 'contemplative Platonism'. The Wordsworthian doctrines, he went on to say, are 'at variance with the philosophy at present most fashionable in this country', which is 'directed chiefly towards the laws of intellect and association'.[1] This essay is flatly opposed to Beatty's sweeping generalization that Wordsworth from 1797 until his death was a follower of Hartley and the associationist psychology.

The most telling evidence outside of his poetry that Wordsworth adhered to associationism is to be found in the famous Preface to the *Lyrical Ballads*. Here he states that his purpose is 'above all' to make 'the incidents and situations' of common life 'interesting by tracing in them, truly though not ostentatiously, the primary laws of our nature: chiefly, as far as regards the manner in which we associate ideas in a state of excitement'. This Preface, both in the 1800 version and the 1802 revision, contains other unmistakably associationist language. Finally, Beatty has established the fact that Wordsworth employed the language of associationism in a good many passages of the poetry.

The just conclusion from all this evidence, including the data I have reviewed in Chapter I, is that Wordsworth combined the ideas of Locke and Hartley with other strains of thought. He adhered, not to Hartley pure and simple, but 'Hartley transcendentalized by Coleridge, and at once modified and exalted by Wordsworth's own mystical experience'.[2] Convinced of the great value of the sensory experience of nature, he tried to cling to the Associational psychology, but his growing impulse towards transcendentalism could not be fitted into the confines of the Lockian tradition. This will be evident from subsequent chapters.

4. *Shaftesbury*

Among the writers who must have influenced Wordsworth was Anthony Ashley Cooper, the third Earl of Shaftesbury (1671–1713). An early edition of his works was in the Rydal Mount library. In the 'Essay Supplementary to the Preface'

---

[1] *Blackwood's Edinburgh Magazine*, vol. 4 (Dec. 1818), pp. 257–8.
[2] *The Prelude*, ed. E. de Selincourt and H. Darbishire, op. cit., p. lxix.

(1815) Wordsworth refers to him as 'an author at present unjustly depreciated'.

As the grandson of the first Earl, who had been Locke's friend and patron, Shaftesbury was educated under the philosopher's supervision. He loved the classics, Plato, Aristotle, Plotinus, and the Stoics, and he introduced into English thought the typical Greek view, that beauty and goodness are fundamentally akin. 'Virtue', he said, 'is no other than the love of beauty and order in society.'[1] This 'love of order' is inherent in the human constitution, and is therefore not to be explained by Locke's derivation of all ideas from experience. Wordsworth virtually repeats the words of Shaftesbury when he declares:

> The love of order is a Sentiment
> Inherent in the mind.[2]

Moral goodness consists in the proper harmony and balance of our mental faculties which inwardly reflect the harmony and order of nature. Just as we respond aesthetically to sensory beauty, so we respond morally to spiritual beauty. The soul, he declares, 'must needs find a beauty and a deformity as well in actions, minds and tempers, as in figures, sounds or colours'.[3]

In developing this theory Shaftesbury insists that there is an 'eye of the mind', or visionary power, akin to the bodily eye:

The mind, which is the spectator or auditor of other minds, can not be without its eye and ear; so as to discern proportion, distinguish sound, and scan each sentiment or thought which comes before it. . . . It feels the soft and harsh, the agreeable and disagreeable, in the affections; and finds a foul and fair, a harmonious and a dissonant as really and truly here, as in any musical numbers, or in the outward forms or representations of sensible things. Nor can it withold its admiration and ecstasy, its aversion and scorn, any more in what relates to one than to the other of these subjects.[4]

This idea that there is a 'moral sense', akin to the sense of beauty, is the heart of Shaftesbury's conception of morality.

Whether by accident or deliberate design, Wordsworth

---

[1] Shaftesbury, *Characteristics* (London: 1732), ii, p. 75. (I have modernized the spelling and punctuation.)

[2] *The Prelude*, ed. E. de Selincourt and H. Darbishire, pp. 612–13.

[3] *Characteristics*, ii. 43.

[4] Ibid., p. 29.

appears to be echoing Shaftesbury in a number of passages. He uses such phrases as 'my inward eye', the 'eye of love', 'an eye . . . which spake perpetual logic to my soul', 'a quiet eye That broods and sleeps on his own heart'; and he contrasts this spiritual faculty with 'the bodily eye', 'outward sense', and the 'fleshly ear'. It is characteristic of both Wordsworth and Shaftesbury that the spiritual eye probes not only the moral depths of life but the profounder meanings of nature:

> . . . with an eye made quiet by the power
> Of harmony, and the deep power of joy,
> We see into the life of things.[1]

> Resolving into one great faculty
> Of being bodily eye and spiritual need,
> The converse which he holds is limitless;
> Not only with the firmament of thought,
> But nearer home he looks with the same eye
> Through the entire abyss of things.[2]

> I seemed about this time to gain clear sight
> Of a new world—a world, too, that was fit
> To be transmitted, and to other eyes
> Made visible; as ruled by those fixed laws
> Whence spiritual dignity originates.[3]

> . . . living things, and things inanimate,
> Do speak, at Heaven's command, to eye and ear,
> And speak to social reason's inner sense,
> With inarticulate language.[4]

The phrase 'social reason's inner sense' corresponds very aptly to Shaftesbury's view that the virtuous man combines social sympathy with reason. To possess the social affections is, in the words of Shaftesbury, 'to live according to Nature and the Dictates and Rules of supreme Wisdom'.

The ancient phrase, 'to live according to Nature', takes on a religious and cosmological meaning in Shaftesbury. Sharply rejecting the theory of a mechanical universe, he maintains that

---

[1] *Tintern Abbey*, ll. 47–49. *Poetical Works*, ii. 259.
[2] *The Prelude*, ed. E. de Selincourt and H. Darbishire, p. 575.
[3] *Prelude*, XIII. 369–73.   [4] *Excursion*, IV. 1204–7.

there is a Spirit diffused through all things, and that the human soul should blend harmoniously with the Universal Soul. He thus addresses the God in nature: 'Thee, the All-True, and Perfect, who hath thus communicated thy-self more immediately to us, so as in some manner to inhabit within our Souls; Thou who art Original Soul, diffusive, vital in all, inspiriting the Whole. . . . How glorious is it to contemplate him, in this noblest of his Works apparent to us, The System of the Bigger World!'[1] The resemblance to Wordsworth's more pantheistic sentiments is obvious. When the poet speaks of the 'sense sublime Of something far more deeply interfused', or 'the one interior life That lives in all things', or 'A soul divine that we participate', he is far closer to Shaftesbury than to Locke or Hartley.

Both poet and philosopher share the sense of 'a mighty unity' that binds together men and animals and material objects. In a typical passage Shaftesbury declares:

All things in this world are united. For as the branch is united with the tree, so is the tree as immediately with the earth, air, and water, which feed it. As much as the fertile mould is fitted to the tree, as much as the strong and upright trunk of the oak or elm is fitted to the twining branches of the vine or ivy; so much are the very leaves, the seeds, and fruits of these trees fitted to the various animals; these again to one another, and to the elements where they live, and to which they are, as appendices, in a manner fitted and joined, as either by wings for the air, fins for the water, feet for the earth, and by other correspondent inward parts of a more curious frame and texture. Thus in contemplating all on earth, we must of necessity view all in one, as holding to one common stock.[2]

Similarly Wordsworth felt that all things in nature are 'like workings of one mind, the features Of the same face, blossoms upon one tree'.[3]

It should now be clear why he retained his respect for Shaftesbury at a time when the latter had lost his main hold on British thought. The basic creed of both men is the oneness of sense and spirit, the natural goodness of man, the presence of God in nature, and the harmony of things with one another.

---

[1] *Characteristics*, ii. 370.
[2] Ibid., ii. 287.
[3] *Prelude*, VI. 636–7.

E

5. *Rousseau*

Among the romantic spirits that responded to the influence of Shaftesbury was Jean Jacques Rousseau (1712–78). Shaftesbury's *An Inquiry Concerning Virtue* had been translated into French and Rousseau owned a copy of this translation. He also imbibed the ideas of Shaftesbury indirectly through the writings of Voltaire, Diderot, d'Holbach, and other French writers.

The extent to which Rousseau in turn may have influenced Wordsworth is not easy to determine. Émile Legouis contends that the poet is intellectually 'a son of Rousseau'.[1] George McLean Harper, the poet's biographer, also declares: 'Rousseau it is, far more than any other man of letters, either of antiquity or of modern times, whose works have left their trace in Wordsworth's poetry.'[2] Rousseau's influence has likewise been pointed out by Joseph Warren Beach and recently by Herbert Lindenberger.[3] But it would appear from the available evidence that the extent of this influence is questionable.

We can be sure that Wordsworth was familiar with the works of Rousseau. *Émile* and the *Confessions* were among the books in the Rydal Mount library. In his *Descriptive Sketches* (1791) and the *Letter to the Bishop of Llandaff* (1793) the youthful Wordsworth used the language of Rousseau to express his radical sentiments. Also in the Preface to *The Borderers* and in *The Convention of Cintra* he mentions Rousseau by name. During the revolutionary period in France the poet must have discussed Rousseau with his philosophically minded friend, Michel Beaupuy. Moreover, Godwin was a great admirer of Rousseau, and Wordsworth fell under the spell of Godwin.

This evidence indicates an early familiarity with Rousseau, but it is hard to demonstrate a lasting admiration. The conclusion of the well-known sonnet, 'Great men have been among us' (1802), indicates a generally low estimate of French writers. Comparing the England of the age of Milton with modern France, Wordsworth declares:

---

[1] *The Early Life of William Wordsworth* (London: Dent, 1921), pp. 54–67.

[2] *William Wordsworth*, revised edition (New York: Russell & Russell, 1960), i, p. 84.

[3] Cf. Beach, *The Concept of Nature in Nineteenth-Century English Poetry* (New York: Macmillan, 1936), and Lindenberger, *On Wordsworth's 'Prelude'* (Princeton University Press, 1963).

France, 'tis strange
Hath brought forth no such souls as we had then.
Perpetual emptiness! unceasing change!
No master spirit, no determined road;
But equally a want of books and men!

In *The Convention of Cintra* (1808) Wordsworth similarly denounced 'the pestilential philosophism of France' and coupled
Rousseau's name with that of Voltaire, whom he despised: 'The
Spaniards are a people with imagination: and the paradoxical
reveries of Rousseau, and the flippancies of Voltaire, are plants
which will not naturalize in the country of Calderon and Cer-
vantes'.[1] In the face of this over-reaction against French thought,
it is impossible to maintain that the mature Wordsworth was
'a son of Rousseau'. The poet nevertheless retained the typical
Rousseauistic conviction of the need to 'draw out' human nature,
the equality of human rights, and the common brotherhood of
man. He may also have retained some trace of Rousseauism
in his preference for the rustic, the untutored, the innocent,
as against the sophisticated and urban. The introspective preoccupation with time and memory in Rousseau's *Confessions*
and *Reveries of a Solitary Walker* foreshadows Wordsworth's
time-consciousness in *The Prelude*.

There is one characteristic doctrine of Rousseau's early *Discourses* to which Wordsworth did not subscribe. This is the
picture of the 'innocent savage' uncorrupted by the vices and
artificialities of civilization. Wordsworth was a great reader of
travel literature, and in the realistic narratives of travellers he
had found a truer account. He knew that primitive men were
in an even worse state than the slum-dwellers that he had
observed in London—that 'monstrous ant-hill on the plain'.[2]
In *The Excursion* the Solitary contrasts 'Primeval Nature's
child', the idyllic uncivilized man of Rousseau's *Discourses*,
with the crude savage that he discovered on the banks of the
Mississippi:

> . . . that pure archetype of human greatness,
> I found him not. There, in his stead, appeared
> A creature, squalid, vengeful, and impure;

---

[1] *Prose Works*, ed. Grosart, i, pp. 161–2. For Wordsworth's opinion of Voltaire
see *Excursion*, II. 437–86.
[2] *Prelude*, VII. 149.

Remorseless, and submissive to no law
But superstitious fear, and abject sloth.[1]

In fairness to Rousseau it should be pointed out that in the
Social Contract, as distinguished from the *Discourses*, there is
little to suggest the idyllic character of primitive life. As a
result of civic institutions a human being ceases to be 'a stupid
and unimaginative animal' and becomes 'an intelligent being
and a man'.[2] Wordsworth, if he had chosen to do so, could have
quoted the later Rousseau to refute the earlier.

The problem of tracing influences is complicated by the con-
vergence of doctrines among a number of writers. Rousseau
and Shaftesbury, for example, share fundamental tenets: that
one should venerate 'nature' in nearly all the senses of the word;
that Hobbes' account of the 'state of nature' and the rise of the
social contract is false; that the child's mental constitution is
innocent; that conscience or the moral sense is an original
affection in the soul; that the merely intellectual processes of the
mind are suspect, and hence there must be an ample cultivation
of the senses and the feelings; and that nature, especially wild
and untamed nature, declares the glory of God. Consequently
it is difficult to distinguish between Wordsworth's indebtedness
to Rousseau and his indebtedness to Shaftesbury. In certain
respects he appears to be nearer to the English thinker. For
example, he is in closer accord with Shaftesbury's tendency to
regard God as the soul of nature than with Rousseau's relatively
sharp distinction between God and his creation. He shares with
Shaftesbury an idea not developed in Rousseau, that the aesthetic faculties are very important instruments in the search for
truth. In considering ideas of such wide currency it is difficult
to be sure about the specific influence of either Rousseau or
Shaftesbury upon Wordsworth. Moreover, in his theory of
education and the natural virtues of childhood, the poet probably
owed less to books than to the memories of his boyhood and the
carefree days at Hawkshead.

6. *Spinoza*

Although the catalogue of the Rydal Mount library listed
no work of Baruch Spinoza (1632–77), Wordsworth must have

---

[1] *Excursion*, III. 951–5.
[2] *The Social Contract*, trans. G. D. H. Cole (New York: Dutton, 1913), p. 6.

been familiar with at least the gist of his philosophy. Coleridge's enthusiasm for Spinoza, which was surely communicated to Wordsworth, lasted a long time. Henry Crabb Robinson made this entry in his Diary on 20 December 1810: 'Coleridge warmly praised Spinoza, Jacobi on Spinoza, and Schiller "Ueber die Sendung Moses", &c. And he concurred with me in thinking the main fault of Spinoza to be his attempting to reduce to demonstration that which must be an object of faith.'[1] In another entry, dated 3 October 1812, Robinson described a dramatic scene when Coleridge kissed the portrait of Spinoza in front of an edition of his works, exclaiming: ' "This book is a gospel to me." But in less than a minute he added: "His philosophy is nevertheless false." '[2] During the days of his closest intimacy with Wordsworth, Coleridge did not consider the philosophy of Spinoza 'false', and he must often have discoursed about it. Indeed, Carlyon testified: 'Coleridge used frequently to make [Spinoza's doctrines] the subject of our conversation, and took pains to explain them to us.'[3] Then there is the amusing anecdote, related in the *Biographia Literaria*, concerning the government spy who overheard Coleridge and Wordsworth talking repeatedly about 'one Spy Nozy, which he was inclined to interpret of himself, and of a remarkable feature belonging to him'.[4]

It is important to know what aspects of Spinoza's philosophy Wordsworth would have thus learned about from Coleridge. The latter's concentrated definition of Spinozism, according to Carlyon, was that 'each thing has a life of its own, and we are all one life'.[5] This definition embraces two aspects of Spinoza's thought. First, we have his doctrine of psycho-physical parallelism: of the infinite attributes of God, man grasps but two, thought and extension; God or nature always has these two aspects, body and mind. One cannot occur without the other, because both are essential to the nature of universal substance. Hence everything has an inner life as well as an outward bodily form. Second, we find in Spinoza a monistic pantheism, or (as some would prefer to say) panentheism; God is not an external

---

[1] *Diary, Reminiscences, and Correspondence of Henry Crabb Robinson*, ed. Sadler, op. cit., i, p. 309.   [2] Ibid., pp. 399–400.

[3] Clement Carlyon, *Early Years and Late Reflections*, op. cit., i, p. 193.

[4] *Biographia Literaria*, i, p. 127. This story may indicate a pronunciation of 'Spinoza' different from that of today.

[5] *Early Years and Late Reflections*, i, p. 193.

contriver, but an immanent, all-pervading, and indivisible presence.

These ideas are reflected in Wordsworth's poetry, whether he derived them from Spinoza or not. His mature pantheistic view is formulated in the lines from *Tintern Abbey* which are the most perfect expression in English of this philosophy:

> And I have felt
> A presence that disturbs me with the joy
> Of elevated thoughts; a sense sublime
> Of something far more deeply interfused,
> Whose dwelling is the light of setting suns,
> And the round ocean and the living air,
> And the blue sky, and in the mind of man:
> A motion and a spirit, that impels
> All thinking things, all objects of all thought,
> And rolls through all things.

I quote these familiar lines because I wish to place the exact wording of a disputed passage before the reader. Protests have been made against calling the lines pantheistic: it has been pointed out that they imply a spirit *dwelling* in things, and therefore distinguished from them.

I think Wordsworth means to suggest that the 'spirit' is to be distinguished from 'extension' (Spinoza's term), that is, from mere matter. This distinction was always insisted upon by Spinoza. The proper way to interpret the lines, I believe, is to regard them as no more than a partial expression of pantheism; the 'presence' is not God, but a part of God. Besides the 'motion and the spirit' there is the outer form of the world, or matter; but both spirit and body are ultimately included in the all-embracing unity which is God. This interpretation seems to me consonant with the other ideas expressed by Wordsworth in the period when this poem was written.

According to Hazlitt, the lines that I have quoted from *Tintern Abbey* (including 'impels' as a key word) set forth Wordsworth's necessitarianism. 'Perhaps the doctrine of philosophical necessity', declared Hazlitt, 'was never more finely expressed.'[1] This creed was deeply rooted in Wordsworth's mind, and he did not easily shed it. When Coleridge tried to convert him to the

---

[1] 'Philosophical Necessity', *Collected Works of William Hazlitt*, op. cit., xi, pp. 277-8.

idea of free will, he stubbornly resisted because some of his
most fervent convictions were bound up with the necessitarian
doctrine. His ardent faith—the creed of idealistic youth—was
that mankind would progress inevitably towards freedom and
perfection. Stirred to the depths by the French Revolution, he
joyously discovered this optimistic creed when he listened to
Beaupuy and read Godwin and Hartley. Wordsworth evidently
believed that necessary progress is part of 'nature's holy plan'
and that the mind's communion with nature is its *modus oper-
andi*. He finally revolted against Godwinian rationalism, but
still clung tenaciously to the doctrine of necessity. He needed
to fit necessitarianism into a new intellectual framework, and
it was at this opportune moment that Coleridge extolled the
gospel of Spinoza. Wordsworth found in it a form of determinism that was much less mechanistic and more teleological
than the corresponding doctrine of Godwin or Hartley.

In Spinoza's *Ethic*, the forces that make for necessity are
represented as indwelling and not as operating mechanically
from outside. God is free, because He is the totality, and His
nature is not limited by anything external to it. In so far as man
shares in God's nature, he also is free—not in the sense of being
undetermined, but in the sense of participating in God's free
and infinite being. This sort of determinism did not exclude
the remarkable tribute in the *Ethic* to 'the power of the intellect'
and its capacity for achieving a noble kind of freedom.

I am suggesting that Wordsworth found in Spinoza a theory
intermediate between Godwin's mechanistic determinism and
Coleridge's doctrine of free will. As a bridge, Spinoza's philosophy enabled him to cling to his intense naturalism and social
idealism while he moved towards his later libertarian convictions. Even when, under Coleridge's prodding, he finally came
to believe in free will, the spirit of teleological determinism
lingered on. To illustrate, let me quote an early manuscript in
which Wordsworth expressed his necessitarian creed:

> Thus deeply drinking in the soul of things,
> We shall be wise perforce, and we shall move
> From strict necessity along the path
> Of order and of good.[1]

---

[1] *Poetical Works*, v, pp. 402–3.

It is instructive to see how these lines were altered when they were finally incorporated in *The Excursion*:

> So build we up the Being that we are;
> Thus deeply drinking-in the soul of things,
> We shall be wise perforce; and, while inspired
> By choice, and conscious that the Will is free,
> Shall move unswerving, even as if impelled
> By strict necessity, along the path
> Of order and of good.[1]

Apropos of this revised version, Helen Darbishire has written:

> The word 'impelled' here accompanies 'strict necessity,' yet the idea is significantly yoked with free will. Here is another of Wordsworth's paradoxes. Godwin's idea of necessity is bound up with an inherited Calvinistic strain in his thought. With Wordsworth it goes with a natural identification of himself with the forms and movements of Nature. He recalls 'the breeze of Nature stirring in my soul,' and speaks of the river of his mind: 'Whate'er I saw, or heard, or felt, was but a stream, that flowed into a kindred stream.' He has a strong sense of the *inevitability* of this deeper life that he shared with the universe. This is the paradox: to live according to the order of Nature is to be free. He found the idea corroborated by Spinoza.[2]

Thus Wordsworth's belief in freedom represents not so much an outright abandonment of Spinozistic determinism as a shift in emphasis.

The doctrine of freedom is linked in the *Ethic* with the concept of 'the intellectual love of God'. Apropos of a remark by Sir Thomas Browne, Coleridge wrote: 'This recalls a sublime thought of Spinosa [*sic*]. Every true virtue is a part of that love, with which God loveth himself.'[3] According to the doctrine to which Coleridge refers, happiness depends upon the quality of the object of one's love, and love towards the greatest of objects, God or Nature, feeds the mind with a profound joy. This joy, accompanied with a clear apprehension of its cause, is intellectual love. He who has clear knowledge of himself and the natural world loves God: his intellectual love is that very love of God whereby God loves himself. The finite human being

[1] *Excursion*, IV. 1264–70.
[2] *The Poet Wordsworth* (Oxford University Press, 1950), p. 163.
[3] T. M. Raysor, *Coleridge's Miscellaneous Criticism* (Harvard University Press, 1936), p. 263.

is then vitally at one with the eternal nature of things. His life is a communion with that sublime and marvellous order in which God is manifest. He who loves God in this 'intellectual' way is a free man; he is caught up into the impersonal infinite of being, and knows the deepest happiness of which human life is capable.

Wordsworth's sympathy with this doctrine has been pointed out by Samuel Alexander and Newton P. Stallknecht. The latter has cited a passage from the final book of *The Prelude* (1805 version) in which Wordsworth identifies intellectual love with the highest flight of the human imagination:

> This love more intellectual cannot be
> Without Imagination, which, in truth,
> Is but another name for absolute strength
> And clearest insight, amplitude of mind,
> And reason in her most exalted mood.
> This faculty hath been the moving soul
> Of our long labour: we have traced the stream
> From darkness, and the very place of birth
> In its blind cavern, whence is faintly heard
> The sound of waters; follow'd it to light
> And open day, accompanied its course
> Among the ways of Nature, afterwards
> Lost sight of it, bewilder'd and engulph'd,
> Then given it greeting, as it rose once more
> With strength, reflecting in its solemn breast
> The works of man and face of human life,
> And lastly, from its progress have we drawn
> The feeling of life endless, the great thought
> By which we live, Infinity and God.
> Imagination having been our theme,
> So also hath that intellectual love,
> For they are each in each, and cannot stand
> Dividually.[1]

In this important passage, which states the main theme of *The Prelude*, Wordsworth uses the term 'imagination' in place of Spinoza's term 'intuition', but his intent resembles that of the philosopher—to denote the joyful intuitive grasp of the cosmic unity. As Alexander says: 'Two great men may have like

---

[1] *Prelude* (1805), XIII. 166–88. See Newton P. Stallknecht, *Strange Seas of Thought* (Duke University Press, 1945), Chapter VI, for an illuminating discussion of Spinoza's influence on Wordsworth.

emotions and the one be a poet and the other a philosopher, and the expression of each be perfect in its kind.'[1]

While recognizing the truth of Alexander's remark, one must guard against overestimating this resemblance. Wordsworth has a strong sense of the moral life in nature, and sometimes applies to natural processes a curiously anthropomorphic interpretation.[2] Spinoza's flat refusal to apply human predicates to God, or to interpret nature in the light of human ethics or teleological concepts, sharply distinguishes him from the author of such poems as *Nutting* or *Hart-leap Well*. Another un-Wordsworthian aspect of Spinoza's thought is his abstract rationalism and disparagement of imagination.

The poet's later divergence from Spinoza is apparent from a letter of 1814. Wordsworth has been discussing a criticism of the recently published *Excursion* made by a Miss Patty Smith:

She talks of my being a worshipper of nature, a passionate expression uttered incautiously in the Poem upon the Wye has led her into this mistake. She, reading in cold heartedness and substituting the letter for the Spirit—Unless I am mistaken there is nothing of this kind in the Excursion—There is indeed a passage towards the end of the 4th Book where the Wanderer introduces the Simile of the Boy and the Shell. And what follows—That has something ordinarily but absurdly called Spinosistic—But the intelligent reader will easily see the *dramatic* propriety of the passage. . . . She condemns me for not distinguishing between Nature as the work of God and God himself—But where does she find this Doctrine inculcated? Whence does she gather that the author of the Excursion looks upon Nature and God as the same? He does not indeed consider the Supreme Being as bearing the same relation to the Universe as a Watch maker bears to a watch —In fact there is nothing in the course of religious education adopted in this country and in the use made by us of the Holy Scriptures that appears to me so injurious as the perpetually talking about *making* by God—Oh! that your Correspondent had heard a conversation which I had in bed with my sweet little boy four and a half years old upon this subject the other morning. 'How did God make me? Where is God? How does he speak? He never spoke to *me*.' I told him that God was a *spirit*, that he was not like his flesh which he could touch; but more like the thoughts in his mind which he could not touch—The

[1] *Beauty and Other Forms of Value* (London: Macmillan, 1933), p. 60.
[2] For a discussion of this aspect of Wordsworth's thought, see W. A. Raleigh, *Wordsworth* (London: Arnold, 1912).

wind was tossing the fir trees and the sky and light were dancing about in their dark branches as seen through the Window. Noting these fluctuations he exclaimed eagerly 'There is a bit of him—I see it there.' This is not meant entirely for Father's prattle; but for Heaven's sake in your religious talk say as little as possible about *making*.[1]

The letter not only denies the identification of nature and God but repudiates the charge that *The Excursion* is Spinozistic. It must be remembered, however, that the letter was written in 1814 after Wordsworth had turned towards Church of England orthodoxy. It is no accurate index of his earlier convictions.

The latter part of the letter suggests that his position still coincided with Spinoza in two important respects. First, the philosopher also inveighed against the idea of 'making by God', and sought to prove that 'God is the indwelling and not the transient cause of all things'.[2] Second, the child's remark about the wind tossing the fir trees is admirable from the viewpoint of Spinoza, who identified God, as active principle and immanent source, with the vital, moving processes of nature. In contrast to the passive, material content of the world, the *'natura naturata'*, or God as product, stands the *'natura naturans'*, or God as action, motion, and life. As Helen Darbishire remarks: 'Wordsworth seems to find in motion the very essence of life. God Himself, the divine principle in things, *is* motion.'[3] The poet's 'sweet little boy', from the standpoint of both his father and Spinoza, was penetrating to the meaning of God as source.

Patty Smith had good reason for thinking that there was pantheism even in *The Excursion*, for Wordsworth had not managed to expunge all traces of his earlier creed. As a foe of pantheism, Coleridge complained that the later poetry of Wordsworth still bore the mark of a 'vague, misty rather than mystic, confusion of God with Nature . . . while the odd introduction of the popular, almost vulgar, religion in his later publications (the popping in . . . of the old man with a beard), suggests the painful suspicion of worldly prudence . . . carried into religion. At least it

---

[1] *The Correspondence of Henry Crabb Robinson with the Wordsworth Circle*, ed. Edith J. Morley (Oxford University Press, 1927), i, pp. 79-80.
[2] Spinoza, *Ethic*, I, prop. xvii.
[3] *The Poet Wordsworth*, op. cit., p. 127.

conjures up to my fancy a sort of *Janus* head of Spinosa and
Dr. Watts, or "I and my brother the Dean."'[1] Thus Coleridge
felt that Wordsworth had never entirely divested himself of the
Spinozistic creed, however incongruous it might be with his
later orthodoxy.

7. *Kant*

The philosophers we have so far considered, such as Hartley,
Rousseau, and Spinoza, appear to have affected Wordsworth
most deeply in the period from 1797 to 1803. Thereafter the
poet's outlook gradually suffered a sea change. His point of
view shifted from the nature-mysticism and associationism of
the early period to the more transcendentalist doctrines of his
later years. Perhaps the major philosophical influences to be
detected in this second stage are Kant, Platonism, the Roman
Stoics, and Christianity.

Although Immanuel Kant has been frequently mentioned as a
source of Wordsworthian doctrines, the evidence is divided and
uncertain. From Henry Crabb Robinson, who knew intimately
both Germany and Wordsworth, we have two statements which
would tend to show that he regarded the poet's knowledge of
German philosophy as superficial. Although he recorded a
'German bent' in Wordsworth's mind,[2] he did not believe that
this similarity was based upon first-hand knowledge of German
thinkers. Apropos of a conversation with the poet concerning
'imagination' the diarist reports: 'He represented . . . *much as,
unknown to him the German philosophers have done*, that by the
imagination the mere fact is exhibited as connected with that
infinity without which there is no poetry.'[3] Referring to the
passage 'in which Wordsworth talks of *seeing Jehovah unalarmed*'
Robinson also states: 'If Wordsworth means that all notions
about the personality of God, as well as the locality of hell, are
but attempts to individualize notions concerning Mind, he will

---

[1] Thomas Allsop, *Letters, Conversations and Recollections of S. T. Coleridge*,
op. cit., pp. 57–58. The 'Dr. Watts' referred to was an orthodox theologian, and
'the Dean' was the poet's brother, Christopher Wordsworth, Master of Trinity
College, Cambridge—an important personage in ecclesiastical circles.

[2] *Diary, Reminiscences, and Correspondence of Henry Crabb Robinson*, ed. Sadler,
op. cit., i, p. 482.

[3] Ibid. ii. 24 (11 Sept. 1816). My italics.

be much more of a metaphysical philosopher *nach deutscher Art*, than I had any conception of.'[1] Clearly Robinson regarded Wordsworth's knowledge of German thought as not very detailed, although he recognized a parallelism in ideas.

The poet himself lent support to the view that the Kantian influence was slight. In a letter of 1840 that he wrote to Robinson he thus comments upon a 'serious charge of Plagiarism brought against Coleridge in the last number of Blackwood': 'With the part concerning the imputation of thefts from Schelling, having never read a word of German metaphysics, thank Heaven! though I doubt not that they are good diet for some tastes, I feel no disposition to meddle.'[2] This declaration is not as conclusive as it appears, for Wordsworth may have discovered the vital ideas of the German thinkers through his conversations with Coleridge rather than through the cloudy pages of the Teutonic philosophers, who wrote in a language scarcely known to him.

Another bit of evidence is of the same tenor. On one occasion Wordsworth told Captain Hamilton, the brother of the philosopher Sir William Hamilton, that he had no knowledge of Kant. ' "I asked Wordsworth," says Captain Hamilton, writing from the Lakes, where he resided latterly, "about that passage in the 'Excursion' which William says contains the doctrine of Kant. Wordsworth says he is utterly ignorant of everything connected with Kant or his philosophy. So that it could not have come from that source, but is a casual coincidence." '[3] Perhaps we should not take Wordsworth's disavowal too literally, since in his old age he was doggedly provincial in denying such foreign influences. Also it is quite possible that he had forgotten the original source of some of the Kantian ideas that he derived from Coleridge.

The evidence from an earlier period is of a more positive nature. In a sonnet composed in 1809 Wordsworth expressed his conviction that the intellectual interests of the world were being jeopardized by Napoleon's subjugation of 'sapient Germany':

[1] Ibid. i. 465 (19 Dec. 1814).
[2] *The Correspondence of Henry Crabb Robinson with the Wordsworth Circle*, op. cit., i, p. 401.
[3] John Veitch, *Memoir of Sir William Hamilton* (Edinburgh and London: Blackwood, 1869), p. 89.

Alas! what boots the long laborious quest
Of moral prudence, sought through good and ill;
Or pain abstruse—to elevate the will,
And lead us on to that transcendent rest
Where every passion shall the sway attest
Of Reason, seated on her sovereign hill;
What is it but a vain and curious skill,
If sapient Germany must lie deprest,
Beneath the brutal sword?

The poem defines leading elements in two of the principal German philosophical systems: the teaching of both Kant and Fichte sought 'to elevate the will'; and Kant endeavoured to bring passion under the sway of the Practical Reason, as expressed in the law of duty. The same fear that French aggression would damage German philosophy is expressed in *The Convention of Cintra*.[1] Elsewhere in the tract, when Wordsworth considers the chance of Spanish resistance, he does not mention the thinkers of Spain, but the Spanish literary tradition as constituting the spiritual strength which would generate its own independence. In the case of Germany he trusts in the solid worth of the inhabitants and the vitality of the philosophy.

A similar opinion of German thought is conveyed in a letter concerning the Cintra tract, posted 31 March 1809. The poet herein contrasts the degradation of 'moral philosophy' in England with 'the voice of reason and nature' to be heard in Germany before the French invasion.[2] This statement was made at a time when the utilitarianism of Bentham, Paley, and Adam Smith was regnant in England, and the categorical ethics of Kant and Fichte were dominant in Germany. The letter indicates Wordsworth's sympathies in one important branch of philosophy. I have already cited Wordsworth's statement that Kant, Fichte, and Schelling, although 'dreary' writers, 'have much of Plato in them, and for this I respect them'. Wordsworth appears to have had a somewhat favourable impression of their ideas if not of their style.

All the evidence so far cited is overshadowed by Wordsworth's intimacy with Coleridge, who was intensely devoted to

---

[1] *Prose Works*, ed. Grosart, i, pp. 171–2.
[2] *Letters From the Lake Poets to Daniel Stuart* (London: West, Newman, 1889), pp. 334–5. (Letter of 31 Mar. 1809.)

Kant. As I have pointed out in Chapter I, Coleridge's serious study of the Kantian philosophy began as early as March 1801, in time to affect the first version of *The Prelude* and a large body of additional poetry. Undoubtedly Kant's doctrines, as refracted through Coleridge's mind, were well known to Wordsworth, and must have been impressed upon him by many conversations. Robinson wrote of a first meeting: 'Coleridge kept me on the stretch of attention and admiration from half-past three till twelve o'clock. On politics, metaphysics, and poetry, more especially on the Regency, Kant, and Shakespeare, he was astonishingly eloquent.'[1] Wordsworth must have listened to many such performances. He may not have found them very intelligible, but the salient ideas probably sank in.

Coleridge gave his own twist to the Kantian doctrines, largely eliminating the sceptical elements. Reason, as he interpreted it, returns to its old meaning of intellectual intuition, apprehending the nature and properties of ultimate reality. Coleridge expounded this tender-minded version of Kant in his lectures on Æsthetics (1808) and his articles in *The Friend* (1809), but Wordsworth must have heard about these ideas long before they were presented to the general public.

We have a few clues to indicate what Kantian doctrines impressed Wordsworth. I have already cited his commendation of the moral philosophy of Germany in the letter concerning the Cintra tract and the sonnet in praise of German thought. The sonnet's mention of the inadequacy of moral prudence and the need to 'elevate the will' is pure Kantianism. Also the philosopher's intent was to seek

> that transcendent rest
> Where every passion shall the sway attest
> Of Reason, seated on her sovereign hill.

The control of feeling and impulse by the dictates of practical reason is at the heart of the Kantian ethics. In this period of Wordsworth's life (1809) he felt a profound need for the 'transcendent rest' represented by Kant and the Stoics.

The poem that is usually cited as an example of Kantian influence is the *Ode to Duty*. Here Wordsworth invokes the

---

[1] *Diary, Reminiscences, and Correspondence of Henry Crabb Robinson*, ed. Sadler, i, p. 313. (Quoted in 1810 as having been jotted down on Robinson's first acquaintance with Coleridge in 1808.)

'firm support' of duty and longs 'for a repose that ever is the same':

> Stern Lawgiver! yet thou dost wear
> The Godhead's most benignant grace;
> Nor know we anything so fair
> As is the smile upon thy face:
> Flowers laugh before thee on their beds
> And fragrance in thy footing treads;
> Thou dost preserve the stars from wrong;
> And the most ancient heavens, through Thee, are fresh
> and strong.

Kant similarly compared the austere sublimity of the stars with the categorical imperative, and maintained that moral law is binding upon all thinking beings including God.

The identification of the poem with Kantian doctrine is made more likely by the character of the third stanza, which seems to be based upon Friedrich Schiller's idea of the 'beautiful soul', a conception advanced in controversy with Kant. Schiller's *schöne seele* combines the grace of spontaneous virtue with the rigour of moral discipline. In still another stanza, one that he withdrew after 1807, Wordsworth tempered the austerity of the categorical imperative in a manner highly reminiscent of Schiller:

> Yet not the less would I throughout
> Still act according to the voice
> Of my own wish; and feel past doubt
> That my submissiveness was choice:
> Not seeking in the school of pride
> For 'precepts over dignified,'
> Denial and restraint I prize
> No farther than they breed a second Will more wise.[1]

If Wordsworth's attempt was to characterize Schiller's doctrine of the 'beautiful soul', he could not have done so more aptly than in this concept of 'a second Will more wise'.

On the other hand, we know that Wordsworth read Henry Vaughan, and in two of the poems of Vaughan we find ideas that might explain the apparent echoing of Kant and Schiller. In *Misery* occurs the contrast between being to oneself a guide and being a happy bondsman of God. In *The Constellation* appears

[1] *Poetical Works*, iv. 85.

the declaration that the same laws that are exemplified by 'Thy whole creation', and by the stars in particular, should be binding upon the individual human heart. Other possible sources mentioned by scholars are the Stoics, Newton's *Opticks*, Jacob Boehme, and the nineteenth Psalm. But Mary Moorman has revealed that the *Ode* had its origins in conversations with Coleridge about the relation between duty and inclination[1]—a topic that he would instantly associate with Kant and Schiller. Hence the resemblance of Wordsworth's poem to their doctrines is surely not fortuitous.

Kant maintained that his concept of a Kingdom of Ends was another way of formulating his conception of duty. This doctrine, that every rational being should be treated as an end, never as a means merely, is precisely summarized in a passage of *The Excursion*:

> Our life is turned
> Out of her course, wherever man is made
> An offering, or a sacrifice, a tool
> Or implement, a passive thing employed
> As a brute mean, without acknowledgment
> Of common right or interest in the end;
> Used or abused, as selfishness may prompt.
> Say, what can follow for a rational soul
> Perverted thus, but weakness in all good,
> And strength in evil?[2]

Thus Wordsworth appears to have accepted two main principles of the Kantian ethics: the categorical imperative and the doctrine of ends.

I have already discussed, in Chapter I, the role that Kant played in shaping the anti-necessitarianism and transcendentalism of Coleridge and the indirect effect of these doctrines upon Wordsworth. Perhaps a similar influence can be attributed to Kant's criticism of associationism and his alternative theory of transcendental imagination (I shall discuss this question in Chapter V). But enough has already been said to suggest an important, if somewhat conjectural, Kantian influence.

8. *Platonism*

There can be no doubt that Coleridge communicated to his friend many Platonic conceptions. His two great philosophical

---

[1] Cf. *William Wordsworth: A Biography* (Oxford: Clarendon Press, 1965), ii, pp. 1–7. [2] *Excursion*, IX. 113–22.

passions were German metaphysics and Platonism, and his deepest allegiance was to the latter. Except for a few years when he was intellectually entangled with Godwin and Hartley, he sought to redirect English thought to the deep bed in which it ran in the days of Hooker and Jeremy Taylor and the Cambridge Platonists. This was the main labour of his life.[1]

If we can judge from the large number of books on Platonism in the Rydal Mount library, Coleridge must have struck a sympathetic chord when he discussed his favourite philosophy with Wordsworth. Not only Plato, but others in the Platonic tradition, were represented in the collection. We note such authors as Paracelsus, Clement of Alexandria, Ralph Cudworth, Jeremy Taylor, and Friedrich Schleiermacher (the latter by his *Introduction to the Dialogues of Plato*). Among the works with a Platonic flavour must also be counted the poems of Edmund Spenser, Henry Vaughan, and Michelangelo. Spenser was one of Wordsworth's favourite poets, and in such Spenserian poems as 'An Hymne in Honour of Beautie' Platonism was never more beautifully expressed. 'Wordsworth read Plato in Nature, not in books', remarks one writer.[2] If so, it was not for want of relevant sources in his own library.

The references to Plato in the *Poetical Works* are uniformly complimentary. Wordsworth speaks of 'Plato's genius', his 'lore sublime', and the 'everlasting praise' that is his due. Five references to Plato (more than to any other thinker) are listed in the *Concordance* of Wordsworth's poetry; and one of the drafts of *The Prelude* contains an additional reference.[3] In *The Convention of Cintra* Wordsworth declares that in the persons of Plato, Demosthenes, Homer, Shakespeare, Milton, and Lord Bacon 'were enshrined as much of the divinity of intellect as the inhabitants of this planet can hope will ever take up its abode among them'.[4] The poet also remarked in conversation that Plato's *Phaedo*, Shakespeare's *Othello*, and Walton's *Life of George Herbert* were 'the most pathetic of human composi-

---

[1] Cf. Norman Wilde, 'The Development of Coleridge's Thought', *The Philosophical Review*, vol. 28 (1919), pp. 149–50, and Roberta Florence Brinkley, *Coleridge on the Seventeenth Century* (Duke University Press, 1955).

[2] G. P. H. Pawson, *The Cambridge Platonists* (London: Society for Promoting Christian Knowledge, 1930), p. 92.

[3] *The Prelude*, ed. E. de Selincourt and H. Darbishire, p. 609.

[4] *Prose Works*, ed. Grosart, i, p. 312.

tions'.[1] I have already quoted his comment that Plato represents that 'half of truth' most neglected in England.

Let us now consider some of Wordsworth's doctrines that bear the Platonic stamp. In the scheme of the Platonists the universe is not only a rational universe, but God Himself is eternal Reason. Wordsworth writes in this vein when he addresses his apostrophe to the

> Wisdom and Spirit of the universe!
> Thou Soul that art the eternity of thought.[2]

Neither in Wordsworth nor in the Platonists is rationality conceived narrowly as mere intellectualism. In both the *Symposium* and *Phaedrus* Plato maintains that reason is one with spiritual love. Likewise Benjamin Whichcote, the Cambridge Platonist, declares: 'I oppose not rational to spiritual—for spiritual is most rational.'[3] John Smith, another of the Cambridge group, draws out the religious implications of this position: 'God is not better defined to us by our understandings than by our wills and affections: he is not only the eternal reason, that almighty mind and wisdom which our understandings converse with; but he is also that unstained beauty and supreme good which our wills are perpetually catching after: and wheresoever we find true beauty, love, and goodness, we may say, Here or there is God.'[4] Similarly Wordsworth affirms that imagination and intellectual love are identical with 'reason in her most exalted mood'.

Another favourite doctrine of the Platonists was the concept of a Soul of the World. In the *Timaeus*, of which Wordsworth possessed Thomas Taylor's English edition with much commentary, Plato described the creation of this soul, so fashioned that it is one and many, changing and changeless. By endowing the world soul with antipodal qualities, the Demiurge bridges the gulf between the world of ideas and the world of formlessness or prime matter.

This conception of a world soul was re-expressed by Coleridge's favourites, the Cambridge Platonists, among whom one

---

[1] Christopher Wordsworth, *Memoirs of William Wordsworth* (London: Moxon, 1851), ii, p. 482.

[2] *Prelude*, I. 401–2.

[3] Quoted by John Herman Randall, Jr., *The Career of Philosophy* (Columbia University Press, 1962), p. 472.

[4] E. T. Campagnac, *The Cambridge Platonists* (Oxford University Press, 1901), pp. 173–4.

of the most important is Ralph Cudworth, represented in Words-worth's library. The world as Cudworth described it is no giant clockwork created by a Divine Mechanic: rather there is spirit everywhere at work. The concept of immanent spirit, or 'plastic nature', is necessary 'for the defence of Theism':

Forasmuch as without such a nature, either God must be supposed to do all things in the world immediately, and to form every gnat and fly, as it were, with his own hands; which seemeth not so becoming of him, and would render his providence, to human apprehensions, laborious and distractious; or else the whole system of this corporeal universe would result only from fortuitous mechanism, without the direction of any mind: which hypothesis once admitted, would un-questionably, by degrees, supplant and undermine all Theism.[1]

Henry More, the best known of the Cambridge Platonists, de-fines this inward-working force:

The spirit of nature is . . . a substance incorporeal but without sense and animadversion, pervading the whole matter of the universe, and exercising a *plastical power* therein . . . raising such phenomena in the world . . . as cannot be resolved into mere mechanical powers.[2]

In the books of both Plato and the Cambridge men all movement and activity are explained by the dynamical influence of soul or spirit.

'Power' and 'soul' are the favourite nouns, and 'plastic' or 'plastical' the favourite adjective, of both More and Cudworth in characterizing this immanent force. The same key words appear in the poetry and notes of Coleridge written during or immediately after his study of Cudworth. From 15 May to 6 June 1795 and 9 November to 13 December 1796 Coleridge borrowed Cudworth's *The True Intellectual System of the Universe* from the Bristol Library, and he jotted down in his notebook a number of quotations from this volume.[3] His philosophical poem, *The Eolian Harp*, written on 24 August 1795, clearly echoes the Cambridge philosopher:

[1] *The True Intellectual System of the Universe* (London: 1743), pp. xxxiv–xxxv.
[2] *The Immortality of the Soul*, Book III, ch. xii, sec. 1, in *Philosophical Writings of Henry More*, ed. Florence Isabel MacKinnon (Oxford University Press, 1925). My italics. Compare Plato on motion: *Phaedrus*, 245, and *Laws*, X, 894–6.
[3] *Notebooks*, ed. Coburn, op. cit. i, entries 200, 201, 203, with the editor's explanatory comment in the accompanying volume.

And what if all of animated nature
Be but organic harps diversely framed,
That tremble into thought, as o'er them sweeps
Plastic and vast, one intellectual breeze,
At once the *Soul* of each, and God of all?

In *Religious Musings*, written during Coleridge's sojourn in Bristol, the same kind of language is used:

. . . ye of *plastic power* that interfused
Roll through the grosser and material mass
In organizing surge! Holies of God![1]

Both of these poems appeared in Coleridge's first volume of verse, *On Various Subjects* (1796). Wordsworth obtained this book as soon as it was published, and he picked out *Religious Musings* as particularly worthy of praise. Perhaps not altogether by accident the words 'plastic power' appear in Book II of *The Prelude*.[2] It would appear to be a safe inference that Wordsworth imbibed the ideas of Cudworth from Coleridge. We know that in course of time he acquired *The True Intellectual System of the Universe* for his own library.

The conception of 'plastic power' is that of an unconscious creative energy akin to Bergson's *élan vital*. In sketching this notion Cudworth points out 'two imperfections of the plastick nature':

First, that though it act for ends artificially, yet itself neither intends those ends, nor understands the reason of what it doth, and therefore cannot act electively. . . . The second imperfection of the plastick nature, that it acts without animal fancy, . . . express consense [*sic*], and consciousness, and is devoid of self-perception and self-enjoyment.[3]

Cudworth was aware of unconscious depths in both nature and the human mind:

It is certain that our human souls themselves are not always conscious of whatever they have in them; for even the sleeping geometrician hath, at that time, all his geometrical theorems and knowledges some way in him; as also the sleeping musician, all his musical skills and songs: and therefore why may it not be possible for the soul

---

[1] My italics. According to Cottle, a great part of *Religious Musings* was written in Bristol in 1796. See *The Poetical Works of Samuel Taylor Coleridge*, ed. James Dykes Campbell (London: Macmillan, 1914), p. 579.

[2] *Prelude*, II. 362.

[3] *The True Intellectual System of the Universe*, pp. 179–80.

to have likewise some actual energy in it, which it is not expressly conscious of? We have all experience, of our doing many animal actions non-attendingly, which we reflect upon afterwards; as also that we often continue a long series of bodily motions, by a mere virtual intention of our minds, and as it were by half a cogitation.[1]

Here is a clear statement that the mind includes actions that are semi-conscious or unconscious.

Coleridge shared these basic ideas, although he probably derived them quite as much from his own experience as from books. The author of *Kubla Khan*, the most famous dream poem in the English language, was not inclined to overlook 'the outgoing pre-existent ghosts of many feelings' and other subliminal states.[2] But it may be that his reading of Cudworth and other Platonists strengthened his belief, not only in the subconscious depth of the human mind, but in 'the spirit of unconscious life In tree and wild flower'.[3] Likewise Wordsworth was cognizant of the limits and shadowy fringes of consciousness. In *The Prelude*, for example, we find him alluding to the great 'underconsciousness' that lies deep beneath all explicit awareness.[4] It would be hazardous to claim more than resemblance to Cudworth's doctrine, but this at least is manifest.

The 'life within us or abroad' can be conceived as either one or many. The Platonists believed that both conceptions are true. In Plato's *Timaeus* the world soul is made up of two levels of being, that which is undivided and always self-same, and that which is divisible in bodies. The same concept of the one and many is repeated by Plotinus, Proclus, Bruno, Eckhart, Boehme, and the Cambridge Platonists. Henry More, for example, recognized not only the universal soul but also 'created spirits', 'seminal forms', or '*archei*' which may or may not be incorporated in the world soul: 'To the last puzzle propounded, whether these archei be so many sprigs of the common soul of the world, or particular subsistences of themselves, there is no great inconvenience in acknowledging that it may be either way.'[5]

---

[1] *The True Intellectual System of the Universe*, p. 162.
[2] *Anima Poetae*, op. cit., pp. 152–3.
[3] Coleridge, *The Picture*, ll. 20–21. (This poem was first published 6 Sept. 1802.)   [4] Cf. *The Prelude*, ed. E. de Selincourt and H. Darbishire, pp. 622–3.
[5] *Antidote Against Atheism*, Appendix XI, sec. 9, in *Philosophical Writings of Henry More*, op. cit.

This doctrine must have been congenial to Wordsworth. As John Jones has argued in *The Egotistical Sublime*, it is characteristic of Wordsworth's genius that he is equally concerned with solitude and relationship. On the one hand, he speaks of

> . . . the one Presence, and the Life
> Of the great whole.[1]

On the other hand, he writes

> Of the individual Mind that keeps her own
> Inviolate retirement.[2]

His strong sense of oneness is combined with an equally insistent sense of individual identity:

> Points have all of us within our souls
> Where all stand single; this I feel, and make
> Breathings for incommunicable powers.[3]

There is more than one point where *all* stand *single*; the phrasing deftly suggests that both the unity and the multiplicity are indefeasible and ultimate. Note how similar is the language of Plotinus: 'For every one has all things in himself and again sees in another all things, so that all things are everywhere and all is all and each is all, and infinite the glory. For each of them is great, since the small also is great.'[4]

This sentiment, when applied to external nature, would explain Wordsworth's pervasive sense of the significance of small things:

> To me the meanest flower that blows can give
> Thoughts that do often lie too deep for tears.

The following lines are in the spirit of William Blake's *Auguries of Innocence*, or many another work touched by neo-Platonic mysticism:

> I would not strike a flower
> As many a man would strike a horse; at least,
> If, from the wantonness in which we play
> With things we love, or from a freak of power,
> Or from involuntary act of hand

[1] *Prelude* (1805), III. 130–1.
[2] *Recluse*, 772–3. *Poetical Works*, v. 313.
[3] *Prelude*, III. 188–90.
[4] Translation of Thomas Whittaker, *The Neo-Platonists* (Cambridge University Press, 1901), p. 63.

Or foot unruly from excess of life,
It chanc'd that I ungently used a tuft
Of meadow-lillies, or had snapp'd the stem
Of foxglove bending o'er his native rill,
I should be loth to pass along my way
With unreprov'd indifference.[1]

Each little thing is an integral part of the living cosmos: hence the sacredness of the whole is instinct in every part.

This mystical conviction found expression in Wordsworth's pantheism; but as he grew older, partly as a result of Coleridge's entreaties, he abandoned pantheism for an immanent theism. Neither in Plato, nor the Cambridge Platonists, nor the later Wordsworth, is the world soul identified with the Deity. In the *Timaeus* this soul is created by the Demiurge, under commission of eternal God. For More and Cudworth God is likewise removed from space and time, and clearly distinguished from 'the spirit of nature'. In typical Platonic fashion Wordsworth likewise rose from the abstractions of 'geometric science' to the concept of a transcendent Deity:

Yet from this source more frequently I drew
A pleasure calm and deeper, a still sense
Of permanent and universal sway
And paramount endowment in the mind,
An image not unworthy of the one
Surpassing Life, which out of space and time,
Nor touched by welterings of passion, is
And hath the name of God.[2]

This passage was written by Wordsworth when he resumed the composition of *The Prelude* in 1804. We may therefore conclude that by this date the poet was no longer a pantheist but conceived a God that is 'out of space and time'. The spirituality of nature, as he then expressed it, is more akin to Platonic theism than to Spinozistic pantheism.

His vision ascended 'From earth to heaven, from human to divine', intent upon 'the forms Whose kingdom is where time and space are not'.[3] Thus he adopted the most characteristic of all the Platonic doctrines, the conception of 'forms' or arche-

---

[1] *The Prelude*, ed. E. de Selincourt and H. Darbishire, p. 612.
[2] *Prelude* (1805), VI. 150–7.
[3] *Prelude*, XIV. 118, and *Excursion*, IV. 75–76.

typal 'ideas'. In the sonnet 'Brook! whose society the Poet seeks', composed in 1806, the stream manifests an aspect of the eternal order:

> It seems the Eternal Soul is clothed in thee
> With purer robes than those of flesh and blood.

Perhaps the clearest expression of the Platonic conception of 'form' is to be found in Sonnet XXXIV in the series entitled *The River Duddon*. Forced to forsake his old haunts by the river, the poet sees, in the transitoriness of his attachment, the sign of life's impermanence, but comforts himself with the reflection that the 'form' of the stream is eternal. From this thought, he ascends, as Socrates does in the *Phaedo*, to faith and hope in immortality:

> I thought of Thee, my partner and my guide,
> As being past away.—Vain sympathies!
> For, backward, Duddon! as I cast my eyes,
> I see what was, and is, and will abide;
> Still glides the Stream, and shall for ever glide;
> The Form remains, the Function never dies;
> While we, the brave, the mighty, and the wise,
> We Men, who in our morn of youth defied
> The elements, must vanish;—be it so!
> Enough, if something from our hands have power
> To live, and act, and serve the future hour;
> And if, as toward the silent tomb we go,
> Through love, through hope, and faith's transcendant
>   dower,
> We feel that we are greater than we know.

Wordsworth is in vital accord with Plato in his 'intimations of immortality'. Not only did he make use, in the famous *Ode*, of the Platonic 'recollection' of pre-existence, but the entire poem follows the *Phaedo* in emphasizing the 'high instincts' by which our 'mortal Nature' appears a pensioner upon the immortal elements of the mind. To find a similar glorification of childhood 'trailing clouds of glory' we cannot do better than to read the Platonists—Proclus, Hermes Trismegistus, Henry Vaughan, Thomas Traherne, and Thomas Taylor. However, Plato himself rejects the 'wisdom' of the child in favour of the rigorously disciplined mind of the philosopher.

In this chapter I have indicated some of the main philosophical sources and affinities of Wordsworth's poetry, but I have not examined several influences that other scholars have discussed at length. Newton P. Stallknecht, in *Strange Seas of Thought*, has found that many of the ideas of Wordsworth resemble those of the nature-mystics, Jacob Boehme and William Law, both favourites of Coleridge and represented in Wordsworth's library. Two other influences—Stoicism and Christianity—are marked in the later poetry. So revealingly has Jane Worthington written of the one, and Edith Batho of the other, that there is no need for me to enlarge upon these themes.[1] I would differ only in emphasis: Miss Batho, I believe, has over-estimated the extent to which Wordsworth, especially in the great decade from 1797 to 1807, was under the sway of the Anglican Church.

What emerges from our study is a curiously complex thinker. James Logan has characterized the poet well:

The extreme complexity of Wordsworth arises from these causes: (1) in his earlier period he was more boldly naturalistic, but his attitude shifted and he became more markedly spiritual; (2) he attempted to unite the naturalistic with the transcendental; and (3) he embodied elements of both the eighteenth-century sensational school of philosophy, and the mystical and suprasensuous thought of the Neoplatonists and of the German transcendentalists.[2]

This interpretation of Wordsworth will be confirmed by my whole argument.

The purpose of the present chapter has been manifold: to define more precisely the influence of Coleridge as mediator between books and the poet; to clarify the meaning of various elements in Wordsworth's thought by exhibiting their philosophical analogues; to prevent any categorizing of a mind that must have owed its inspiration to a considerable variety of sources; and to prove that Wordsworth's philosophical devotions were not antithetical to the interpretation that I shall sketch in the following pages.

[1] See Jane Worthington, *Wordsworth's Reading of Roman Prose* (Yale University Press, 1946), and Edith Batho, *The Later Wordsworth* (Cambridge University Press, 1933). For a brief but excellent account of the Christian influence on Wordsworth, see *The Prelude*, ed. E. de Selincourt and H. Darbishire, pp. lxix–lxxiv.

[2] James V. Logan, *Wordsworthian Criticism* (Ohio State University Press, 1961), p. 112.

III. GROWTH OF A POET'S MIND

1. *Stages of Development*

I N the previous chapters we have looked to books and Coleridge for the sources of Wordsworth's thought. We have now to investigate a still more important source, the poet's own experience as he develops from childhood to maturity. Studying his mind in its unfoldment, we can the more readily discern the strength and character of the forces influencing him.

The most common formula for interpreting the growth of Wordsworth's mind is 'the three ages of man'. In expounding this chronological scheme Arthur Beatty has greatly influenced subsequent interpretations. To quote Beatty:

The psychology of the eighteenth century, and especially that of Hartley, provided [Wordsworth] with a most important idea, by which he was able to give significance to the autobiographical and reminiscent habit of the time. . . . The Hartleian psychology had noted that the mind is a developing organism marked by three principal stages of progress: (1) sensations derived directly from objects; (2) simple ideas, derived from sensations; and (3) complex ideas, or intellectual ideas, derived from simpler ideas, under the power of association. Wordsworth fully accepted this analysis of the mind's history; and, following the hints given him by numerous psychologists, he gave to these three stages a definitely autobiographical and chronological interpretation; and so we have in his *Tintern Abbey*, *Intimations of Immortality*, *The Prelude*, and many other poems, (1) Childhood, the age of sensation, developing into (2) Youth, the age of direct emotional responses to life, of aching joys and dizzy raptures, an age that leads on to (3) Maturity, the period of thought, but also the period when the immediate joy of childhood and youth has departed. Yet, so much greater is the perception of 'the philosophic mind' to see into the significance and life of things, than the mind in either of the earlier stages, that the resulting mood is not melancholy, but optimism.[1]

[1] Arthur Beatty, *Romantic Poetry of the Early Nineteenth Century* (New York: Scribner's, 1928), pp. 4–5. See Beatty's detailed statement in his *William Wordsworth: His Doctrine and Art in Their Historical Relation*, op. cit., ch. v.

The doctrine of the three ages is presented as an integral part of associationism. In writers such as Hume and Hartley, we find the distinction between sensations, simple ideas, and complex ideas. Except in the very early stages of infancy, all three classes of ideas are present in the human mind during every period of development. Hence, in its original form, this is not primarily a pattern of biographical development. It can be converted into such a pattern if we regard the child's life as predominantly made up of sensations, the youth's mental processes as consisting mainly of simple ideas, and the adult's mind as preoccupied with complex intellectual ideas. Something of this sort has crept into Hartley's book, but it would be hazardous to conclude that Wordsworth must have derived his conception from this source. His view of the growth of his own mind is so decidedly autobiographical in its application, so deeply based upon his own experience, that any search for bookish sources seems nearly superfluous. Also the doctrine of the three ages, as Havens has remarked, 'would naturally occur to anybody', and it is 'one often made in tracing the development of painters and writers'.[1]

If philosophical sources are nevertheless demanded, there are other sources besides Hartley that are plausible. Rousseau in *Émile* had thoroughly popularized the belief that the mind develops in stages; that each stage has its characteristic virtues and qualities that should be fully developed before the mind moves on to the next stage; and that the development of sensation and emotion naturally precedes the ripening of intellect.[2] The idea is also advanced in a famous passage of Plato's *Symposium* that the soul normally develops from the concrete to the abstract, from a life of sensation to a far more philosophical development. Likewise in a widely known passage of the *Phaedrus*, Plato indicates that 'dizzy raptures' are characteristic of youth, or the second age.

The basic principle that the higher elements in the soul depend upon the lower and more original elements is a recurrent notion in the history of ideas. For example, we find that it was central to the thought of Jacob Boehme: 'If the higher is to govern the

---

[1] Robert Dexter Havens, *The Mind of a Poet* (Baltimore: Johns Hopkins Press, 1941), p. 463.
[2] Cf. *Émile* (London: Dent; New York: Dutton, 1911), pp. 131, 134, 165, 220.

lower, it is not to substitute itself therefor and annihilate it, for the lower is its reality and its very existence; deprived of this support, the higher element would be dissipated. . . .'[1] This doctrine is not far removed from a passage in *The Convention of Cintra* selected by Beatty as an expression of Wordsworth's theory of the three ages: 'The higher mode of being does not exclude, but necessarily includes, the lower; the intellectual does not exclude, but necessarily includes, the sentient; the sentient, the animal; and the animal, the vital—to its lowest degrees.'[2] In quoting this passage, Beatty has omitted the last nine words, thus enabling the reader to discover *three stages* of mental development rather than *four divisions* of human nature. If we make this correction, there is nothing peculiarly Hartleian in the quotation.

The concept that the higher mode of being includes the lower was also expressed by Milton, whose poetry Wordsworth not only read but largely memorized. In the following passage from *Paradise Lost* the angel Raphael explains that angels can eat the same food that God gives to man, and that in general the higher capacity includes the lower:

> Therefore what he gives
> (Whose praise be ever sung) to man in part
> Spiritual, may of purest Spirits be found
> No ingrateful food: and food alike those pure
> Intelligential substances require
> As doth your Rational; and both contain
> Within them every lower faculty
> Of sense, whereby they hear, see, smell, touch, taste,
> Tasting concoct, digest, assimilate,
> And corporeal to incorporeal turn.
> For know, whatever was created, needs
> To be sustain'd and fed; of Elements
> The grosser feeds the purer. . . .[3]

In a second closely related passage Milton uses the tree as a microcosmic symbol of the origin, growth, and destiny of man. Again Raphael is speaking:

---

[1] Émile Boutroux, *Historical Studies in Philosophy* (London: Macmillan, 1911), p. 198.
[2] *The Convention of Cintra*, in *Prose Works*, ed. Grosart, i, p. 171.
[3] *Paradise Lost*, V. 404–16.

O *Adam*, one Almighty is, from whom
All things proceed, and up to him return,
If not deprav'd from good, created all
Such to perfection, one first matter all,
Indu'd with various forms, various degrees,
Of substance, and in things that live, of life;
But more refin'd, more spiritous, and pure,
As nearer to him plac't or nearer tending,
Each in thir several active Spheres assign'd,
Till body up to Spirit work, in bounds
Proportioned to each kind. So from the root
Springs lighter the green stalk, from thence the leaves
More aery, last the bright consummate flow'r
Spirits odorous breathes; flow'rs and thir fruit
Man's nourishment, by gradual scale sublim'd
To vital spirits aspire, to animal,
To intellectual, give both life and sense,
Fancy and understanding, whence the Soul
Reason receives, and reason is her being,
Discursive, or Intuitive.[1]

There can be no doubt that these passages attracted Wordsworth's attention. The phrase 'bright consummate flower' is
quoted in *The Convention of Cintra* immediately following the
sentence from this tract that I have reproduced on page 83.
Milton's key words—'vital', 'animal', 'sense', and 'intellectual'—are echoed in 'vital', 'animal', 'sentient', and 'intellectual' in Wordsworth's phrasing. The last line in the second
quotation, 'Discursive, or Intuitive', is repeated by Wordsworth in *The Prelude* (XIV. 120) in close proximity to another
Miltonic phrase ('a universe of death'). The recurrent Miltonic
adjectives 'pure', 'purer', and 'purest' appear frequently and
with comparable meaning in Wordsworth. The *thought*, and
not merely the phraseology, of Milton is recurrent in the later
poet's work. They have the same interpretation of the levels
of man's soul: the lower sustains the higher, and the higher
includes and develops out of the lower. Thus Wordsworth appears to be partially indebted to Milton for a conception that
makes possible a reconciliation of the sensationist and idealistic
strains in his interpretation of man.

It may be objected that the theory of 'the three ages' is much

[1] *Paradise Lost*, V. 469–88.

more central to Wordsworth's thought than any similar doctrine to be found in Milton, Rousseau, Boehme, or the Platonists. Let us see.

In *Tintern Abbey*, which is cited as a prime expression of the theory, the three stages are supplemented by a fourth and independent phase. This is the mystical experience, which is so far differentiated from the three stages that it deserves separate attention. At the time of writing *Tintern Abbey* Wordsworth attributed this mystical state to the influence of the 'beauteous forms' of nature. It is nevertheless important to note that in addition to the period of animal sensation, to the stage in which the love of nature was a 'hunger' and a 'passion', and to the mature period of thought, Wordsworth recognized another phase of consciousness in which 'the body is laid asleep', and thought itself is transformed into a 'living soul'. This mystical element in the poem simply refuses to be brought into harmony with the Hartleian scheme.

Similar disturbing elements thrust themselves forward in *The Prelude* and the general body of Wordsworth's work. In the most searching study that has yet been made of *The Excursion*, Judson Stanley Lyon states: 'Professor Beatty makes some effort to show that the doctrine of the three ages of man is one associationistic tenet which plays an important part in *The Excursion*, but his examples fail to bear out this contention. . . . In *The Excursion* the ages of man are usually four or more, and a great deal more spiritual insight is conceded to the child than any mechanical system of the mind's growth could allow.'[1]

What I find most impressive about Wordsworth's development is *not* its differentiation into chronological divisions but its *inner cohesion and continuity*. We shall nevertheless find it convenient, for the sake of a fuller analysis, to consider a provisional schematization based upon *The Prelude*:

1. *Childhood: The Stage of Sensation* (Age 1–10). This is the period of glad animal movements. The reflective faculties are undeveloped. The visionary gleam rests on the child's perceptions, and an incipient mysticism appears. The child tends to be wrapped up in his own body and mind.

2. *Boyhood: The Stage of Emotion* (Age 10–17). At first there is an unconscious drinking in of beauty, of which the

[1] Judson Stanley Lyon, *The Excursion* (Yale University Press, 1950), p. 92.

mind gradually becomes conscious. Fear and awe are uppermost, and the creative and mystical tendencies persist. Nature is at the focus of attention.

3. *Youth: The Stage of Fancy* (Age 17–22). The mind, self-consciously attempting to be creative, indulges in conceits and forced associations. Nature, which remains in the focus, is interpreted fancifully, and a moral life is imputed to natural objects.

4. *Early Manhood: The Stage of Reason as an Analytical Faculty* (Age 22–26). This is the period of republican ardour. In the later stages, Godwinism is accepted, and a crisis follows. Nature and life are approached analytically and the senses become despotic. Man, rather than nature, is the prime object of concern.

5. *Maturity: The Stage of Imagination and Synthetic Reason* (Age 26–34). Man is still primary, but the old love of nature is renewed and deepened. Fear no longer dominates; calm and meditation are in control. There is a sense of the oneness of man and nature, a oneness in God; and also a new sense of the value of the homely and familiar.

It is to be understood that no stage has an exclusive set of characteristics. There may be anticipation in one period of traits that become pronounced only at a later time. The values developed in the successive periods tend to persist, so that in the last stage there is completeness, synchronization, and mutual protection among the mental powers. Finally, Wordsworth's optimistic interpretation of his own development is subject to certain strains and inconsistencies, leading to the bleaker and more Stoical outlook of his later years.

2. *Childhood: The Stage of Sensation*

At the earliest time of life the germs are present which will develop into the highest faculties of being. From the very first, creative sensibilities are at work; there is an initial activity—a 'poetic spirit' which works in alliance with the stimulation from the encircling world. The infant is eager, prompt, and watchful, or the stuff of his experience will be loath to coalesce. Endowed with this original fund of sensitivity, he proceeds to gather passion from his mother's eye, and pleasure in her arms and

at her breast; these feelings send an awakening breeze through
his perceptions; they irradiate and exalt the objects of sensation.

> Blest the infant Babe,
> (For with my best conjecture I would trace
> The progress of our Being) Blest the Babe,
> Nurs'd in his Mother's arms, the Babe who sleeps
> Upon his Mother's breast, who, when his soul
> Claims manifest kindred with an earthly soul,
> Doth gather passion from his Mother's eye!
> Such feelings pass into his torpid life
> Like an awakening breeze, and hence his mind
> Even in the first trial of its powers
> Is prompt and watchful, eager to combine
> In one appearance, all the elements
> And parts of the same object, else detach'd
> And loath to coalesce. Thus, day by day,
> Subjected to the discipline of love,
> His organs and recipient faculties
> Are quicken'd, are more vigourous, his mind spreads,
> Tenacious of the forms which it receives.
> In one beloved Presence, nay and more,
> In that most apprehensive habitude
> And those sensations which have been deriv'd
> From this beloved Presence, there exists
> A virtue which irradiates and exalts
> All objects through all intercourse of sense.
> No outcast he, bewilder'd and depress'd;
> Along his infant veins are interfus'd
> The gravitation and the filial bond
> Of nature, that connect him with the world.
> Emphatically such a Being lives,
> An inmate of this *active* universe;
> From nature largely he receives; nor so
> Is satisfied, but largely gives again,
> For feeling has to him imparted strength,
> And powerful in all sentiments of grief,
> Of exultation, fear, and joy, his mind,
> Even as an agent of the one great mind,
> Creates, creator and receiver both,
> Working but in alliance with the works
> Which it beholds.—Such, verily, is the first
> Poetic spirit of our human life;
> By uniform control of after years

In most abated or suppress'd, in some,
Through every change of growth or of decay,
Pre-eminent till death.[1]

Thus the tiny mind, 'even as an agent of one great mind', creates as well as receives; for it is 'an inmate of an *active* universe'. The infant is mainly receptive, of course, but if he develops naturally, the inward, creative contribution will steadily grow in significance. All too often the development is otherwise. The concluding six lines, which express this latter thought, scarcely fit the temper of Hartleian optimism.

As the child advances, his body seeks expression in 'glad animal movements' and his senses expand with a fresh vitality. Nothing clouds these early sensations, because perception is unrigidified by the 'frost' of 'custom', and the mind interposes no haze of abstraction between itself and its objects. Typical is the account of the boy William as 'a naked savage', swimming in a side-channel of the River Derwent, or clambering over rocky hills:

> Oh, many a time have I, a five years' child,
> In a small mill-race severed from his stream,
> Made one long bathing of a summer's day;
> Basked in the sun, and plunged and basked again
> Alternate, all a summer's day, or scoured
> The sandy fields, leaping through flowery groves
> Of yellow ragwort; or, when rock and hill,
> The woods, and distant Skiddaw's lofty height,
> Were bronzed with deepest radiance, stood alone
> Beneath the sky, as if I had been born
> On Indian plains, and from my mother's hut
> Had run abroad in wantonness, to sport
> A naked savage, in the thunder shower.[2]

He and his friends 'were a noisy crew'—whether it was chasing butterflies, or winding along mountain brooks with rod and line, or hissing across the polished ice 'all shod with steel'. He was a true boy, daring and untamed:

> While yet an innocent little one, with a heart
> That doubtless wanted not its tender moods,

---

[1] *Prelude* (1805), II. 237–80. The wording of the 1850 version is more orthodox.
[2] *Prelude*, I. 288–300.

I breathed (for this I better recollect)
Among wild appetites and blind desires,
Motions of savage instinct my delight
And exaltation. Nothing at that time
So welcome, no temptation half so dear
As that which urged me to a daring feat,
Deep pools, tall trees, black chasms, and dizzy crags,
And tottering towers: I loved to stand and read
Their looks forbidding, read and disobey,
Sometimes in act and evermore in thought.[1]

But there is another aspect of the poet's childhood. This is its 'all-soulness': 'In my Ode on the "Intimations of Immortality in Childhood," [Wordsworth explains] I do not profess to give a literal representation of the state of the affections and of the moral being in childhood. I record my own feelings at that time, my absolute spirituality, my "all-soulness," if I may so speak. At that time I could not believe that I should lie down quietly in the grave, and that my body would moulder into dust.'[2] Wordsworth remarked on several occasions that there were times in his childhood when he lost himself in an 'abyss of idealism', intervals when he was sure only of his own mind; 'everything else fell away, and vanished into thought'.[3] So complete was his abstraction that he had to clench the top bar of a gate or tightly grasp a tree in order to recall himself to reality. Similar is the account in the Ode of those

> Fallings from us, vanishings;
> Blank misgivings of a Creature
> Moving about in worlds not realized.

This profundity of idealism was manifested in sensation as well as in withdrawal from external stimulation. Hence Wordsworth emphasized the 'glory and dream' of childhood. The objects of sense were clothed with a strange radiance because sensations were informed by 'the immortal mind'. The 'celestial' brightness of impressions was due to their immersion in the 'clouds of glory' which the mind trails with it from its 'home'.

---

[1] *Recluse*, 703–14.
[2] *Prose Works*, ed. Grosart, iii, p. 464.
[3] Letter of Professor Bonamy Price, quoted by William Knight, *Poetical Works of William Wordsworth*, pp. 201–2; see also Fenwick note to *Ode: Intimations of Immortality*, and *Prose Works*, ed. Grosart, iii, p. 467.

All that he beheld shone in pure light, because his spirit shed its own radiance over the apparitions of sense.

The child, in its perception of the 'visionary gleam', penetrates into the eternal order. He does this by intuiting a beauty simple and calm and happy, the highest pledge of the mind's kinship with God. For this temporal beauty is heightened by its participation in eternal beauty, which the mind brings 'from afar'. It is precisely because the child thus sees with the eye of the soul that he can be entitled the 'best Philosopher'. He deserves this title only in a restricted sense: not by virtue of intellectual penetration, but by reason of those powers which infect sensation with absolute beauty, a possession inborn.

In the great Ode the child's idealistic spirit is represented as investing objects of sense with this dreamlike vividness and splendour. The other poetry of Wordsworth provides similar evidence. Something of the boy's inward life, for example, is captured in the famous account of the stealing of the boat, with its aftermath of foreboding when his brain 'for many days . . . Worked with a dim and undetermined sense Of unknown modes of being'.[1] Similarly, when he snatched the bird that was in another boy's snare, he

> heard among the solitary hills
> Low breathings coming after me, and sounds
> Of undistinguishable motion, steps
> Almost as silent as the turf they trod.[2]

Not only guilt and fear but silence and solitude evoked these visionary moods. He would walk alone under the quiet stars, listen in the shadow of some giant rock to the ghostly language of the wind, or drink in 'a pure Organic pleasure from the silver wreaths Of curling mist'.

> Oft in these moments such a holy calm
> Would overspread my soul, that bodily eyes
> Were utterly forgotten, and what I saw
> Appeared like something in myself, a dream,
> A prospect in the mind.[3]

In a poem composed in 1817 Wordsworth tells of a mood then rare but common in childhood—a sublime transport, a pure love,

---

[1] *Prelude*, I. 392–3.   [2] Ibid. I. 322–5.
[3] Ibid. II. 348–52.

a supreme peace, a solemn harmony, a wonderful radiance, an exquisitely clear vision. It seemed to him a second birth:

> Such hues from their celestial Urn
> Were wont to stream before mine eye,
> Where'er it wandered in the morn
> Of blissful infancy.[1]

We thus have abundant evidence of the mind informing the senses and shedding a glory from its mystical intuitions. Wordsworth portrayed childhood not as a period of sensation merely, but as a joyous period in which the spirit had its internal prospects and its immortal light. Though the body was the focus of being, the mind might either dwell in abstraction or clothe the external world with the 'glory and freshness of a dream'.

To conclude this account of childhood we cannot do better than to quote a manuscript version of a passage in Book I of *The Prelude*. These lines clarify Wordsworth's attitude towards the two aspects of the child's life: the side that may be expressed in such associationistic language as 'collateral interest' and 'extrinsic passion', and the other side which emerges in 'naked feelings' and 'first sympathies' imparted by the Eternal Spirit:

> I tread the mazes of this argument, and paint
> How nature by collateral interest
> And by extrinsic passion peopled first
> My mind with beauteous objects: may I well
> Forget what might demand a loftier song,
> For oft the Eternal Spirit, He that has
> His life in unimaginable things,
> And he who painting what He is in all
> The visible imagery of all the World
> Is yet apparent chiefly as the *Soul*
> Of our first sympathies—O bounteous power
> In Childhood, in rememberable days
> How often did thy love renew for me
> Those *naked feelings*, which, when thou would'st form
> A living thing, thou sendest like a *breeze*
> Into its infant being![2]

It is interesting to compare the last few lines, especially the

---

[1] *Composed upon an Evening of extraordinary Splendour and Beauty*, IV. *Poetical Works*, iv. 10.

[2] *The Prelude*, ed. E. de Selincourt, first edition, p. 508.

words that I have italicized, with the letter of Coleridge pre-
viously quoted (page 26): 'I almost think, that Ideas *never*
recall Ideas, as far as they are Ideas—any more than Leaves in a
forest create each other's motion. The Breeze it is that runs
through them—it is the Soul, the state of Feeling.' As we shall
see in Chapter V, Wordsworth gave an un-Hartleian interpretation to the visitings of the Eternal Spirit. Even in this passage,
he contrasts the feelings, naked of associations, with 'the visible
imagery' of Berkeley's idealism and with the associational factors
of Hartley's psychology. He suggests that the purely inward
power might demand the loftier song.

3. *Boyhood: The Stage of Emotion*

The difference between the first period and the second is to be
found in the more turbulent emotions of adolescence and the
emergence of self-consciousness. In contrast to the self-aware-
ness of the boy, the child's feelings are objectified—the inner
brightness is attached to the external world—sense and soul
are one. (This is not true of the fits of abstraction, but these
are only occasional.) In boyhood, on the contrary, Wordsworth
awakened to a sense of the *independence* and creativeness of the
mind.

The transition to the second stage may conveniently be
placed at ten years, in accordance with Wordsworth's suggestion:

> Twice five years
> Or less I might have seen, when first my mind
> With conscious pleasure opened to the charm
> Of words in tuneful order, found them sweet
> For their own *sakes*, a passion, and a power.[1]

The wording of the 1805 version, which substitutes 'thirteen
years' in place of 'twice five years', indicates that we must
not regard the change as abrupt or definitely marked. From this
time onward, Wordsworth adopted a more conscious attitude
toward his creative faculties. He lived in a 'delicious world of
poesy', where 'images, and sentiments, and words . . . Kept
holiday'.[2] Although at first his 'intercourse with beauty' was

---

[1] *Prelude*. V. 552–6.   [2] Ibid. V. 577–83.

'unconscious', he gradually became more aware of natural love-liness and less absorbed in mere 'animal movements'.

This broadening of his consciousness was not characterized by any break with the spirituality of childhood. He thus writes of the period of his school days between his tenth and his seventeenth years:

> But let this
> Be not forgotten, that I still retained
> My first creative sensibility;
> That by the regular action of the world
> My soul was unsubdued. A plastic power
> Abode with me; a forming hand, at times
> Rebellious, acting in a devious mood;
> A local spirit of his own, at war
> With general tendency, but, for the most,
> Subservient strictly to external things
> With which it communed. An auxiliar light
> Came from my mind, which on the setting sun
> Bestowed new splendour; the melodious birds,
> The fluttering breezes, fountains that run on
> Murmuring so sweetly in themselves, obeyed
> A like dominion, and the midnight storm
> Grew darker in the presence of my eye.[1]

Sometimes the imaginative remoulding of experience passed over into moments of a distinctly mystical quality. He could still return to 'the abyss of idealism' that he had experienced as a child.

His 'rebellious' imagination and 'devious mood' were expressed in a mounting restlessness:

> In youth from rock to rock I went,
> From hill to hill in discontent
> Of pleasure high and turbulent,
> Most pleased when most uneasy.[2]

Although Wordsworth uses the term 'youth' in this passage, the truculence to which he refers emerged in the period of boyhood.

William's wise and kindly mother died when he was only eight years old, and his morose father died five years later. The difficult period of puberty coincided with the death of the latter.

---

[1] Ibid. II. 358–74.   [2] *To the Daisy, Poetical Works*, ii. 135.

The boy was taken under custody by his maternal grandfather, William Cookson, principal draper in the little Cumberland town of Penrith. Cookson and his wife appear to have been unlovely characters—philistine, avaricious, puritanical, and repressive. Writing at a later period, Dorothy told a friend and confidante, Jane Pollard, the woes of the Wordsworth children:

Many a time have William, John, Christopher, and myself shed tears together, tears of the bitterest sorrow, we all of us, each day, feel more sensibly the loss we sustained when we were deprived of our parents, and each day do we receive fresh insults. . . . We have been told thousands of times that we were liars but we treat such behaviour with the contempt it deserves. We always finish our conversations which generally take a melancholy turn, with wishing we had a father and a home.[1]

But it was William, not Dorothy, who mainly suffered from this unfriendly environment. During a nine-year separation Dorothy was reared in far-distant Yorkshire by their mother's cousin, and William's loneliness was intensified by her absence.

How deeply the boy was affected by these circumstances is indicated by a comment in his *Autobiographical Memoranda*: 'I was of a stiff, moody, and violent temper, so much so that I remember going once into the attics of my grandfather's house at Penrith, upon some indignity having been put upon me, with an intention of destroying myself with one of the foils which I knew was kept there. I took the foil in hand, but my heart failed.'[2] On another occasion, William and his brother Richard, two years older, had been whipping tops in their grandfather's drawing-room. Pointing to a large ancestral portrait hanging on the wall, William asked his brother, 'Dare you strike your whip through that old lady's petticoat?' Richard, for whom discretion was the better part of valour, refused the challenge. 'Then', cried William, 'here goes!' And seizing the cord, which he had been using to whip the top, he lashed through the hooped petticoat. 'No doubt', he remarked in telling the incident seventy years later, 'I was properly punished.'[3] Fortunately he escaped the dour atmosphere of Penrith most months of the year, attending school at Hawkshead, in the heart of the Lake

---

[1] *Early Letters*, ed. E. de Selincourt, pp. 2, 4.
[2] Christopher Wordsworth, *Memoirs of William Wordsworth*, op. cit., i, p. 9.
[3] Ibid.

District. There he lived with a kindly dame, Anne Tyson, enjoying the country sports and nature's 'lovely forms'.

His violent moods and the punishment meted out by his grandfather must have contributed to the sense of terror that he mentions in many passages. Even in childhood, but characteristically in adolescence, William's mind was filled with

> Images of danger and distress,
> Man suffering among awful Powers and Forms;
> Of this I heard, and saw enough to make
> Imagination restless; nor was free
> Myself from frequent perils; nor were tales
> Wanting,—tragedies of former times,
> Hazards and strange escapes, of which the rocks
> Immutable and everflowing streams,
> Wher'er I roamed, were speaking monuments.[1]

This 'fever of the heart', felt in association with the awesome aspects of nature, contributed to the ripening of his imagination.[2]

During this period his life was characterized by depth of thought as well as feeling. We can apply to his own mind the characteristic that he attributed to William Taylor, the headmaster of the Hawkshead School:

> Yet, sometimes, when the secret cup
> Of still and serious thought went round,
> It seemed as if he drank it up—
> He felt with spirit so profound.[3]

It is false to separate thought and emotion as if they were necessarily antithetical.

4. *Youth: The Stage of Fancy*

Between the second and third stage there is no sharp cleavage. Nevertheless Wordsworth does mention his seventeenth year as marking the point at which fancy began to dominate his outlook. During the early ripening of his genius his spirit expressed itself in the less profound operations of the poetic faculty. The trouble at this stage was that he had not learned

> . . . from . . . timely exercise to keep
> In wholesome separation the two natures,
> The one that feels, the other that observes.[4]

---

[1] *Prelude*, VIII. 164–72.
[2] See ibid. I. 340–50.
[3] *Matthew, Poetical Works*, iv. 68.
[4] *Prelude*, XIV. 345–7.

He was frequently guilty of the pathetic fallacy, transferring to 'unorganic natures' his own emotions. With joy or fear in his own heart, he freely projected such moods into the outer world. This play of fancy took quite immature forms: 'the yew tree had its ghost'; the forlorn widow drenched 'the turf with never-ending tears'; the sunlight on a wet rock was a 'burnished silver shield Suspended over a knight's tomb'.[1]

But fancy, enforced by a deeper imaginative insight, sometimes succeeded in attaining to a plane of vision which was highly significant to the developing youth:

> To every natural form, rock, fruit or flower,
> Even the loose stones that cover the high-way,
> I gave a moral life: I saw them feel,
> Or linked them to some feeling: the great mass
> Lay bedded in a quickening soul, and all
> That I beheld respired with inward meaning.[2]

This conception of reality was still crude; the youth forced nature to 'put on' a 'daily face' corresponding to some 'transitory passion', and impressed his own moral life upon rocks and flowers and 'every natural form'. Hence he made his own world, a world that only lived for him and for God who pierces into the heart; but nevertheless a world that was a fit subject for lofty verse, because he was beginning to see deeply into 'the life of things'.[3]

In *The Prelude*, Wordsworth breaks the thread of his narrative at this point to comment on the significance of the material that he has been relating:

> And here, O Friend! have I retraced my life
> Up to an eminence, and told a tale
> Of matters which not falsely may be called
> The glory of my youth. Of genius, power,
> Creation and divinity itself
> I have been speaking, for my theme has been
> What passed within me. Not of outward things
> Done visibly for other minds, words, signs,
> Symbols or actions, but of my own heart
> Have I been speaking, and my youthful mind.

[1] *Prelude*, VIII. 376–420.   [2] Ibid. III. 130–5.
[3] Cf. ibid. III. 149–96.

O Heavens! how awful is the might of souls,
And what they do within themselves while yet
The yoke of earth is new to them, the world
Nothing but a wild field where they were sown.
This is, in truth, heroic argument,
This genuine prowess, which I wished to touch
With hand however weak, but in the main
It lies far hidden from the reach of words.
Points have we all of us within our souls
Where all stand single; this I feel, and make
Breathings for incommunicable powers;
But is not each a memory to himself,
And, therefore, now that we must quit this theme,
I am not heartless, for there's not a man
That lives who hath not known his god-like hours,
And feels not what an empire we inherit
As natural beings in the strength of Nature.[1]

These words convey an uncommon profundity of conviction.
They clearly indicate that Wordsworth has been dealing with
more than an untrue world of fancy; he has been speaking of
genius, power, creation and divinity itself, of genuine prowess
and godlike hours, of points within our soul where all stand
single. The 'abyss of idealism' was reappearing, but with a
more philosophic interpretation of its meaning.

It was in this period, after his first year in Cambridge, that
the memorable state of exaltation flooded his consciousness
when he became a 'dedicated spirit'. He had passed the night in
'gaiety and mirth' at a country dance and was walking homeward
as the sun came up over Helvellyn:

Magnificent
The morning rose, in memorable pomp,
Glorious as e'er I had beheld—in front,
The sea lay laughing at a distance; near,
The solid mountains shone, bright as the clouds,
Grain-tinctured, drenched in empyrean light;
And in the meadows and the lower grounds
Was all the sweetness of a common dawn—
Dews, vapours, and the melody of birds,
And labourers going forth to till the fields.[2]

In this moment of vision, he 'made no vows but vows were then

[1] Ibid. III. 170–96.   [2] Ibid. IV. 323–32.

made' for him in the unconscious depths of his mind. His devotion to beauty and its imaginative re-creation was henceforth fixed.

Another intense experience befell him during the same summer vacation. So beautiful were the lake and the woods in the evening light that he felt a most deep and holy calm.

> Gently did my soul
> Put off her veil, and, self-transmuted, stood
> Naked, as in the presence of her God.[1]

Out of an experience that at least bordered on the mystical, a philosophy emerged that was more than naturalistic. Once again there was an attempt to rationalize the occurrence, but we miss the suggestion of immaturity:

> —Of that external scene which round me lay,
> Little, in this abstraction, did I see;
> Remembered less; but I had inward hopes
> And swellings of the spirit, was rapt and soothed,
> Conversed with promises, had glimmering views
> How life pervades the undecaying mind;
> How the immortal soul with God-like power
> Informs, creates, and thaws the deepest sleep
> That time can lay upon her.[2]

The soul, Wordsworth announces, is eternal and triumphs over the temporal order. It is this immortal soul which 'informs' and 'creates'.

These glimmering views were certain to work a change in the youth's outlook. Until now nature had been first and man had been second in his regard. But during the period of his early sojourn at Cambridge, his sympathies began to shift:

> Then rose
> Man, inwardly contemplated, and present
> In my own being, to a loftier height;
> As of all visible natures crown.[3]

If this state of mind had continued, he would soon have advanced to the fifth stage, although certain important values would have been lacking if the fourth period had been omitted.

---

[1] *Prelude*, IV. 150-2.   [2] Ibid. IV. 160-8.
[3] *Prelude* (1805), VIII. 630-3.

He had already left mere fancy behind, and was ready to lift man to a primary place in his affections.

But there were intervals of retrogression before and after the memorable summer vacation. At Cambridge, which he had entered at the age of seventeen, he was less happy than at Hawkshead, feeling that 'he was not for that hour, Nor that place'. He disliked, seriously and deeply, the competitive examination system and compulsory chapel, and found it difficult to settle down to study or to planning for the future. Thus adrift, he found himself an 'idler among academic bowers', his attention being absorbed with 'little bustling passions' and the 'vice and folly' which, so he tells us, were characteristic of student life. From the 'timid course' of 'scholastic studies' he turned 'to travel with the shoal of . . . unthinking natures', and fell under the sway of an unidentified companion who encouraged 'a treasonable growth of indecisive judgments'. This impairment of 'the mind's simplicity' was the beginning of a change to the next period in Wordsworth's life. The alteration was considered retrogressive by the mature poet. But all was not a waste of time —his imagination responded to the historic charm of the old University town, and his somewhat desultory reading was congenial to the ripening of his poetic nature.

> I lov'd, and I enjoy'd, that was my chief
> And ruling happiness, happy in the strength
> And loveliness of imagery and thought.[1]

Perhaps such intellectual truancy was what he most needed at this stage in his development.

The higher life at times flashed back into consciousness. A notable instance is the soaring of his imagination during a vacation ramble in the Alps with a friend, Robert Jones. The passage is familiar, but so magnificent that it can be read anew with pleasure:

> The immeasureable height
> Of woods decaying, never to be decayed,
> The stationary blasts of waterfalls,
> And in the narrow rent at every turn
> Winds thwarting winds, bewildered and forlorn,
> The torrents shooting from the clear blue sky,

[1] Ibid. VI. 77–79.

The rocks that muttered close upon our ears,
Black drizzling crags that spake by the way-side
As if a voice were in them, the sick sight
And giddy prospect of the raving stream,
The unfettered clouds and region of the Heavens,
Tumult and peace, the darkness and the light—
Were all like workings of one mind, the features
Of the same face, blossoms upon one tree;
Characters of the great Apocalypse,
The types and symbols of Eternity,
Of first, and last, and midst, and without end.[1]

The experience is recorded in the very language of a monistic idealism, the philosophy upon which transcendentalism is usually based. The last line defines the timelessness and infinity of the Absolute Mind. It should be recognized, however, that this passage was written long after the original experience, and that the interpretation may owe much to intervening reflection.

On this same trip the two friends came into contact with the rising tide of the French Revolution, which was soon to sweep the poet into a new period in his development.

5. *Early Manhood: The Stage of Reason as an Analytical Faculty*

By the age of 22 Wordsworth had reached a state in which man was foremost in his affections. Although he had spent a period in London during the early months of 1791, the shifting of his love from nature to man did not occur until the following winter. It coincided with his plunge into radical politics and his love for Annette during a visit to France in December 1791–January 1792.[2] Fresh from college, with very little money and no definite plans, he was caught up in the mighty drama of the Revolution. He remained in France for more than a year, mostly at Orleans and Blois, as an ardent supporter of the Girondist party. To Wordsworth the French upheaval opened a whole new world of possibilities:

. . . Europe at that time was thrilled with joy,
France standing on the top of golden hours,
And human nature seeming born again.[3]

[1] *Prelude*, VI. 624–40.
[2] *The Prelude*, ed. E. de Selincourt and H. Darbishire, p. 580.
[3] *Prelude*, VI. 339–41.

Even when the blood-baths of the Revolutionary terror piled horror upon horror, he clung tenaciously to his revolutionary faith.

In the midst of his intial excitement, he fell head over heels in love with Annette Vallon, a young Frenchwoman living in Blois. To the enraptured young poet it seemed that

> Earth breathed in one great presence of the spring;
> Life turned the meanest of her implements,
> Before his eyes, to price above all gold;
> The house she dwelt in was a sainted shrine;
> Her chamber-window did surpass in glory
> The portals of the dawn; all Paradise
> Could, by the simple opening of a door,
> Let itself in upon him:—pathways, walks,
> Swarmed with enchantment, till his spirit sank,
> Surcharged within him, overblest to move
> Beneath a sun that wakes a weary world
> To its dull round of ordinary cares:
> A man too happy for mortality![1]

Annette gave birth to a daughter whose paternity Wordsworth acknowledged and who was baptized Anne Caroline Wordsworth. In December 1792 the young and needy poet returned to England hoping to persuade his guardians to continue his allowance for further residence in France. But to his horror, the sudden outbreak of war between France and England interposed a formidable barrier to his return to Annette and Caroline. There were also barriers of belief and commitment: Annette was French, he was English and patriotic; she was a Catholic, he was a rather free-thinking Protestant; she was a passionate Royalist, he an ardent Republican. Nevertheless, the ensuing long separation from Annette must have contributed greatly to the crisis in his mental history. The tragic theme of the unwed or deserted mother—as expressed in such early poems as *The Ruined Cottage*, *The Thorn*, *The Mad Mother*, *Vaudracour and Julia*, and *Ruth*—bears witness to his feelings of pity and remorse.

When the war between England and France broke out in February 1793 Wordsworth was still pro-French and prayed for

---

[1] *Vaudracour and Julia*, 41–53. *Poetical Works*, ii. 59.

the defeat of his own countrymen. But gradually the terror and dictatorship in France filled his mind with profound revulsion:

> Through months, through years, long after the last beat
> Of those atrocities . . .
> I scarcely had one night of quiet sleep,
> Such ghastly visions had I of despair
> And tyranny, and implements of death,
> And long orations which in dreams I pleaded
> Before unjust Tribunals, with a voice
> Labouring, a brain confounded, and a sense
> Of treachery, and desertion in the place
> The holiest that I knew of, my own soul.[1]

Although disillusioned with the French excesses, he clung tenaciously to his Republican principles. As late as 1804, when he was writing the later books of *The Prelude*, he denounced the repressive British officials as 'vermin', scorning them with an intensity 'that would profane the sanctity of verse'.[2]

In reacting against both the excesses of the French dictatorship and the reactionary government of Britain he found himself adrift in a sea of perplexity. The only beacon that he could find to guide him was Godwinism. He not only read Godwin's books, *Political Justice* and *Caleb Williams*, but repeatedly called upon the author in person. Entries found in Godwin's diaries record nine meetings with Wordsworth between February and August 1795. Years later, defending himself against Hazlitt's charge that he was a dull conversationalist, Godwin wrote: 'I had the honour, in the talk of one evening, to convert Wordsworth from the doctrine of self-love to that of benevolence—ask him.'[3] The doctrine of benevolence, which pitted Godwin against the cynics of the age, must have done much to restore Wordsworth's faith in the dignity and goodness of human nature. But another strain in Godwin's philosophy—its dry and narrow rationalism—worked havoc with the young poet's mind. Godwin had no use for nature, for sentiment, for tradition, for civil society, and he recognized no guide except individual reason. Embracing this rationalist dogma, Wordsworth tried to solve

---

[1] *Prelude* (1805), X. 371–81. [2] Cf. ibid. X. 636–57.
[3] Quoted by Ben Ross Schneider, Jr., *Wordsworth's Cambridge Education*, op. cit., p. 222. The original letter, along with Godwin's Diary, is among Godwin's papers now in microfilm at Duke University.

all moral problems through 'the human Reason's naked self'. He 'magisterially' adopted

> One guide, the light of circumstances, flashed
> Upon an independent intellect.[1]

This was contrary to the whole tenor of his mental history from earliest childhood. So narrow a rationalism was bound to clash with his deeper self:

> Thus strangely did I war against myself;
> A Bigot to a new Idolatry
> Did like a Monk who hath forsworn the world
> Zealously labour to cut off my heart
> From all the sources of her former strength;
> And, as by simple waving of a wand
> The wizard instantaneously dissolves
> Palace or grove, even so did I unsoul
> As readily by syllogistic words
> Some charm of Logic, ever within reach,
> Those mysteries of passion which have made,
> And shall continue evermore to make . . .
> One brotherhood of all the human race.[2]

His mind was possessed by the faculty of analysis and judgement, not inglorious but below the higher type of reason. This is made clear in a passage which, although poetically inferior, is important for the understanding of his thought.

> There comes (if need be now to speak of this
> After such long detail of our mistakes)
> There comes a time when Reason, not the grand
> And simple Reason, but that humbler power
> Which carries on its no inglorious work
> By logic and minute analysis
> Is of all Idols that which pleases most
> The growing mind. A Trifler would he be
> Who on the obvious benefits should dwell
> That rise out of this process; but to speak
> Of all the narrow estimates of things
> Which hence originate were a worthy theme
> For philosophic Verse; suffice it here
> To hint that danger cannot but attend
> Upon a Function rather proud to be

---

[1] *Prelude*, XI. 243–4.   [2] *Prelude* (1805), XI. 74–88.

> The enemy of falsehood, than the friend
> Of truth, to sit in judgment than to feel.[1]

Just as fancy, an inferior faculty of the poetic spirit, precedes imagination in order of mental evolution, so also mere logical reason, a lower faculty of the intellect, appears in advance of the synthetic reason, which integrates thought and feeling. The contrast between these two types of reason serves to differentiate this transitional phase, when thought worked at variance with feeling, from what I have termed the fifth stage.

The result of this licentiousness of the purely logical intellect was nothing less than a withering of the imaginative life. Wordsworth carried the spirit of judgement into the midst of all his perceptions: 'giving way to a comparison of scene with scene'; 'disliking here, and there liking' according to 'rules of mimic art'; 'roaming from hill to hill, from rock to rock', craving 'combinations of new forms'; until his intellect suppressed his deeper feelings, but left his 'bodily eye' unfettered.[2]

A number of critics have supposed that the resultant 'absolute dominion' of sensation applies to the period of youth and fancy, when the mind was still very undeveloped. Instead, this state commences subsequent to Wordsworth's return from France, a whole year after the age of reason had set in. As the months went by, the rule of sensation became more tyrannical, until, at the time of the moral crisis of 1795, his personality was reft in a 'twofold frame of body and of mind'. This, said Wordsworth, was a period

> When the bodily eye, in every stage of life
> The most despotic of our senses, gained
> Such strength in *me* as often held my mind
> In absolute dominion.[3]

Thus the clearest expression in *The Prelude* of the tyranny of sensation refers to the time when an excess of analytical reason had caused his 'soul's last and lowest ebb'.[4]

Incidentally, we must now clear up a misunderstanding concerning *Tintern Abbey*. Arthur Beatty, Herbert Read, and others

---

[1] *Prelude* (1805), XI. 121–37.
[2] Cf. *Prelude*, XII. 106–21, 140–7.
[3] Ibid. XII. 127–31. See the explanatory notes in the E. de Selincourt and H. Darbishire edition, pp. 603–6 and 610–11.
[4] *Prelude*, XI. 307.

consider the poem to be an exposition of 'the three ages of man'.
I have already asked whether Wordsworth's mystical experiences, as reported in the poem, can be fitted into the Hartleian
scheme. But the point I now wish to make is different. According to the doctrine of the three ages, the stage of pure sensation
is that of childhood, the stage of strong emotion is that of youth,
and the stage of philosophic thought is that of maturity. This
interpretation when applied to *Tintern Abbey* is tidy but too re-
strictive.

As its full title indicates, the poem was composed on 13 July
1798. The first lines are:

> Five years have past; five summers, with the length
> Of five long winters! and again I hear
> These waters, rolling from their mountain springs
> With a soft inland murmur.

The initial visit was thus five years before, in 1793. It is to *this*
earlier period that Wordsworth refers in the lines:

> And now, with gleams of half-extinguished thought,
> With many recognitions dim and faint,
> And somewhat of a sad perplexity,
> The picture of the mind revives again:
> While here I stand, not only with the sense
> Of present pleasure, but with pleasing thoughts
> That in this moment there is life and food
> For future years. And so I dare to hope,
> Though changed, no doubt, from what I was when first
> I came among these hills; when like a roe
> I bounded o'er the mountains, by the sides
> Of the deep rivers, and the lonely streams,
> Wherever nature led: more like a man
> Flying from something that he dreads than one
> Who sought the thing he loved. For nature then
> (The coarser pleasures of my boyish days,
> And their glad animal movements all gone by)
> To me was all in all.—I cannot paint
> What then I was. The sounding cataract
> Haunted me like a passion: the tall rock,
> The mountain, and the deep and gloomy wood,
> Their colours and their forms, were then to me
> An appetite; a feeling and a love,
> That had no need for a remoter charm,

By thought supplied, nor any interest
Unborrowed from the eye.—That time is past,
And all its aching joys are now no more,
And all its dizzy raptures.

This account tallies with a similar description in *The Prelude*.[1]
According to the schematism of 'the three ages', one would
expect to find 'the bodily eye' predominant in boyhood and
'dizzy raptures' characteristic of youth. Instead one finds these
states most clearly embodied in the crisis of early manhood.
Life, with its unforeseeable exigencies, has a way of refusing to
fit into any *a priori* scheme. Once we abandon a rigid schematism, we can admit that certain characteristic traits can appear
in boyhood or youth and *reappear* in later years. Hence Wordsworth, and later Beatty, could cite this passage as descriptive
of a 'youthful mind'.[2]

Characteristic of Wordsworth's restlessness after his return
from France was the fluctuation between opposite poles. On the
one hand, there is the feverish return to nature described in
Tintern Abbey; on the other hand, there is a hankering to escape
from the country into the bustling activity of the city. On
7 November 1794 he wrote to his friend William Mathews:
'I begin to wish much to be in Town. Cataracts and mountains
are good occasional society, but they will not do for constant
companions.'[3] Turning away from nature represents a derelic-
tion from his primary loyalties.

In this mood he moved to London, arriving in the metropolis
in early February 1795 and remaining until August. There were
other visits to London both before and after this sojourn. In
his poetic account of that bustling world he includes the whole
'motley imagery' of fairs, circuses, theatres, parliament, shops,
factories, slums, and fashionable promenades. Although he found
much to interest and delight him, his lasting impression was
that of suffering and alienation:

He truly is alone,
He of the multitude whose eyes are doomed
To hold a vacant commerce day by day
With objects wanting life, repelling love;

[1] *Prelude*, XII. 140–7.
[2] See Beatty, *William Wordsworth*, op. cit., pp. 95–96, for the poet's comment.
[3] *Early Letters*, p. 128.

He by the vast Metropolis immured,
Where pity shrinks from unremitting calls,
Where numbers overwhelm humanity,
And neighbourhood serves rather to divide
Than to unite.[1]

Unless with nature we have sympathy, Wordsworth tells us, we shall find little for our fellow man. He eventually returned to the countryside to rediscover not only the loveliness of natural forms but the deep roots of human fraternity:

From crowded streets remote,
Far from the living and dead wilderness
Of the thronged World, Society is here
A true Community, a genuine frame
Of many into one incorporate.[2]

There is much to indicate that he found a certain grandeur in the multifarious life of the great city and thereby attained a deeper understanding of humanity. He became aware not only of the gaiety but of

the fierce confederate storm
Of sorrow, barricadoed evermore
Within the walls of cities.[3]

This awareness, however painful, served to deepen and humanize his soul.

So likewise, in transcending the stage of analytical reason, he did not turn his back on scientific research nor wholly deny the value of intellectual analysis. 'Poetry', he said in his famous Preface, 'is the breath and finer spirit of all knowledge; it is the impassioned expression which is in the countenance of all science.' In *The Prelude* he traced the growth of a mind which fought its way through incomplete loyalties to a rich and integrated personality. The faculty of judgement and comparison, like the analogous gift of fancy, is an indispensable but subordinate constituent of the good life. It is below the synthetic reason because it introduces, when in command, a sharp division into consciousness; for it becomes 'sequestered' from the feelings and the imagination. After the same fashion, the 'bodily

---

[1] Early version of *The Recluse*, in *Poetical Works*, v. 333 (ll. 593–601).
[2] Ibid., pp. 333–4 (ll. 612–16).
[3] *Recluse*, 831–3.

eye' is to be subordinated to the 'intellectual eye', because the latter eliminates the 'twofold frame' of the divided personality.

6. Maturity: The Stage of Imagination and Synthetic Reason

Freed from worldly cares by a legacy from Raisley Calvert and deeply inspired by Coleridge and Dorothy, Wordsworth finally emerged from his moral depression. I have written in Chapter I of the profound influence of Coleridge and the deep love that united the two poets. But Dorothy also was a spirit of rare genius, with great delicacy of intuition and a most penetrating eye for natural beauty. She and Wordsworth loved one another with very tender devotion.

> Witness thou
> The dear companion of my lonely walk,
> My hope, my joy, my sister, and my friend,
> Or something dearer still, if reason knows
> A dearer thought, or in the heart of love
> There be a dearer name.[1]

Bateson believes that this love eventually attained incestuous intensity, the guilty possibilities being repressed into the subconscious, there to remain a secret source of melancholia. However that may be, the immediate influence of his sister in helping Wordsworth to recover was wholesome and strong.

The restoration was gradual, and cannot be said to have been completed until the summer of 1797 or later. It brought with it a return of those 'serene and blessed moods' that he had occasionally known in his youth. One way that he interpreted these renewed experiences is indicated by a fragment of poetry taken from a manuscript notebook and published for the first time in the variorum edition of *The Prelude*. Upon the basis of internal evidence afforded by the notebook, Mr. Ernest de Selincourt decided that these lines were probably written between the summer of 1798 and February 1800:

> I seemed to learn [   ][2]
> That what we see of forms and images
> Which float along our minds, and what we feel

---

[1] *Poetical Works*, v. 347.
[2] The remainder of the line is illegible in the present state of the manuscript.

Of active or recognizable thought,
Prospectiveness, or intellect, or will,
Not only is not worthy to be deemed
Our being, to be prized as what we are,
But is the very littleness of life.
Such consciousness I deem but accidents,
Relapses from the one interior life
That lives in all things, sacred from the touch
Of that false secondary power by which
In weakness we create distinctions, then
Believe that all our puny boundaries are things
Which we perceive and not which we have made;
—In which all beings live with god, themselves
Are god, Existing in the mighty whole,
As indistinguishable as the cloudless East
At noon is from the cloudless west, when all
The hemisphere is one cerulean blue.[1]

This fragment, which is so revealing that we shall return to it repeatedly, proves that Wordsworth was very deeply affected by a mystical conception of reality. Forms and images represent the very littleness of life; and intellective processes are mere relapses from the unitary life in which all beings share. Our puny boundaries are man-made; the true reality is the ineffable unity. The '*one interior* life lives *in* all things'; therefore sensations, with their report of the external world, are mere 'accidents' in comparison with the inward sense that we are god. Thus Wordsworth presents a sweeping denial of the external senses and the reason and an assertion of a completely mystical point of view.

It may be objected that the poet did not finally include this manuscript fragment in *The Prelude*, and that the thought must have represented, therefore, an aberration which was rejected in a more reasonable mood. Fortunately we can give this objection its proper weight.

We have reason to hope that the passage in *The Prelude* which reproduces four of the lines might furnish some indication why the substance of the entire first draft was not incorporated. Turning to this passage, we find a tribute to Coleridge which was quoted in our first chapter. The two lines immediately following the lines reproduced are these:

[1] *The Prelude*, ed. E. de Selincourt, first edition, pp. 512–13.

To thee, unblinded by these formal arts,
The unity of all hath been revealed.[1]

It appears from this statement that Wordsworth agreed with
Coleridge in asserting the unity that he so positively affirmed in
the fragment. This declaration, however, is much more moderate
than the lines which follow the denunciation of 'the false secondary
power' in the first manuscript version. Why did the poet thus
temper his statement? We suspect that it was due to Coleridge's
influence, because the entire passage as it appears in Book II
is concerned with Coleridge and his ideas. We therefore turn to
another passage which sums up Wordsworth's indebtedness
to his friend. Here we find a statement, also reproduced in our
first chapter, describing the transition from pantheism to an immanent theism:

> And so the deep enthusiastic joy,
> The rapture of the Hallelujah sent
> From all that breathes and is, was chasten'd, stemm'd
> And balanced by a Reason which indeed
> Is reason; duty and pathetic truth;
> And God and Man divided, as they ought,
> Between them the great system of the world
> Where Man is sphered, and which God animates.[2]

Thus it becomes clearer than ever that Wordsworth had an
early period of mystical and radically pantheistic conviction,
and that Coleridge finally converted him to a decided modification of this philosophy. The influence of Coleridge is a partial,
but not a complete, explanation for Wordsworth's revision of
the sentiments contained in the manuscript fragment.

A more complete explanation can be found in the inconsistency of the manuscript fragment with the development
of Wordsworth as a man and poet. In the fragment the sense of
unity is so absolute that ideas and images of particular things
are dismissed as illusory. This kind of mysticism can be called
'negative' because it turns away from all the wealth of nature
to seek identification with an undifferentiated unity. Carried to
its limits, this position differs in no way from the contention
of extreme Oriental pantheism that 'the distinction of objects

[1] *Prelude*, II. 220–1.   [2] *Prelude* (1805), XIII. 261–8.

known, knowers, acts of knowledge, . . . is fictitiously created by Nescience'.[1] Its votaries teach the unreality of earthly things; they often regard the flesh and spirit as at war; they view the ordinary world as a prison; and they reject science as a basis of belief. Wordsworth could not permanently rest in any such creed without forsaking his love of nature and individual human beings.

Hence this negative mysticism was soon abandoned and re-placed by the positive mysticism of *Tintern Abbey*. Here he speaks of trance-like experiences in which the body is laid to sleep and 'we . . . become a living soul', while, with 'an eye made quiet' by the power of joy and harmony, we 'see into the *life* of *things*'. The unitary 'life' does not negate 'things' in the plural. There is no turning away from individual forms and the copious variety of nature. Because of the mystic vision, natural objects and individual persons are more precious rather than less. Con-sequently, Wordsworth is

> A lover of the meadows and the woods
> And mountains, and of all that we behold
> From this green earth. . . .[2]

This attitude separates Wordsworth decisively from the negative mystics, but his outlook upon the world is none the less mystical for being positive. Whenever he portrays these 'blessed' moods his words quicken with heightened vitality. It may be that we are here touching upon his genius, approaching the great 'hiding place' of his power. In the following lines from *The Recluse*, written in 1800, we are permitted to peer deep into his mind:

> Of ill-advised Ambition and of Pride
> I would stand clear, but yet to me I feel
> That an internal brightness is vouchsafed
> That must not die, that must not pass away . . .
> Possessions have I that are solely mine,
> Something within which yet is shared by none,
> Not even the nearest to me and most dear,
> Something which power and effort may impart:
> I would impart it, I would spread it wide.[3]

---

[1] Sankara Acharya (*c.* A.D. 789–820) in *Sacred Books of East*, ed. F. Max Müller (Oxford University Press, 1890), xxxiv, pp. 14–15.

[2] *Tintern Abbey*, 103–5.   [3] *Recluse*, 673–90.

What is this 'internal brightness' which none shares, not even the nearest to him and the dearest? Not mere sensitive acuteness to the external world, because he shared this with Dorothy:

She gave me eyes, she gave me ears.[1]

Not simply philosophical insight, because he recognized Coleridge's pre-eminence in this respect. Not poetical genius, because this could never be transferred. It was, I think, nothing less than the deep pervasive joy that pulsed through his being as a result of the mystical intuitions that neither Dorothy, nor Coleridge, nor any of his friends, could quite share with him. The aspiration that troubled his dreams and irradiated his whole moral being was to impart the vision which his lonely spirit had captured.

He had now attained a maturity of insight and a breadth of personality for which all his experience had prepared him. The excesses of fancy, sensationism, analytical reason, and mysticism had been rooted out, but not before new values had been sown by each phase. The higher faculties of imagination and synthetic reason controlled the lower, but they did not substitute themselves in place of the inferior powers. There was no annihilation of the lesser faculties, no swamping out of fancy, analysis, and sensuousness, for this suppression would have deprived the greater functions of their support, dissipating them in a vacuous idealism. Instead there was complete representation of the several aspects of the personality—sense, emotion, reason, and spirit—of which the higher were not earth-spurning. Even though man was now primary in Wordsworth's regard, he was still 'wedded to this goodly universe In love and holy passion'. I have been presenting, to be sure, the ideal extension and correction of his real self; but to a remarkable degree he approximated this state in creation and practice. To do so was his greatest achievement, of which *Tintern Abbey*, the *Intimations of Immortality*, and *The Prelude* offer the record which will 'look Time's leaguer down'.

I have traced the development of Wordsworth's mind through the various stages of its growth to the point represented by the final book of *The Prelude*.

---

[1] *The Sparrow's Nest. Poetical Works*, i. 227.

> Imagination having been our theme,
> So also hath that intellectual Love,
> For they are each in each, and cannot stand
> Dividually.[1]

Love and imagination and reason all coalesce in the apprehension of reality:

> Imagination, . . . in truth,
> Is but another name for absolute power
> And clearest insight, amplitude of mind,
> And Reason in her most exalted mood.[2]

His long struggle to achieve psychic integration had culminated in a majestic but precarious synthesis.

7. *The Ebbing of Inspiration*

This richness without confusion, this fullness of harmony, was altogether too rare and difficult to remain for long the organizing principle of Wordsworth's personality. One of the first constituents to drop out of his life was his mystical experience. At the age of about thirty his trance-like moments seemed to have ceased. There is a suggestion of this change in *The Prelude*:

> The days gone by
> Return upon me almost from the dawn
> Of life: the hiding-places of man's power
> Open; I would approach them, but they close.
> I see by glimpses now; when age comes on,
> May scarcely see at all; and I would give,
> While yet we may, as far as words can give,
> Substance and life to what I feel.[3]

In the *Intimations of Immortality* (1802–4) he recognized the departure of the raptures that he had known, but he takes comfort in the reflection that faith and thought can even more completely reconcile him to life than did his old intense experiences.

Probably one reason why he so emphasized the role of memory in the poetry written in his maturity, is that he found that his ecstasy was departing or had already departed; and that only the brooding processes of recollection could secure values

---

[1] *Prelude*, XIV. 206–9.   [2] Ibid. XIV. 189–92.
[3] Ibid. XII. 277–84.

deep enough to take its place. So was created a new mood somewhat like the first, but perhaps even richer and deeper. Yet the conscious effort involved in remembrance was not permanently to sustain him at the height of his power.

We need not trace the change in heart and mind which he underwent in later years. It will be enough to indicate a poem that records his alteration. In *Composed Upon an Evening of Extraordinary Beauty and Splendour*, written in 1817, Wordsworth describes the 'fervent rapture' that suddenly visits him and recalls to his mind the glories of childhood. He then proceeds:

> This glimpse of glory, why renewed?
> Nay, rather speak with gratitude;
> For if a vestige of those gleams
> Survived, 'twas only in my dreams.
> Dread Power! whom peace and calmness serve
> No less than Nature's threatening voice,
> If aught unworthy be my choice,
> From Thee if I would swerve;
> Oh, let Thy grace remind me of the light
> Full early lost, and fruitlessly deplored;
> Which, at this moment, on my waking sight
> Appears to shine, by miracle restored;
> My soul, though yet confined to earth,
> Rejoices in a second birth!
> —'Tis past, the visionary splendour fades;
> And night approaches with her shades.

It becomes evident upon a careful reading of the poem that the 'second birth' is simply the 'glimpse of glory' that immediately departs. This rebirth is merely 'the dower bestowed on this transcendent hour'; it is only the 'visionary splendour' that 'fades' while 'night approaches with her shades'. He 'fruitlessly deplored' 'the light full early lost' because he was powerless to regain the visionary gleam of that far-off time. By 1819 he had lost touch with the complete synthesis of manhood as well as the fervent raptures of childhood.

There have been many attempted explanations of the slackening in his poetic powers. Not only Wordsworth, but many other poets, have suffered this sort of change. As he himself noted, not only in the Ode on Immortality but in the last book of *The*

Prelude, 'the frost of custom' dulls all but the hardiest of spirits. Poets, as well as ordinary people, suffer from

> The tendency, too potent in itself,
> Of use and custom to bow down the soul
> Under a growing weight of vulgar sense,
> And substitute a universe of death
> For that which moves with light and life informed,
> Actual, divine, and true.[1]

The peculiar nature of Wordsworth's genius may help to explain his difficulties. His mind was distinguished by the combination of very sharp perception and very intense subjectivity. The 'fallings from us, vanishings' and the ecstasies of mystical experience represent one side of his nature. But no less remarkable was the acuteness of his sensory perceptions. In his old age he remarked with justifiable pride: 'I have hardly ever known anyone but myself who had a true eye for nature.'[2] This minute accuracy of his visual and auditory impressions was preserved by a most retentive memory. From both these sources, 'the abysses of idealism' and the vivid apprehension of natural appearances, he drew the matter of most of his poems. As Bateson suggests, 'the efficient cause, so far as the poetry had a single originating source, was the impelling need Wordsworth felt to integrate the more subjective or inward-looking and the more objective or outward-looking aspects of his personality'.[3] All his greatest poetry was written in the moments when he succeeded in this endeavour. In the following passage we can see how his mind worked:

> There is creation in the eye,
> Not less in all the other senses; powers
> They are that colour, model, and combine
> The things perceived with such an absolute
> Essential energy that we may say
> That those most godlike faculties of ours
> At one and the same moment are the mind
> And the mind's minister. In many a walk
> At evening or by moonlight, or reclined
> At midday upon beds of forest moss
> Have we to Nature and her impulses

---

[1] Ibid. XIV. 157–62.   [2] *Prose Works*, ed. Grosart, iii, p. 488.
[3] F. W. Bateson, *Wordsworth*, op. cit., p. 186.

Of our whole being made free gift, and when
Our trance had left us, oft have we, by aid
Of the impressions which it left behind,
Looked inward on ourselves, and learned, perhaps,
Something of what we are. Nor in those hours
Did we destroy. . . .
The original impression of delight,
But by such retrospect it was recalled
To yet a second and a second life,
While in this excitation of the mind
A vivid pulse of sentiment and thought
Beat palpably within us, and all shades
Of consciousness were ours.[1]

The right blend of the inner and the outer, of sensory acuteness and the depths of subjectivity, was bound to be a difficult feat. The spirit bloweth where it listeth, and the wonder is not that it departed but that it was so marvellous when it came.

His personal tribulations should also be taken into consideration. The love for Annette and no less the love for Dorothy ran into difficulties, and the man-to-man love for Coleridge likewise suffered. Marrying at the age of thirty-two, Wordsworth dearly cherished his wife Mary but never, it appears, recovered the rapture of his early love for Annette. The drowning (6 February 1805) of his favourite brother John dealt his morale a very severe blow. Again and again the members of the Wordsworth circle were struck by tragedy: the opium-addiction of Coleridge and De Quincey, the double insanity of Charles and Mary Lamb and of Southey and his wife—not to mention similar afflictions among Wordsworth's less intimate friends—must have distressed him sorely. Most heart-rending of all was the mental breakdown of his sister Dorothy, and her living on for twenty-five years a shattered wreck. Then there were the deaths of Wordsworth's children: Catherine in her fourth year, Thomas in his sixth, and his passionately beloved Dora after she had attained to young womanhood.

Wordsworth himself suffered from illness and psychological difficulties. From the age of seventeen he was subject to violent sick headaches, and later plagued by fits of depression. Of his recurrent moods of melancholy, his 'fears' and 'dim sadness'

---

[1] *Poetical Works*, v. 343–4.

and 'blind thoughts', Wordsworth speaks in *Resolution and Independence*:

> We Poets in our youth begin in gladness;
> But thereof come in the end despondency and madness.

Finally he suffered from an eye disease so severe that during 'the last forty years of his life he was living under the threat of blindness, . . . he was frequently in severe pain, and . . . for long periods, twice at least for more than a year at a time, he was physically incapable of reading and writing and of continuous poetic composition'.[1]

He fell back upon the best defences he could muster—vigorous life in the open air and a Stoical philosophy. Even at the age of sixty he was the crack skater on Rydal Lake and one of the hardiest mountain climbers in England. He never gave up his love for wandering and again and again was off on walking tours. Equal to his physical hardihood was his inward strength. His poems abound in figures of heroic endurance, such as Michael, the Leech Gatherer, the Old Cumberland Beggar, and the Happy Warrior. In *Laodamia* he characteristically wrote:

> . . . the Gods approve
> The depth, and not the tumult, of the soul.

As he grew older his Stoicism gradually gave way to a dignified Christianity, but the iron in his soul remained. He was still a poet of consummate skill although no longer of bold originality.

What I have tried to prove in this chapter may be summarized as follows. According to Wordsworth's retrospective account of his own life, there are five periods which severally represent the dominion of one or two major faculties of his mind: sensation, emotion, fancy, analytical reason, synthetic reason, and imagination. It should not be understood by this division that there are distinct stages or mental factors which must always be thought of as separate. What I have called the stage of sensation is very idealistic; the stage of emotion is thoughtful and creative; imagination almost dominates the stage of fancy; the period of analytical reason brings an interval of intense hunger and passion; the stage of imagination and the 'grand' reason is often merely fanciful, and frequently logical in the narrow sense:

[1] Edith Batho, *The Later Wordsworth* (Cambridge University Press, 1933), pp. 319–20.

in other words, the five-fold division is an abstraction employed for the sake of a fuller understanding. By this approach I have sought to make one fact clear: Wordsworth's mind was not a mechanical structure in which one function excluded another; it was a vital evolution in which the early stages were incorporated into the completed economy. The fundamental conception in his ethical theory is the relational and conservative nature of human growth. The values of earlier development are focused in the mature mind, gathered and contained there like rays in a prism; when thus captured they saturate the entire spirit with their reciprocal light. We discover a hierarchy of values, to be sure, but neither the rigidity of 'the three ages of man', nor the benevolent tyranny of reason to be found in rationalistic ethics; the higher state protects the lower because it is constituted thereof. Thus a great inwardness is achieved without the sacrifice of a shrewd outwardness; the poet remains 'true to the kindred points of Heaven and Home'.[1]

[1] 'Ethereal Minstrel! pilgrim of the sky!' *To a Skylark, Poetical Works,* ii. 266.

IV. SENSE AND IMAGINATION

1. *Wordsworth's Reliance on the Associational Psychology*

I n the preceding chapter I have referred to the two poles of
Wordsworth's genius: his intense inwardness and his acute perception of natural objects. These were complementary: the poet's
spirituality cast a visionary splendour over outward things, and
the beauty of nature stirred the depths of subjectivity:

> To gaze
> On that green hill and on those scattered trees
> And feel a pleasant consciousness of life,
> In the impression of that loveliness,
> Until the sweet sensation called the mind
> Into itself, by image from without
> Unvisited, and all her reflex powers
> Wrapped in a still dream of forgetfulness.
> I lived without the knowledge that I lived,
> Then by those beauteous forms brought back again
> To lose myself again, as if my life
> Did ebb and flow with a strange mystery.[1]

Life swings between the two poles, the 'beauteous forms' of
outer perception and the 'still dream of forgetfulness'. 'Sweet
sensation' calls the mind into itself, 'by image from without
unvisited', but then the self again awakens to the loveliness of
natural forms, made still more lovely by the visionary power of
the mind.

Wordsworth tried to understand 'the strange mystery' of
this 'ebb and flow'. The human mind, he concluded, hearkens to
'voices of two different natures', one of them received from sensory experience, the other from inmost modes of being. These
voices are so intimately connected that the second follows from
the first, like an echo 'giving sound . . . for sound'; yet it would
be wrong to confuse the two.[2] In the present chapter we shall

---

[1] *Poetical Works*, v. 341.
[2] 'Yes, it was the mountain Echo,' ibid. ii. 265.

consider Wordsworth's interpretation of the voice of experience, postponing until the next chapter his theory of the inner voice. Since the one voice implicates the other, the division between the two chapters cannot be sharp.

Recognizing that sensation does play momentously upon the mind, Wordsworth was confronted with the problem of the reactions which follow. He early found in Hartleianism, as conveyed to him by Coleridge and independent study, an elaborate account of sensory stimulation and the consequent formation of ideas. Like Coleridge, he rejected Hartley's sensationism as an exclusive theory, but he found that the associational psychology could be applied to one side of mental life.

Hartley's theory is as follows. Sensations or ideas become associated when they appear in the mind 'at the same Instant of Time, or in the contiguous successive instants'.[1] The strength of the linkage depends also upon the vividness of the associated impressions and the frequency of repetition. For example, if I see a cat hissing at a dog, especially if the sight is frequently repeated or makes an intense original impression, I shall remember the dog when I again catch sight of the cat. All such associations may become increasingly complex: around one's idea of the cat may collect many notions—of milk, catmint, scratches, maternity, bad luck. In the case of highly 'intellectual ideas' the elements that contribute to the associational clusters are often so numerous and so faded that the complex idea may balk all attempt to analyse it. The idea of justice, for example, is such a composite, in which the ideas and feelings gained from a great range of experience have coalesced into a most abstract notion. We cannot trace back all the associated elements; but Hartley, as a strict associationist, believes that the concept of justice, or any other abstract idea, is formed by the same associational process as the notion of the cat.

The several stages in the association of ideas are set forth in the form of propositions:

Sensations, by being often repeated, leave certain Vestiges, Types, or Images, of themselves, which may be called, Simple Ideas of Sensation.[2]

---

[1] Hartley, *Observations on Man*, prop. x. (All references in this chapter are to Book I of Hartley's text. Again, since the pagination differs in various editions, I shall refer to propositions rather than pages.)   [2] Ibid., prop. viii.

Any Sensations A, B, C, &c., by being associated with one another a sufficient Number of Times, get such a Power over corresponding Ideas, a, b, c, &c., that any one of the Sensations A, when impressed alone, shall be able to excite in the Mind, b, c, &c., the Ideas of the rest.[1]

And upon the whole, it may appear to the reader, that the simple ideas of sensation must run into clusters and combinations, by association; and that each of these will, at last, coalesce into one complex idea, by the approach and commixture of the several compounding parts.[2]

In this process of association, sensations may be associated with either ideas of sensation or intellectual ideas; any type of mental content with any other type; or the association may be within one type, sensation with sensation, simple idea with simple idea, or complex idea with complex idea.

The development of thought is further enriched by the use of language. From an early age 'many sensible impressions and internal feelings are associated with particular words and phrases, so as to give these the power of raising the corresponding ideas', as, for example, the association of the sound 'nurse' with the picture of the nurse on the retina. 'Since words thus collect ideas from various quarters, unite them together, and transfer them both upon other words, and upon foreign objects, it is evident, that the use of words adds much to the number and complexness of our ideas, and is the principal means by which we make intellectual and moral improvements.'[3] Thus, little by little, the mind acquires its complex ideas.

By similar reasoning Hartley traces complex emotions back to the simple feelings that accompany the original sensations. As a hedonist, he puts primary stress upon pleasure and pain, maintaining that 'the sensible pleasures and pains . . . are the common source from whence all the intellectual pleasures and pains are ultimately derived'.[4] We begin, then, with sensation, and proceed by associating pleasure with ever loftier objects and more intellectual ideas, until we reach the stage of moral and religious maturity.

This development, as Hartley optimistically conceives it, is the natural progress of the human mind towards perfection. 'Some

[1] Ibid., prop. x.   [2] Ibid., prop. xii, case 5.
[3] Ibid., prop. lxxx.   [4] Ibid., chap. iv, second paragraph.

degree of spirituality is the necessary consequence of passing through life. . . . Association . . . has a tendency to reduce the state of those who have eaten of the tree of the knowledge of good and evil, back again to a paradisiacal one.'[1] Hartley argues that 'our sensible pleasures are far more numerous than our sensible pains', and that in the process of association the pains tend to be cancelled out, so that 'the remainder . . . will be pure pleasure'. By devising a sound education and a wholesome environment we can control the associational process and make the human race happy. Thus Hartley's argument arrives at 'some pleasing presumptions':

> . . . that we have a power of suiting our frame of mind to our circumstances, of correcting what is amiss, and improving what is right: that our ultimate happiness appears to be of a spiritual, not corporeal nature . . . : that association tends to make us all ultimately similar; so that if one be happy, all must: and lastly, that the same association may also be shewn to contribute to introduce pure ultimate spiritual happiness, in all. . . .[2]

The pleasures and pains are ranged under seven classes: sensation, imagination, ambition, self-interest, sympathy, theopathy (love of God), and the moral sense. The progress of the human mind is the movement from the lower sorts of pleasure to the higher, the pleasures of sympathy, theopathy, and morality being the proper objects of human aspiration. All of these noble feelings are the resultant, not of some innate faculty, but of experience transmuted by association.

As in Godwin's works, the doctrine of human perfectibility is combined with necessitarianism. Hartley thus defines his mechanistic conception of human behaviour: 'By the mechanism of human actions I mean, that each action results from the previous circumstances of body and mind, in the same manner, and with the same certainty, as other effects do from their mechanical causes; so that a person cannot do indifferently either of the actions A, and its contrary a, while the previous circumstances are the same; but is under an absolute necessity of doing one of them, and that only.'[3] In explaining the nature of this mechanical action he brings in his theory of physical vibrations, maintaining that 'every action, or bodily motion, arises from previous

---

[1] Hartley, op. cit., prop. xiv, cor. viii and ix.
[2] Ibid., prop. xiv, cor. xii.   [3] Ibid., Conclusion, seventh paragraph.

circumstances, or bodily motions, already existing in the brain, *i.e.* from vibrations. . .'.[1] Inconsistently, the *laissez-faire* doctrine that the higher states of consciousness are 'generated necessarily and mechanically' is combined with the activist creed that we should control and alter circumstances so as to perfect the human mind.

Several features of Hartley's psychology must have appealed deeply to Wordsworth during the impressionable period (1795–8) when he was recovering from mental crisis. His strong humanitarianism, after the French dictatorship and reign of terror had so disappointed his hopes, found a new release in the doctrine of perfectibility. Having repudiated Godwin's dry intellectualism and scorn for personal sentiment, he welcomed the Hartleian emphasis upon the values of sympathy and the moral sense. His renewed faith in the healing power of nature was confirmed by the notion that the human mind is a kind of refinery distilling spirituality out of the raw materials of sensation. The doctrine of the association of ideas seemed to explain how the child is father of the man: it rationalized the search backward through time for the sources of his spiritual life. The emphasis upon memory satisfied the need for psychic distance from his personal sufferings: emotion was to be recollected in tranquillity and calmly transmuted into verse.

The following passage represents a typical expression of Wordsworth's associationism:

> Thus oft amid those fits of vulgar joy
> Which, through all seasons, on a child's pursuits
> Are prompt attendants, 'mid that giddy bliss
> Which, like a tempest, works along the blood
> And is forgotten; even then I felt
> Gleams like the flashing of a shield;—the earth
> And common face of Nature spake to me
> Rememberable things; sometimes, 'tis true,
> By chance collisions and quaint accidents
> (Like those ill-sorted unions, work supposed
> Of evil-minded fairies), yet not vain
> Nor profitless, if haply they impressed
> Collateral objects and appearances,
> Albeit lifeless then, and doomed to sleep

---

[1] Ibid., Conclusion, eighth paragraph.

Until maturer seasons called them forth
To impregnate and to elevate the mind.
—And if the vulgar joy by its own weight
Wearied itself out of the memory,
The scenes which were a witness of that joy
Remained in their substantial lineaments
Depicted on the brain, and to the eye
Were visible, a daily sight; and thus
By the impressive discipline of fear,
By pleasure and repeated happiness,
So frequently repeated, and by force
Of obscure feelings representative
Of things forgotten, these same scenes so bright,
So beautiful, so majestic in themselves,
Though yet the day was distant, did become
Habitually dear, and all their forms
And changeful colours by invisible links
Were fastened to the affections.[1]

The emphasis upon fear and pleasure 'so frequently repeated' is in accordance with Hartley's doctrine that repetition and emotional vivacity strengthen the associational linkages.

It is interesting to compare such passages with Hartley's explanation of the manner in which fear and horror ultimately contribute to the pleasures of imagination:

If there be a precipice, a cataract, a mountain of snow, &c. in one part of the scene, the nascent ideas of fear and horror magnify and enliven all the other ideas, and by degrees pass into pleasures by suggesting the security from pain. In like manner the grandeur of some scenes, and the novelty of others, by exciting surprise and wonder, *i.e.* by making a great difference in the preceding and subsequent states of mind, so as to border upon, or even enter the limits of pain, may greatly enhance the pleasure.[2]

This passage may help to explain Wordsworth's emphasis upon fear and wonder in recounting the incidents of his childhood, as for instance in the stealing of the boat, the robbing of the bird's nest, and the sight of the gibbet where a man had been hanged. But, instead of offering a simple explanation, Wordsworth speaks of the inscrutability and strangeness of the mental processes involved:

[1] *Prelude*, I. 581–612.   [2] Hartley, op. cit., prop. xciv.

Dust as we are, the immortal spirit grows
Like harmony in music; there is a dark
Inscrutable workmanship that reconciles
Discordant elements, makes them cling together
In one society. How strange that all
The terrors, pains, and early miseries,
Regrets, vexations, lassitudes interfused
Within my mind, should e'er have borne a part,
And that a needful part, in making up
The calm existence that is mine when I
Am worthy of myself![1]

Wordsworth retained Hartley's belief in the happy outcome of these mental processes, but he found no easy explanation in terms of associational psychology.

The association of ideas, however, helped the poet to explain how man became exalted in his boyish eyes, when he saw shepherds glorified by the deep radiance of the setting sun or silhouetted against the sky on the mountain height. He at first 'looked at man through objects that were great or fair'; hence the human form was loved because it was to be seen on the glowing hills or along the winding streams; the sight of man evoked emotions derived from his environment. In the period of maturity the association was often the reverse: the poet heard in nature the still sad music of humanity; the common haunts of the green earth were more dear for the sake of love and friendship. No other writer has expressed so frequently and so subtly this reciprocity of relationship through which the love of man is ennobled and the sympathy with nature is intensified.

The associational psychology served partially to explain the interdependence that pervaded consciousness. Wordsworth could find little disconnexion in the well-fashioned soul; every part of the mind seemed to implicate all the rest in itself. Relatedness bound his days each to each with natural piety. Association also created within the mind a body of sympathetic responses, so that each mental process was enriched by its affiliations; if one string of the soul was plucked, the other strings vibrated in unison. Wordsworth frequently illustrated the growth of these systems of relationships which involve each other in their

---

[1] *Prelude*, I. 340–50.

interplay. He revealed, in particular, how nature intertwined for him

> The passions that build up our human soul;
> Not with the mean and vulgar works of man,
> But with high objects, with enduring things—
> With life and nature.[1]

When the mind became 'a mansion for all lovely forms', life itself took on something of the integration of a well-knit poem.

We should recognize that Wordsworth penetrated through emotion to thought, and not vice versa. He had initially felt and lived the relations, and he subsequently utilized associationism to explain them. In his own life he achieved something of an organic interfusion of elements; perhaps otherwise he would not have been so attracted to Hartley's psychology. As soon as he found that this body of thought was inadequate, he leaped beyond it into supplementary or even contradictory notions. His attachment to Hartley was strongest when he wrote the *Lyrical Ballads*, the 1800 Preface, and Books I and II of *The Prelude*. After this period the more idealistic and transcendentalist strain in his thinking gradually became paramount. But even during his greatest attachment to associational psychology his insight was too keen and original to remain within the strict confines of Hartley's system.

2. *Necessity and Freedom*

To indicate Wordsworth's independence of Hartley, I shall compare the latter's necessitarianism with the poet's emphasis upon freedom and imaginative creativity. As I have already explained, Hartley thought that the associational clusters *must* run into higher and higher forms. From the pleasures and pains of sensation, the grossest form of life, are generated the pleasures and pains of imagination, which Hartley put much lower in the scale than did Wordsworth. Thus each class of pleasures generates the next succeeding class until completion of the seven stages: sensation, imagination, ambition, self-interest, sympathy, theopathy, and the moral sense. Each class, once brought into being, reacts upon the previous classes; but the higher and

---

[1] *Prelude*, I. 407–10.

more general classes 'never alter and new-model the particular ones so much, as that there are not many traces and vestiges of their original mechanical nature and proportions remaining'.[1]

That this progression retains its deterministic and mechanical nature is indicated by Hartley's statement that the process, if indefinitely prolonged, would reduce everybody exposed to the same environment to identical mentalities!

If beings of the same nature, but whose affections and passions are, at present, in different proportions to each other, be exposed for an indefinite time to the same impressions and associations, all their particular differences will, at last, be overruled, and they will become perfectly similar, or even equal. They may also be made perfectly similar, in a finite time, by a proper adjustment of the impressions and associations.[2]

If by manipulation of stimuli men can be reduced to perfectly similar creatures, the inward factors must be of no account except as derivative from outside. This view makes man a machine. The reader should never allow Hartley's dithyrambs about God to obscure the essentially mechanistic character of his system. Unless Wordsworth believed that the human personality is a kind of automaton, his outlook cannot be made to tally with this theory.

As I have pointed out in Chapter I (pp. 19–20), there is some evidence that he was for a time a necessitarian. In addition, Coleridge indicates that an optimistic and necessitarian approach was part of Wordsworth's original design for *The Prelude* and its sequels: '. . . He was to infer and reveal the proof of, and necessity for, the whole state of man and society being subject to, and illustrative of, a redemptive process in operation, showing how this idea reconciled all anomalies, and promised future glory and restoration.'[3] Nevertheless, it would be a mistake to identify Wordsworth's mature thought with the general tenor of Hartley's necessitarianism. The belief in determinism was after a time rejected, and even in the poet's most Hartleian period there was a much larger recognition accorded to 'vital accidents' and inward determination.

Several references to freedom appear in the early version of *The Prelude*. The first occurs in Book I, which Ernest de Selincourt

---

[1] Hartley, op. cit., prop. lxxxix. [2] Ibid., prop. xiv.
[3] Coleridge, *Table Talk*, ed. T. Ashe, op. cit., p. 171. (20 July 1832.)

thinks was completed in the latter half of 1799. Here Words-worth speaks of singling out 'with steady choice' the 'time, place and manners' propitious for poetic composition. Perhaps he held that a necessity lay behind that choice, but there is no indication that he did. The tenor of his other references to freedom is illustrated by a later passage referring to the power of his own mind to work changes independently of sensation:

> I was a chosen Son.
> For hither I had come with holy powers
> And faculties, whether to work or feel:
> To apprehend all passions and all moods
> Which time, and place, and season do impress
> Upon the visible universe, and work
> Like changes there by force of my own mind.
> I was a Freeman; in the purest sense
> Was free, and to majestic ends was strong.[1]

Here is the true Wordsworthian ring!

Even during his most naturalistic period he insisted that the mind must make its independent contribution. In the poem *Ruth*, composed in 1799 not long after the supposed conversion to Hartleianism, Wordsworth writes of a wild youth who was only encouraged in his sinful irregularity by natural objects. Arthur Beatty comments upon this poem as follows: 'Ruth's husband lived in the open air, in England, in Georgia, and on the ocean; but he got nothing but evil. Why is this? Because he *gave* nothing in the way of feeling, so that his mind had nothing to transmute into the higher forms of feeling, and he developed into a savage, and never reached the moral heights of a man.'[2] According to this interpretation, the associational processes were blocked because no feeling was present to be associated with the materials of sensation. But Wordsworth's description of 'this Stripling, sportive, gay, and bold' does not for a moment suggest that he was deficient in feeling. Does not this poem constitute an important qualification to Hartley's doctrine of optimistic necessitarianism? If the associational processes lead to good only when the individual is not too 'impetuous', too 'irregular', what happens to the 'necessity' for development toward a higher spiritual plane?

[1] *Prelude* (1805), III. 82–90.
[2] Beatty, *William Wordsworth*, op. cit., p. 213.

An analysis of *Peter Bell* leads to the same question. Before his conversion Peter was a hardy ruffian made still more savage by the natural environment.

> There was a hardness in his cheek,
> There was a hardness in his eye,
> As if the man had fixed his face,
> In many a solitary place,
> Against the wind and open sky![1]

His inward faculties were pitted *against* nature, and hence he was impervious to her gentler influences:

> . . . Nature could not touch his heart
> By lovely forms, and silent weather,
> And tender sounds.[2]

The trouble was that Peter's mind was filled with

> . . . all the unshaped half-human thoughts
> Which solitary Nature feeds.[3]

There must be an inward shaping and humanization of impressions before they can be made fruitful. It was only after his traumatic experiences had wrought a profound spiritual conversion that Peter could behold a yellow primrose by the river's brink in all its loveliness.

> And now is Peter taught to feel
> That man's heart is a holy thing;
> And Nature, through a world of death,
> Breathes into him a second breath,
> More searching than the breath of spring.[4]

Thus in this poem, first written in 1798 and later revised, Wordsworth insisted upon inward creativeness, without which there can be no progression towards a higher personality. This is his consistent attitude and his recurrent theme.

By the time that he completed the early version of *The Prelude* nothing remained of the necessitarian creed. The supposition that underlies passage after passage, the supreme article of his faith, is his belief in the free and creative character of the human mind. If imagination is once active, if in the exercise of our faculties we have been strong and free, then a genuine and

---

[1] *Peter Bell*, 316–20. *Poetical Works*, ii. 331.   [2] Ibid. 286–8.
[3] Ibid. 296–7.   [4] Ibid. 1071–5.

imperishable increment of power is added to life. This is the meaning of those 'spots of time' to which Wordsworth refers:

> There are in our existence spots of time,
> Which with distinct pre-eminence retain
> A vivifying Virtue, whence . . .
> 　　　　　　　　　　　　　our minds
> Are nourished and invisibly repair'd. . . .
> This efficacious spirit chiefly lurks
> Among those passages of life in which
> We have had deepest feeling that the mind
> Is lord and master, and that outward sense
> Is but the obedient servant of her will.[1]

The earliest of these incidents, which we may take as typical of the entire class, concerns an experience of childish fear. When William was barely six years old his father's servant James took him out for a riding lesson. By mischance the boy got separated from his instructor. Dismounting in fear and leading his horse across stony ground, he came upon the remains of a mouldering gibbet where a murderer had been hanged and later someone had cut the name of the victim in the turf. The sight of the gibbet and the strange name excited and terrified the little boy. As he turned and climbed back up the common, all that he beheld took on the eerie intensity of vision:

> . . . forthwith I left the spot
> And, reascending the bare Common, saw
> A naked Pool that lay beneath the hills,
> The Beacon on the summit, and more near,
> A Girl who bore a Pitcher on her head
> And seem'd with difficult steps to force her way
> Against the blowing wind. It was, in truth,
> An ordinary sight; but I should need
> Colours and words that are unknown to man
> To paint the visionary dreariness
> Which, while I look'd all round for my lost Guide,
> Did at that time invest the naked Pool,
> The Beacon on the lonely Eminence,
> The Woman, and her garments vex'd and toss'd
> By the strong wind.[2]

---

[1] *Prelude* (1805), XI. 258–73.　　　　[2] Ibid. XI. 302–16.

When Wordsworth as a grown man revisited this scene it still exercised a powerful spell:

> Upon the naked pool and dreary crags,
> And on the melancholy Beacon, fell
> The spirit of pleasure and youth's golden gleam;
> And think ye not with radiance more divine
> From these remembrances, and from the power
> They left behind? So feeling comes in aid
> Of feeling, and diversity of strength
> Attends us, if but once we have been strong.[1]

This insistence that the mind should inform the senses explains Wordsworth's concern that sensation should not become too exclusive and tyrannical. A rejected passage in the *Intimations of Immortality* Ode expresses the wish to

> Throw off from us, or mitigate, the spell
> Of that strong frame of sense in which we dwell.[2]

In *The Prelude* Wordsworth similarly expresses a fear of the senses' despotism, and rejoices that some men are blessed with creative imagination.

> . . . In a world of life they live,
> By sensible impressions not enthrall'd,
> But quickened, rouz'd and made thereby more apt
> To hold communion with the invisible world.[3]

In maintaining the delicate balance between sense and imagination, Wordsworth insisted that the senses and the inner faculties must both be aroused to the quick and lend each other aid.

Some readers have misunderstood his references to the 'happy stillness of the mind', or the 'holy indolence' of the receptive imagination, finding in such lines as the following an expression of Hartley's sensism:

> Nor less I deem that there are Powers,
> Which of themselves our minds impress;
> That we can feed this mind of ours,
> In a wise passiveness.[4]

These lines and kindred passages are similar to the literature of Chinese mysticism, whether Taoist or Zen Buddhist: 'When

[1] Ibid. XI. 321–8.   [2] *Poetical Works*, IV, p. 283.
[3] *Prelude* (1805), XIII. 102–5.
[4] *Expostulation and Reply. Poetical Works*, iv. 56.

water is still, it is like a mirror, reflecting the beard and the eyebrows. It gives the accuracy of the water-level, and the philosopher makes it his model. And if water thus derives lucidity from stillness, how much more the faculties of the mind? The mind of the sage being in repose becomes the mirror of the universe, the speculum of all creation.'[1] Lest the world be too much with us, lest we lay waste our powers getting and spending, we must learn to achieve the stillness of inner repose. Then with an eye made quiet by the power of harmony, we shall see into the life of things.

3. *Creative Syntheses and Natural Configurations*

In his recognition of the creativeness of mental operations Wordsworth definitely abandoned the assumption that underlies most psychology of the seventeenth and eighteenth centuries. This traditional preconception was that the mind can produce nothing genuinely new in fusing or relating mental content. The components in a complex whole were not thought to undergo any intrinsic modification as the result of their combination. These early psychologists recognized the addition of new elements drawn from experience and they realized that the old elements were compounded in numerous ways, but they seldom discerned that mental syntheses gave rise to radically new content. The prevalent doctrine was expressly accepted by Locke:

The dominion of man, in this little world of his own understanding, being muchwhat the same as it is in the great world of visible things; wherein his power, however managed by art and skill, reaches no farther than to compound and divide the materials that are made to his hand; but can do nothing towards the making the least particle of new matter, or destroying one atom of what is already in being. The same inability will every one find in himself, who shall go about to fashion in his understanding one simple idea, not received in by his senses from external objects, or by reflection from the operations of his own mind about them.[2]

In working out his doctrines, however, Locke again and again

---

[1] 'The Works of Chuang Tze', in Robert O. Ballou, *The Bible of the World* (New York: Viking Press, 1939), p. 532.
[2] John Locke, *Essay Concerning Human Understanding*, Book III, ch. iii, sec. 2.

transcended the limitations of the theory. In the account that he gave of abstractions, universals, and relations, he was forced to recognize tacitly that absolutely new states of consciousness are generated within the mind. In the discussion of self-identity, he also escaped from the confines of the prevailing theory.[1]

Likewise Hartley's premises did not entirely harmonize with the superstructure of his thought. He was committed to the view that there is nothing before the mind that was not first present in sensation. Characteristically, he believed that it is theoretically possible 'to analyse all that vast variety of complex ideas, which pass under the name of ideas of reflection, and intellectual ideas, into their simple compounding parts, *i.e.* into the simple ideas of sensation, of which they consist'.[2] Similarly, he declared 'that our passions or affections can be no more than aggregates of simple ideas united by association'.[3] But he recognized that the affections influence one another, and that as a result of these reciprocal influences they 'arrive at that degree of complexness . . . which makes them so difficult to be analysed'.[4] In pursuance of his theory of psycho-physical parallelism he explained the alteration in mental content by the diffusion of vibratory motions in the brain: 'Since the vibrations A and B are impressed together, they must, from the diffusion necessary to vibratory motions, run into one vibration; and consequently, after a number of impressions sufficiently repeated, will leave a trace, or miniature, of themselves, as one vibration, which will recur now and then, from slight causes.'[5] If Hartley intended to imply that corresponding ideas also run together indistinguishably and *thereby create new qualities*, he was departing from the notion that a whole is merely an aggregate of its parts. In another passage he spoke of simple ideas coalescing into one complex idea in which the simple ideas can no more be separately identified than the several ingredients in a medicine or the primary colours in a white light.[6] But this is a rare statement and there are several statements to the contrary. In general, he clung to psychological atomism, or elementarism, according to which all complex ideas are theoretically analysable

[1] Cf. James Gibson, *Locke's Theory of Knowledge*, pp. 63–70, 115–19.
[2] Hartley, op. cit., prop. xii, cor. ii.
[3] Ibid., prop. lxxxix.   [4] Ibid.
[5] Ibid., prop. xi.   [6] Ibid., prop. xii, cor. 1.

into combinations or recombinations of the unit images of sense.

In one of the psychologists influenced by Hartley there was an explicit recognition of the active power of the mind and the creativeness of fusions. Abraham Tucker, in *The Light of Nature Pursued* (1768), sharply criticized Hartley for regarding the mind as only a passive receiver of impressions. He believed that we have the mental power to fuse ideas together so as to produce a compound of new and unique quality, like water which is different in quality from the hydrogen and oxygen out of which it is compounded. Tucker distinguished between two kinds of 'combination': the first is mere 'association', which does not add anything new and is the mere additive sum of its parts; the second is 'composition', in which there is a genuine alteration of components. ' . . . A compound', he explicitly stated, 'may have properties resulting from its composition which do not belong to the parts singly whereof it consists.'[1] This is an unambiguous statement of the idea of creative synthesis.

In another of the associational psychologists, Joseph Priestley, there was a partial recognition of creation through synthesis. Priestley reiterated Tucker's view, but thought that the effect of creative alteration may be only appearance. He realized that colour mixing apparently produces a new colour. Likewise, 'from the combination of ideas, and especially very dissimilar ones, there may result ideas which, to appearance, shall be so different from the parts of which they really consist, that they shall no more be capable of being analysed by mental reflection than the idea of white.'[2] Thus in Tucker absolutely and in Priestley hesitatingly there was an abandonment of the orthodox theory.

Wordsworth in all probability knew both works. Priestley was so closely associated with Hartley that it was almost impossible to read the one without the other. In 1775 he published an abridged edition of the *Observations on Man*, to which he affixed three essays on the theory of associationism. It is in these that the above statement appears. An influence on Wordsworth is rendered the more probable by his early interest in the repub-

---

[1] *The Light of Nature Pursued* (London, 1765), ch. xii, article 1. The statement occurs in a chapter on 'Imagination and Understanding', a title that must have attracted Wordsworth.

[2] Essay III, in *Miscellaneous Works* (London, 1818), iii, p. 190.

licanism of Priestley and the related group of radicals. There must also have been some contact with Tucker. For several years during the time of Coleridge's closest intimacy with Wordsworth, *The Light of Nature Pursued* was held in high esteem by their circle. So late as 1803 Coleridge still entertained a high opinion of its author.[1] There is every reason to suppose that the same interest that impelled Coleridge and Wordsworth to read Hartley must have led both of them on to a reading of this sequent thinker.

There can be no doubt, at least, that the poet was on the side of the thinkers who recognized the creativeness of the mind. I do not mean that he enunciated the idea of creative synthesis in a doctrinaire manner; I mean that he *saw* nature *en bloc*, each element transfused and modified by the atmosphere of the whole. This is the way his imagination worked; his method as a poet separates him from the traditional psychologists, and this imaginative divergence is just as important as any intellectualistic distinction.

We might select many passages to illustrate his sense of a general tone and quality that emerges from a blending of the particulars in each synthesis. In the following poem one notes that all the sounds are abstracted from their objects, and are fused into one song that seems the 'natural produce of the air':

> Up the brook
> I roamed in the confusion of my heart,
> Alive to all things and forgetting all.
> At length I to a sudden turning came
> In this continuous glen, where down a rock
> The Stream, so ardent in its course before,
> Sent forth such sallies of glad sound, that all
> Which I till then had heard, appeared the voice
> Of common pleasure: beast and bird, the lamb,
> The shepherd's dog, the linnet and the thrush,
> Vied with this waterfall, and made a song
> Which, while I listened, seemed like the wild growth
> Or like some natural produce of the air,
> That could not cease to be.[2]

There is more than a mere summation—there is a genuine

---

[1] Cf. Coleridge, *Biographia Epistolaris* (London: Bell, 1911), i, p. 274.
[2] *Poems on the Naming of Places*, I. *Poetical Works*, ii. 111.

merging that is not to be confused with a simple addition of sounds.

Another example is from the same series of poems:

> And when we came in front of that tall rock
> That eastward looks, I there stopped short—and stood
> Tracing the lofty barrier with my eye
> From base to summit; such delight I found
> To note in shrub and tree, in stone and flower,
> That intermixture of delicious hues,
> Along so vast a surface, all at once,
> In one impression, by connecting force
> Of their own beauty, imaged in the heart.[1]

Wordsworth finds the explanation of the oneness of effect in the intermixture of delicious hues—the connecting force of beauty as imaged in the heart. This way of accounting for the unity of impression is much more profound than Hartley's explanation of association by the temporal or spatial contiguity of the objects involved.

Wordsworth's characteristic method as a poet is to abstract from each object its individuating characteristics, to emphasize its communal properties, and almost to lose it in the reciprocal glow. The cuckoo, for example, is 'No bird, but an invisible thing, A voice, a mystery', which summons to the mind the visionary memories of childhood, and thus so interfuses the past with the present that the earth itself seems an 'unsubstantial, faery place' composed, like the bird, of the stuff of phantoms. In the poem *To A Highland Girl* the maid, the grey rocks, the household lawn, the waterfall, the silent lake, the quiet road, and the half-veiled trees 'together . . . seem like something fashioned in a dream'. In *Resolution and Independence* the old Leech Gatherer is 'not all alive nor dead', and the huge stone to which he is compared 'seems a thing endued with sense'; the environment thus assumes human characteristics, and the old man becomes very nearly elemental and sub-human. The result is a unity, an interfusion, and a visionary and dreamlike atmosphere. It is remarkable that the poet could achieve these syntheses within imagination, and at the same time convince the reader that he had kept his 'eye on the object'.

A passage from *The Prelude* is selected by Alfred North

[1] *Poems on the Naming of Places*, II.

Whitehead as a clear expression of its author's feeling for configurational unities, in which each part is suffused with the atmosphere of the whole:

> Ye Presences of Nature in the sky
> And on the earth! Ye Visions of the hills!
> And Souls of lonely places! can I think
> A vulgar hope was yours when ye employed
> Such ministry, when ye through many a year
> Haunting me thus among my boyish sports,
> On caves and trees, upon the woods and hills,
> Impressed upon all forms the characters
> Of danger or desire; and thus did make
> The surface of the universal earth
> With triumph and delight, with hope and fear,
> Work like a sea?[1]

In such a passage as this, Wordsworth outstrips even the more advanced psychologists in his own day and anticipates the *Gestalt* psychologists of the twentieth century. The significant fact is that the synthesis is not effected by the mind *after* sensation, but the sensations appear to enter into consciousness already synthesized. This aspect of Wordsworth's poetry is characterized by Whitehead:

It is the brooding presence of the hills which haunts him. His theme is nature *in solido*, that is to say, he dwells on that mysterious presence of surrounding things, which imposes itself on any separate element that we set up as an individual for its own sake. He always grasps the whole of nature as involved in the tonality of the particular instance. That is why he laughs with the daffodils, and finds in the primrose 'thoughts too deep for tears'.[2]

In a very important passage in the concluding book of *The Prelude* the poet recognizes the two kinds of blending, the one found in nature and the other created in the mind. He has been describing a climb to the summit of Snowdon:

> With forehead bent
> Earthward, as if in opposition set
> Against an enemy, I panted up
> With eager pace, and no less eager thoughts.
> Thus might we wear perhaps an hour away,

---

[1] *Prelude*, I. 464–75.
[2] Alfred North Whitehead, *Science and the Modern World*, op. cit., pp. 120–1.

Ascending at loose distance each from each,
And I, as chanced, the foremost of the Band;
When at my feet the ground appear'd to brighten,
And with a step or two seem'd brighter still;
Nor had I time to ask the cause of this,
For instantly a Light upon the turf
Fell like a flash: I looked about, and lo!
The Moon stood naked in the Heavens, at height
Immense above my head, and on the shore
I found myself of a huge sea of mist,
Which, meek and silent, rested at my feet:
A hundred hills their dusky backs upheaved
All over this still Ocean, and beyond,
Far, far beyond, the vapours shot themselves,
In headlands, tongues, and promonotory shapes,
Into the Sea, the real Sea, that seem'd
To dwindle, and give up its majesty,
Usurp'd upon as far as sight could reach.
Meanwhile, the Moon look'd down upon this shew
In single glory, and we stood, the mist
Touching our very feet; and from the shore
At distance not the third part of a mile
Was a blue chasm; a fracture in the vapour,
A deep and gloomy breathing-place through which
Mounted the roar of waters, torrents, streams
Innumerable, roaring with one voice.
The universal spectacle throughout
Was shaped for admiration and delight,
Grand in itself alone, but in that breach
Through which the homeless voice of waters rose,
That dark deep thoroughfare had Nature lodg'd
The Soul, the Imagination of the whole.[1]

This grand prospect, with all its various constituents, had one
'soul', represented by the blue chasm through which rose the
homeless voice of waters. The mention of 'Imagination' is
significant, because the poet is establishing a similarity between
synthesis in nature and imaginative synthesis in man. The vision
that rose before him on the mountain top was 'the perfect image
of a mighty Mind':

above all
One function of such mind had Nature there

[1] *Prelude* (1805), XIII. 29–65.

Exhibited by putting forth, and that
With circumstance most awful and sublime,
That domination which she oftentimes
Exerts upon the outward face of things,
So moulds them, and endues, abstracts, combines,
Or by abrupt and unhabitual influence
Doth make one object so impress itself
Upon all others, and pervade them so
That even the grossest minds must see and hear
And cannot chuse but feel.[1]

In this passage Wordsworth presents his interpretation of imagination. It is not only a transcendental faculty, as we shall see in the next chapter, but it is essentially a creative one, because the syntheses which it effects give to its objects a wholly new reality.

This description of imagination will be found to agree with the poet's famous distinctions between fancy and imagination. Fancy is mechanical; imagination is creative. Fancy combines without greatly modifying; its associations are forced or superficial. Imagination alters by fusion; it unites and transmutes objects that have deep affinities.

Various answers can be given to the question of how ideas or impressions may be made to cohere. (1) Hartley emphasizes association based on temporal or spatial contiguity; (2) Aristotle and Hume, in addition to recognizing contiguity, point to resemblance and causal or logical sequence; (3) the *Gestalt* psychologists Ehrenfels and Köhler describe the structure of the entire field of which the associated objects are parts; (4) Coleridge stresses 'the power by which one image or feeling is made to modify many others, and by a sort of fusion to force many into one'.[2]

In his theory of the imagination Wordsworth draws upon the third and fourth types of explanation more than upon the first and second. 'Imagination', he declares, 'is . . . that chemical faculty by which elements of the *most different* nature and *distant* origin are blended together into one harmonious and homogeneous whole.'[3] The words that I have italicized exclude the factors

[1] Ibid. XIII. 73–84.
[2] Coleridge, 'Shakespeare as a Poet Generally', in Bate, *Criticism: The Major Texts*, op. cit., pp. 388–9.
[3] *Prose Works*, ed. Grosart, iii, p. 465.

of contiguity and resemblance, and there is no mention of causal
or logical sequence. What remains is the 'chemical faculty' of
genuine creative synthesis. This deeper coherence is achieved
when the imagination accentuates the configurational patterns
already present in nature, or when scattered impressions are
drawn together in the mysterious depths of subjectivity, there
to be fused by passion.

Let us consider another example—the sight of London beheld
from Westminster Bridge as described in a famous sonnet:

> Earth has not anything to show more fair:
> Dull would he be of soul who could pass by
> A sight so touching in its majesty:
> This City now doth, like a garment, wear
> The beauty of the morning; silent, bare,
> Ships, towers, domes, theatres, and temples lie
> Open unto the fields, and to the sky;
> All bright and glittering in the smokeless air.
> Never did sun more beautifully steep
> In his first splendour, valley, rock, or hill:
> Ne'er saw I, never felt, a calm so deep!
> The river glideth at his own sweet will:
> Dear God! the very houses seem asleep:
> And all that mighty heart is lying still!

Here is no aggregate built up stepwise by the association of
simple constituents, nor a serial order either logical or causal.
Rather there is an intense emotional synthesis achieved in a
single moment of intuition—the vision of a great city wrapped
in a calm so deep that its mighty heart is almost suspended.

It must be admitted that Wordsworth is not always consistent in distinguishing between fancy as based upon the association of ideas and imagination as based upon creative syntheses
and the perception of *Gestalts*. In his Preface to the Edition of
1815 he declares that 'Fancy . . . is also, under her own laws
and in her own spirit, a creative faculty'. In qualifying the sharp
linguistic distinction between the two terms, he asserts not only
that fancy is *creative*, but that imagination is *associative*: 'To
aggregate and to associate, to evoke and to combine, belong as
well to the Imagination as to the Fancy; but either the material
evoked and combined are different; or they are brought together
under a different law, and for a different purpose.' In explaining

this difference, Wordsworth still preserves something of the original distinction:

Fancy does not require that the materials which she makes use of should be susceptible of change in their constitution from her touch; and, where they admit of modification, it is enough for her purpose if it be slight, limited, and evanescent. Directly the reverse of these are the desires and demands of the Imagination. She recoils from everything but the plastic, the pliant, and the indefinite.

'When the Imagination frames a comparison', he goes on to say, the likeness depends 'less upon casual and outstanding than upon inherent and internal properties; moreover, the images invariably modify each other'. Fancy, as the more superficial faculty, is given to us 'to quicken and to beguile the temporal part of our nature'. Imagination, as the more profound and creative faculty, is given 'to incite and support the eternal'.

In the *Biographia Literaria* Coleridge criticized Wordsworth for blurring the distinction between imagination as creative and fancy as associative.[1] Perhaps there is more than a verbal difference here between the two poets. It may be that Wordsworth, as M. H. Abrams maintains, retained more of 'the terminology and modes of thinking of eighteenth-century associationism'.[2] In the light of the evidence presented in this chapter, however, I cannot believe that Wordsworth remained closely attached to the sensationism and elementarism of Hartleian psychology. The remaining chapters will make the difference more apparent.

4. The Mind's Abyss

In the concluding book of *The Prelude* Wordsworth speaks of the imagination as a stream that flows out of a deep cave:

> . . . we have traced the stream
> From darkness, and the very place of birth
> In its blind cavern, whence is faintly heard
> The sound of waters.[3]

In other passages we find similar references to the shadowy

---

[1] *Biographia Literaria*, i, p. 194.
[2] *The Mirror and the Lamp* (New York: Oxford University Press, 1953), pp. 181–2.
[3] *Prelude* (1805), XIII. 172–5.

fringe of consciousness and the mind's subconscious depths.
When, as a child, William stole a boat and saw the mountain
seeming to rise up and pursue him, his brain for days thereafter
'worked with a dim and undetermined sense Of unknown modes
of being'.[1] As he grew older, he held 'unconscious intercourse
with beauty',[2] and his mind was moulded 'by force Of obscure
feelings representative Of things forgotten'.[3] When he became
habituated to Cambridge, the pledges interchanged with his
inner being were forgotten:

> Hush'd, meanwhile,
> Was the under soul, lock'd up in such a calm,
> That not a leaf of the great nature stirr'd.[4]

As a result, '*Caverns* there were within [his] mind Which sun
could never penetrate'.[5] But his life was still nourished by
beauty, because 'the visible scene Would enter unawares into
his mind, With all its solemn imagery'.[6] It was so from childhood onwards in the intertwining of human interests with the
beauteous forms of nature:

> Even then the common haunts of the green earth,
> With the ordinary human interests
> Which they embosom . . .
> . . . are fastening on the heart
> Insensibly, each with the other's help,
> So that we love, not knowing that we love,
> And feel, not knowing whence our feeling comes.[7]

Thus his 'heart was early introduced To an unconscious love and
reverence Of human nature'.[8] All of these quotations imply
semiconscious or subconscious processes.

Even more significant than such scattered references is
Wordsworth's coining of words—under-consciousness, under-
soul, under-powers, under-countenance, under-thirst, and under-
presence—to convey his sense of the depths of the human soul.
As Ernest de Selincourt remarks:

He needed these words to express his profound consciousness of
that mysterious life which lies deep down below our ordinary, every-

[1] *Prelude*, I. 391–3.   [2] Ibid. I. 562.
[3] Ibid. I. 606–7.   [4] *Prelude* (1805), III. 539–41.
[5] *Prelude*, III. 246–7.   [6] Ibid. V. 386–7.
[7] *Prelude* (1805), VIII. 166–72.   [8] *Prelude*, VIII. 278–9.

day experience, and whence we draw our power—that one interior
life:

> In which all beings live with God, themselves
> Are God, existing in the mighty whole.

The relation of this conception to the subconscious or subliminal self
of the modern psychologist is obvious.[1]

Let us return to the passage from which Ernest de Selincourt
quotes the two lines above. After an enumeration of the
ordinary conscious mental processes, the poet declares:

> Such consciousness I deem but accidents,
> Relapses from the one interior life
> That lives in all things.[2]

There is one life of infinite scope. It lives in plants and animals
and men and 'the round ocean and the living air'. In most things
it is unconscious or semiconscious, but in men it quickens into
mystical experience or into more normal thought, feeling, and
imagery. The deep subconscious abyss of the human psyche is
a well connecting the poet's imagination with this cosmic pool
of spirituality.

In advancing the idea of a subconsciousness in which the soul
has its transcendental roots Wordsworth is surely straying far
from the philosophy of Locke and Hartley. In his theory of
knowledge Locke definitely turned away from the psychology
of the subconscious. 'Thinking', he said, 'consists in being
conscious that one thinks.'[3] Even the initial sensation requires
the mind's notice. Although the physical conditions may be
completed, there can be no sensation until there is awareness
upon the part of the 'understanding':

How often may a man observe in himself, that whilst his mind is
intently employed in the contemplation of some objects, and curiously
surveying some ideas that are there, it takes no notice of impressions
of sounding bodies made upon the organ of hearing with the same
alteration that uses to be for the producing of the idea of sound? . . .
Want of sensation, in this case, is not through any defect in the organ,
or that the man's ears are less affected than at other times when he
does hear; but that which uses to produce the idea, though conveyed

---

[1] *The Prelude*, ed. E. de Selincourt and H. Darbishire, pp. 622–3.
[2] *The Prelude*, ed. E. de Selincourt, first edition, p. 512.
[3] John Locke, *Essay Concerning Human Understanding*, Book II, ch. i, sec. 19.

in by the usual organ, not being taken notice of in the understanding, and so imprinting no idea in the mind, there follows no sensation.[1]

Neither in this passage nor elsewhere does Locke admit that there might be an unconscious sensation or idea.

Hartley admits the possibility of unconscious mental processes, but is cautious in doing so. He remarks that if the original 'sensation be faint, or uncommon, the generated idea is also faint in proportion, and, in extreme cases, evanescent and imperceptible'.[2] Thus in *extreme* instances only are there imperceptible ideas, and these are evanescent. There is no inkling of the vast and strange world of the unconscious that we find in modern depth-psychology. Throughout Hartley's argument, in fact, there is the assurance that, just as Newton had found in the principle of gravitation the key to unlock the secrets of the physical universe, so he and Locke had found in the association of ideas the key to throw open the secret chambers of the mind. Quite different is the feeling that permeates Wordsworth's poetry:

> The incumbent mystery of sense and soul,
> Of life and death, time and eternity.[3]

Hartley's neat ratiocinations belong to a different universe of discourse.

Wordsworth's brooding sense of mystery is expressed in a passage of *The Recluse* that states the poet's main theme:

> Urania, I shall need
> Thy guidance, or a greater Muse, if such
> Descend to earth or dwell in highest heaven!
> For I must tread on shadowy ground, must sink
> Deep—and, aloft ascending, breathe in worlds
> To which the heaven of heavens is but a veil.
> All strength—all terror, single or in bands,
> That ever was put forth in personal form—
> Jehovah—with his thunder, and the choir
> Of shouting Angels, and the empyreal thrones—
> I pass them unalarmed. Not Chaos, not
> The darkest pit of lowest Erebus,
> Nor aught of blinder vacancy, scooped out
> By help of dreams—can breed such fear and awe

---

[1] John Locke, *Essay Concerning Human Understanding*, Book II, ch. lix, sec. 4.
[2] Hartley, op. cit., prop. viii. [3] *Prelude*, XIV. 286–7.

As fall upon us often when we look
Into our Minds, into the Mind of Man—
My haunt, and the main region of my song.[1]

Milton's heavens and their hosts are but a veil compared with
the Mind of Man. However deep we may sink or aloft ascend
we cannot exhaust its mysteries. It is more awe-inspiring than
hell or primeval chaos or the shouting angels.

The theory of imagination that Wordsworth constructed
upon this basis is similar to the doctrine of the transcendental
imagination advanced by Kant and Coleridge. The association
of ideas, Kant contended, is inadequate to explain the unity of
the human mind. Even in thinking of the lapse of time from one
noon to another one must first reproduce the images that represent the chain of events in memory; then the images must be
recognized as referring to the past, and this presupposes a self-
consciousness which recognizes past impressions as inhering in
one sequence of experience belonging to oneself. Hence the mind
must grasp not only the idea of a serial order of temporal events
but also the distinction between a subjective or psychological
realm and an objective order. According to Kant, all this implies
a unitary self-conciousness *antecedent* to the experience in question and rendering that experience possible. Kant therefore found
it necessary to supplement the idea of association with another
principle: the 'transcendental' activity of the imagination,
which organizes sensations in accordance with these necessary
forms and categories. It is this working of the transcendental
imagination, mainly at the subconscious level, that comes to
the aid of the associational processes. Imagination thus works
in alliance with reason and understanding; for consciousness is
always an awareness of meanings—not passive contemplation
but active judgement, not mere perception but synthetic interpretation. We can never know things apart from these synthetic
modes of apprehension and judgement, which are the necessary
conditions of all human experience.

Here was the solution that Coleridge discovered when he
sought in German philosophy for an escape from the perplexities
that Hartleianism had brought to his mind. He not only seized
eagerly upon the Kantian conception of imagination as a transcendental faculty, but distinguished between the 'secondary

[1] *Recluse*, 778–94.

imagination', which is the faculty of creative synthesis as exemplified in poetry and art, and the 'primary imagination', which is Kant's transcendental faculty conceived as a repetition in the human mind of the creative act of God. Finally, he distinguished between imagination, in this twofold sense, and fancy:

The IMAGINATION then, I consider either as primary, or secondary. The primary IMAGINATION I hold to be the living power and prime Agent of all human Perception, and as a repetition in the finite mind of the eternal act of creation in the infinite I AM. The secondary Imagination I consider an echo of the former, co-existing with the conscious will, yet still identical with the primary in the *kind* of its agency, and differing only in *degree*, and in the *mode* of its operation. It dissolves, diffuses, dissipates, in order to recreate; or where this process is rendered impossible, yet still at all events it struggles to idealize and to unify. It is essentially *vital*, even as all objects (as objects) are essentially fixed and dead. FANCY, on the contrary, has no other counters to play with, but fixities and definites. The Fancy is indeed no other than a mode of Memory emancipated from the order of time and space; while it is blended with, and modified by that empirical phenomenon of the will, which we express by the word CHOICE. But equally with the ordinary memory the Fancy must receive all its materials ready made from the law of association.[1]

In its metaphysical aspect, the central point in Coleridge's distinction between fancy and imagination is that imagination resembles the radical creativity of God and organizes sensation in accordance with the transcendental principles of reason, whereas fancy operates at the more superficial level of the association of ideas.

It would appear that Wordsworth, at work on his great philosophical poem, and already sure that imagination is the grand faculty of life, embraced the opportunity afforded by Coleridge's new ideas for rationalizing his own experience of the oneness of God and Man. Without accepting every feature of Coleridge's theory, he seized upon the idea of imagination as a transcendental force, giving unity to all life and binding man to God. But he was not content like Kant to suppose that all the main work of the imagination is done in the 'darkness' from whence it emerges. Instead he conceived of imagination as emerging

---

[1] Coleridge, *Biographia Literaria*, ed. Shawcross, i, p. 202.

into the daylight and the common world of men. He went beyond Kant also in identifying the 'blind cavern' of imagination with the 'underpresence' from which wells up 'the sense of God'. Thus he gave to the transcendental imagination a religious colouring. There is a mysterious region which lies deeper than our ordinary experience, a realm of subconsciousness from 'whence we draw our power'. In times of ecstasy we flood this sphere with light, and feel the interior life through which we are in contact with God. But even when man lacks this deeper vision, his imagination may be active, drawing from the infinite depths of being and communicating to human life the oneness which resides at the source of power.

This interpretation would explain why Wordsworth, like Coleridge, regards imagination as

> . . . but another name for absolute power
> And clearest insight, amplitude of mind,
> And Reason in her most exalted mood.[1]

It explains his sense of the omnipresence of the divine spirit in all the workings of nature and in the creative activity of the human mind. It also explains the several processes by which unity in the mind is achieved: association accounts for the linkage of ideas or sensations which occur together; the synthetic imagination produces the more complete fusions; the transcendental imagination lends to the mind an *a priori* unity and self-consciousness, connecting man with that infinite community 'in which all beings live with God'. Although this interpretation is partly conjectural, the concluding book in the 1805 version of *The Prelude* seems consonant with no other interpretation.

To conclude, Wordsworth by no means minimizes the report of the senses. He 'keeps his eye on the object' and faithfully notes its features. As Lascelles Abercrombie has said: 'We must always remember, when we talk of Wordsworth's profound sense of the unity of nature, his perpetual delight in its infinite diversity; as he several times tells us in *The Prelude*, it was the very intensity of his perception of *difference* in nature that gave power and significance to his sense of nature's ultimate unity.'[2] He recognized that a being in communion with natural beauty

---

[1] *Prelude*, XIV. 190–2.
[2] Lascelles Abercrombie, *The Art of Wordsworth* (Oxford University Press, 1952), pp. 123–4.

almost inevitably becomes wiser and nobler. Yet this intimate communion requires for its establishment a free and active mind that vitalizes the processes of association through its inward contribution. The highest manifestation of this mental activity is the work of imagination, which flows from the divine and mysterious underpresence. In this deep subliminal region, and also in the conscious life of the imagination, the disparate elements of experience are grasped together and synthesized. Thus imagination produces a self-consciousness and a unitary life of the whole mind and spirit, whereas association, depending upon contiguity, can introduce connexions only from next to next. When this integral mind seizes upon sensation, it fuses impressions into a new and irrefrangible unity. Consciousness does not always need to create these profounder syntheses; at times sensations enter into the mind in configurations, so that the observer immediately grasps more than individuals or their mere summation. Hence a significant correlation may be established between the ways of nature and the works of the mind.

V. THE INNER VOICE

———

1. *The Question at Issue*

W E approach now the great paradox of Wordsworth as a philosophical poet, his simultaneous attachment to the senses and to an unsensationistic theory of the mind. Some critics have been so impressed by his tenacious hold upon the sensory world that they have denied his belief in ideas or feelings underivative from sensory experience, yet we find in his poetry a good many passages that apparently conflict with a sensationistic account of mental life. Any satisfactory interpretation of his thought must explain this seeming contradiction between his naturalism and his transcendentalism.

The contrast between these two theories of the sources of human knowledge was set forth very clearly by John Stuart Mill in his famous essay on Coleridge, which appeared in the *London and Westminster Review*, March 1840. Here is the way Mill characterized the empiricist doctrine:

The prevailing theory in the eighteenth century . . . was that proclaimed by Locke, and attributed to Aristotle—that all our knowledge consists of generalizations from experience. Of nature, or anything whatever external to ourselves, we know, according to this theory, nothing, except the facts which present themselves to our senses, and such other facts as may, by analogy, be inferred from these. There is no knowledge *a priori*; no truths cognizable by the mind's inward light, and grounded on intuitive evidence. Sensation, and the mind's consciousness of its own acts, are not only the exclusive sources, but the sole materials of our knowledge.

Pitted against this doctrine was the transcendentalism of Coleridge:

He distinguishes in the human intellect two faculties, which, in the technical language common to him with the Germans, he calls Understanding and Reason. The former faculty judges of phenomena, or the appearances of things, and forms generalizations from these:

to the latter it belongs, by direct intuition, to perceive things, and recognize truths, not cognizable by our senses. These perceptions are not indeed innate, nor could ever have been awakened in us without experience; but they are not copies of it: experience is not their prototype, it is only the occasion by which they are irresistibly suggested. The appearances in nature excite in us, by an inherent law, ideas of those invisible things which are the causes of the visible appearances, and on whose laws those appearances depend: and we then perceive that these things must have preexisted to render the appearances possible; just as (to use a frequent illustration of Coleridge's) we see, before we know that we have eyes; but when once this is known to us, we perceive that eyes must have preexisted to enable us to see. Among the truths which are thus known *a priori*, by occasion of experience, but not themselves the subjects of experience, Coleridge includes the fundamental doctrines of religion and morality, the principles of mathematics, and the ultimate laws even of physical nature; which he contends cannot be proved by experience, although they must necessarily be consistent with it, and would, if we knew them perfectly, enable us to account for all observed facts, and to predict all those which are as yet unobserved.[1]

These quotations from Mill make very clear the nature of the issue at stake. One may be a transcendentalist even though one believes the mind dependent upon experience. As Coleridge declared: 'Transcendental knowledge is that by which we endeavor to climb above our experience into its sources by an analysis of our intellectual faculties, still however standing as it were on the shoulders of our experience, in order to reach at truths which are above experience.'[2] Not only the German philosophers to whom Mill referred but Plato and the neo-Platonists believed that sensory stimuli bring into play the transcendental factors in knowledge. According to Plato experience serves to make explicit that which is already implicit within the mind. We have ideals or standards of the true, the good, the beautiful, and nothing in nature entirely corresponds to them. The circle of the mathematician has a perfection that no real circle attains; his lines have no breadth; his points have no dimensions; his cones have no deviations from accuracy; all his

[1] John Stuart Mill, 'Coleridge', *Essays on Politics and Culture* (Garden City, New York: Doubleday, 1963), pp. 128–9.

[2] Reproduced from manuscript in the British Museum by Alice D. Snyder, *Coleridge on Logic and Learning* (Yale University Press, 1929), p. 119.

reasoning concerns perfect points, lines, surfaces, and solids. He is dealing with things that have never been seen or known to sense. But the approximations of nature must be presented to the mind before the absolute mathematical forms may be conceived. In the same way, men have other unlimited, unempirical notions: for example, the idea of a 'beauty absolute, separate, simple, and everlasting', which is not to be found 'in animal, or in heaven, or in earth, or in any other place'.[1] But before any of these forms, these transcendent essences or principles, can be grasped by the mind, sense must present their semblances to the intellect. Thus the issue to be discussed in this chapter, whether Wordsworth was a pure sensationalist or a transcendentalist, does not hinge upon the mind's independence of experience, since a transcendentalist may insist on the necessary co-working of sense and the transcendental faculties.

2. The Argument that Wordsworth was a Naturalist

In stating his fundamental thesis, Arthur Beatty writes of Wordsworth: 'There can be no manner of doubt that he approaches the problem of mind from the angle of Locke, basing his whole theory on the assumption that thought originates in experience, and that out of the product of sensation, or experience, ideas and the more complex forms of mentality are developed.'[2] Beatty represents Hartley as a faithful follower of Locke and Wordsworth of Hartley. But even the first part of this equation is too simple: the Lockian point of view does not coincide with the Hartleian position that sensation is the sole original stuff from which mental states are developed. Locke believed that there is another source—*reflection*, which is the mind's introspective awareness of itself and its operations. Reflection is recognized not only as a source of knowledge, but as a very important one. Locke also maintained, albeit inconsistently, that the mind compounds, abstracts, and relates, and in doing so creates new syntheses and mental relations (a point I have mentioned in the preceding chapter). Consequently he avoided the cruder sort of sensationism, but he was still an

---

[1] Plato, *Symposium*, § 211.
[2] Beatty, *William Wordsworth*, op. cit., p. 108.

L

empiricist in contending that all ideas are generated out of the original stuff of experience, whether sensory or introspective.[1]

Now why does Beatty assert that Wordsworth bases 'his whole theory upon the assumption that thought originates in experience'? He simply says, 'This is so obvious from our fifth chapter that we do not need to develop the matter here.'[2] His fifth chapter is entirely devoted to the theory of 'the three ages of man', which I examined in Chapter III of the present book. There I argued that the doctrine of the three ages was not necessarily derived from Locke or Hartley, and that a fourfold or fivefold division fits Wordsworth's poetry equally well.

Nevertheless, Beatty's contention is plausible in the light of much of the evidence that we examined in Chapter III. We found that Wordsworth conceived of life as evolving from lowest to highest, from 'animal movements' to the noblest exercise of reason and imagination. We discovered that the principle of this evolution was the conservation of values: the grosser mental processes feed the purer, and every lower faculty sustains the higher powers; the genuine values in each stage of development find articulation in the final organization of the personality. This account of the growth of personality suggests that the supersensuous is merely a refinement of the sensuous, that sense is translated into soul without change of essence.

The question whether Wordsworth held such a doctrine should be considered with an open mind; but Beatty's book, it seems to me, contains no evidence of a conclusive nature. For example, he cites Wordsworth's description of the Wanderer:

> Observant, studious, thoughtful, and refreshed
> By knowledge gathered up from day to day.[3]

This method of acquiring knowledge would fit equally a transcendentalist and an empiricist epistemology. *How* is the knowledge obtained? that is the question. By observation, of course, and by thought and study; yet what is the *complete* philosophical explanation? I shall not expend the space and time

[1] Cf. James Gibson, *Locke's Theory of Knowledge and Its Historical Relations* (Cambridge University Press, 1931), especially ch. iii. Gibson's book is a model of clear and accurate exposition.

[2] Beatty, op. cit., p. 108.

[3] *Excursion*, I. 394–5.

required to discuss Beatty's other citations, for if the reader will carefully peruse them, he will find nothing irreconcilable with transcendentalism.

H. W. Garrod, in one of the best studies ever made of Wordsworth, finds in *Tintern Abbey* a fusion of mysticism and a sensationistic theory of mind:

Wordsworth's poetry is essentially mystical. But whereas the mysticism of other men consists commonly in their effort to escape from the senses, the mysticism of Wordsworth is grounded and rooted, actually, *in* the senses. The natural world speaks, not to the intellect, but to that in us which is most 'natural,' viz. our senses. . . . This pure sensationalism of Wordsworth—I use 'sensationalism,' of course, in its philosophical sense, of a theory of mind which regards the senses as the source of truth—this pure sensationalism of Wordsworth is apt to take us by surprise. It surprises us because we are not much in the habit of believing that poets mean what they say. And certainly, in its implications, it appears, at least to our first reflections, a degree naïve. Yet in this sensationalism Wordsworth began, and it is when he passes from it (about 1807) that he ends.[1]

In support of this interpretation Garrod quotes a very famous passage from *Tintern Abbey*:

> For I have learned
> To look on nature, not as in the hour
> Of thoughtless youth, but hearing oftentimes
> The still sad music of humanity,
> Nor harsh nor grating, though of ample power
> To chasten and subdue. And I have felt
> A presence that disturbs me with the joy
> Of elevated thoughts; a sense sublime
> Of something far more deeply interfused,
> Whose dwelling is the light of setting suns,
> And the round ocean and the living air,
> And the blue sky, and in the mind of man:
> A motion and a spirit, that impels
> All thinking things, all objects of all thought,
> And rolls through all things. Therefore am I still
> A lover of the meadows and the woods,
> And mountains; and of all that we behold
> From this green earth; of all *the mighty world*

---

[1] H. W. Garrod, *Wordsworth: Lectures and Essays* (Oxford University Press, 1927), pp. 105–6.

Of eye, and ear,—both what they half create
And what perceive; well pleased to recognize
In nature and the language of the sense
The anchor of my purest thoughts, the nurse,
The guide, the guardian of my heart, and soul
Of all my moral being.　[Garrod's italics.]

This passage is not lightly to be dismissed—it is the very epitome of Wordsworth's thought. Garrod comments:

Note here 'the mighty world of eye and ear'—it is the only world. The poem is addressed to the poet's sister, and it is of her that he says 'she gave me eyes, she gave me ears'—the only gifts for which he had any use. But above all, note the lines where with deliberation, and beyond the chances of misunderstanding, Wordsworth tells us that he recognizes in Nature and the report of sense, not merely the guide of feeling and of heart, but the 'soul of all his moral being.'[1]

It may be that Garrod is correct in this interpretation, but we must take certain things into account.

First, we must remember that *Tintern Abbey* was composed in July 1798, and that a great deal of Wordsworth's most important poetry was not written until a lapse of at least four or five years. There was ample opportunity for a change of viewpoint in time to affect the bulk of his works. The remarks of Coleridge strongly suggest that Wordsworth's views did change. When he first met Wordsworth he said: 'And this man is a Republican, and, at least, a *Semi*-atheist.'[2] After knowing his fellow poet for a year and six months, Coleridge could still state:

On one subject we are habitually silent; we found our data dissimilar, and never renewed the subject. It is his practice and almost his nature to convey all the truth he knows without any attack on what he supposes falsehood, if that falsehood be interwoven with virtues or happiness. He loves and venerates Christ and Christianity. *I wish he did more*, but it were wrong indeed if an incoincidence with one of our wishes altered our respect and affection to a man whom we are, as it were, instructed by our great master to say that not being against us he is for us.[3]

Coleridge wrote this comment during a time which he later looked back upon as something of an apostasy, and when he

---

[1] H. W. Garrod, op. cit., pp. 108–9.
[2] *Collected Letters*, vol. i, p. 216.
[3] Ibid., p. 410. (Letter of 18 May 1798.) My italics.

was still much under the sway of Hartley. Yet the impression
that we gain from this letter is that Wordsworth was distinctly
less orthodox than he. By the time Wordsworth wrote the
last books of *The Prelude* (1804–5), such complaints had ceased,
and Coleridge greeted the poem enthusiastically as a transcendentalist work.[1] One might also note the 'Recollections' of
Aubrey de Vere, who quotes Wordsworth as affirming, in the
last decade of his life, that his 'religious convictions' as a young
man 'were less definite and strong than they had become on
more mature thought'.[2] The truth is that Wordsworth became
more orthodox as he grew older and that his early convictions
were just as strong in their own way. He changed his views in
philosophy and religion, just as we know that he did in politics,
and just as we are certain that Coleridge did in all three areas.
The evidence from *Tintern Abbey* is therefore not binding upon
the later poetry. Even Garrod notes that Wordsworth had
changed his mind by 'about 1807'. I suggest that the change
was not sudden but a gradual process.

Is Garrod's interpretation of *Tintern Abbey* necessarily
correct? Let us remember that Wordsworth, not long before
or after he composed this poem, wrote a sweeping repudiation
of sensationism in a passage that I have already quoted in
Chapter III:

> . . . what we see of forms and images
> Which float along our minds, and what we feel
> Of active or recognizable thought,
> Prospectiveness, or intellect, or will,
> Not only is not worthy to be deemed
> Our being, to be prized as what we are,
> But is the very littleness of life.
> Such consciousness I deem but accidents,
> Relapses from the one interior life
> That lives in all things. . . .[3]

Here the 'forms and images' derived from sensory experience,
as well as all the ordinary processes of thought, are said to
be 'mere accidents' in comparison with the 'one interior life'.

---

[1] Cf. Coleridge's poem *To William Wordsworth*.

[2] Aubrey de Vere, 'Recollections', in Wordsworth, *Prose Works*, ed. Grosart,
iii, p. 491.

[3] *The Prelude*, ed. E. de Selincourt, first edition, pp. 512–13.

These words should make us wary of assuming that Wordsworth was never a believer in the inner light.

Let us now turn back to *Tintern Abbey* and note exactly what he says:

> . . . all the mighty world
> Of eye, and ear,—both what they half create,
> And what perceive.

Wordsworth implies that the creative vision is different from that of the mere 'bodily eye' and that the mind has its own part to play. Notice also the preceding lines, in which he speaks of

> . . . something far more deeply interfused,
> Whose dwelling is the light of setting suns,
> And the round ocean and the living air,
> And the blue sky, and *in* the mind of man:
> A motion and a spirit, *that impels*
> *All thinking things*, all objects of all thought
> And rolls through all things.   [My italics.]

There is a single spirit that pervades all reality and works from within as well as without. It impels all thinking things as well as all objects of all thought. Is this not a fairly clear statement that there are *inward* impelling forces that have their own revelations if we could penetrate to them?

Earlier in the poem he suggests that we *can* penetrate to this inward supersensuous truth:

> . . . we are laid asleep
> In body, and become a living soul:
> While with an eye made quiet by the power
> Of harmony, and the deep power of joy,
> We see into the life of things.

Under any sensationistic account of experience, how could being laid asleep in body enable one to see into the life of things? The clear implication is that some ascertainable truth is attained by a mystical insight that transcends sense-experience. This implication is in no way lessened by the poet's suggestion that these mystical states may be due to the 'beauteous forms of Nature':

> Nor less, I trust,
> To them I may have owed another gift,
> Of aspect more sublime.

It has always been a tenet of Platonism and neo-Platonism, as well as a favourite doctrine of many mystics, that sensibility to natural beauty leads onward to the beauty and truth that is beyond sense.

Wordsworth himself in *The Prelude* writes of those moments of spiritual vision when

> the light of sense
> Goes out, but with a flash that has revealed
> The invisible world.[1]

Commenting on these lines, Ernest de Selincourt remarks:

No passage illustrates better than this at once Wordsworth's relation with the sensationist, empirical philosophy of the eighteenth century and the manner in which he transcends and spiritualizes it. All intellectual and spiritual growth comes from the reaction of the senses, chiefly of eye and ear, to the external world, which is 'exquisitely fitted to the mind', but the highest vision is superinduced upon this in a state of ecstasy, in which the light of sense goes out and the soul feels its kinship with that which is beyond sense.[2]

Let us now turn to the crucial lines emphasized by Garrod:

> well pleased to recognize
> In nature and the language of the sense
> The anchor of my purest thoughts, the nurse,
> The guide, the guardian of my heart, and soul
> Of all my moral being.

The interpretation of these lines partly depends upon the meaning of 'nature'. I suggest that 'nature' includes the 'music of humanity':

> For I have learned
> To look on nature, not as in the hour
> Of thoughtless youth; but hearing oftentimes
> The still, sad music of humanity,
> Nor harsh nor grating, though of ample power
> To chasten and subdue.

Immediately after these lines Wordsworth continues to express his conception of nature:

> And I have felt
> A presence that disturbs me with the joy
> Of elevated thoughts. . . .

[1] *Prelude*, VI. 600–2.
[2] *The Prelude*, ed E. de Selincourt and H. Darbishire, p. 558.

Thus nature includes not only humanity but 'the something far more deeply interfused', which is the 'presence' to which he here refers.

At the time of composing *Tintern Abbey* Wordsworth was a pantheist, or at least had pantheistic leanings. (This is made tolerably clear by the passage that we are now considering.) In its deeper significance, nature meant for him a world soul that includes humanity. It is a mistake to sever it from the language of the sense because it is *one* spirit embracing all things and appearing both within and outside man. The inner characteristics of nature can be known through the ecstasy, just as its outer characteristics can be known through perceptions. The 'soul of all my moral being' should be taken to mean the expression in man of the moral life of nature, conveyed sensuously when we listen to the language of the sense, and supersensuously when the body is laid to sleep and we see into nature's inner self.

The notion that nature speaks with 'two voices' fits the actual wording of *Tintern Abbey* perfectly. To the 'beauteous forms' of outward experience Wordsworth owes 'sensations sweet, Felt in the blood, and felt along the heart'. The language here is strikingly materialistic. But to these same beauteous forms he owes 'another gift, Of aspect more sublime'. This gift springs from an *inward* impulse (since 'the affections', not the senses, 'gently lead us on'). It is the 'privilege' of nature (here personified)

> to lead
> From joy to joy: for she can so inform
> The mind that is within us, so impress
> With quietness and beauty, and so feed
> With lofty thoughts

that the whole moral life is lifted up and transformed. This personification seems perfectly natural, since nature is represented as a 'guide' that informs the mind directly as well as impresses the senses. Or, shifting the metaphor, nature is depicted as a 'nurse' that feeds the soul with 'lofty thoughts':

> The anchor of my purest thoughts, the nurse,
> The guide, the guardian of my heart, and soul
> Of all my moral being.

Thus nature works both outside and inside the mind.

This interpretation is in harmony with the 1805 version of *The Prelude*, in which Wordsworth speaks of the poetic faculty as 'an Element of Nature's *inner* self'.[1] In another passage he expresses the same conception:

> Also, about this time did I receive
> Convictions still more strong than heretofore,
> Not only that the *inner frame* is good,
> And graciously composed, but that, no less,
> *Nature* for all conditions wants not power
> To consecrate, if we have eyes to see,
> The *outside* of her creatures, and to breathe
> Grandeur upon the very humblest face
> Of human life.[2]

The implication is that nature has both an 'outside' and an 'inner frame'. The characteristics of nature can therefore be ascertained by probing into the mind as well as by observing the outer world.

In the light of this conception of nature there is no contradiction in supposing that there are inner transcendental impulses which work in harmony with quite different sensory factors. It is this notion of nature, and of the co-working of the senses and the intuitive faculties, that pervades Wordsworth's greatest poetry. It is this notion that makes him proclaim

> How exquisitely the individual Mind
>   . . . to the external World
> Is fitted:—and how exquisitely, too . . .
> The external World is fitted to the Mind.[3]

With this interpretation in mind, we can explain all of *Tintern Abbey*, including the insight into the life of things when the body is laid asleep.

3. *Transcendentalism*

Let us now consider the additional evidence that Wordsworth maintained transcendentalist doctrines. Only a selection is possible, because much of the poetry bears upon the question.

[1] *Prelude* (1805), VIII. 514.   [2] *Prelude*, XIII. 279–87. My italics.
[3] *Recluse*, 816–21.

In a variant reading of *An Evening Walk* the youthful poet
speaks of the power of nature to heal and cleanse the psyche:

> Its sober charms can chase with sweet controul
> Each idle thought and sanctify the soul,
> And on the morbid passions pouring balm
> Resistless breathe a melancholy calm;
> Or through the mind, by magic influence
> Rapt into worlds beyond the reign of sense,
> Roll the bright train of never ending dreams
> That pass like rivers tinged with evening gleams. . . .[1]

This passage written in 1794 is interesting because of its early
date. It shows that Wordsworth, about the time he first became
acquainted with Hartley, thought that nature could waft the
soul into realms 'beyond the reign of sense'. Thus he early
believed in the visionary powers of the mind and its kinship
with a super-sensory world.

If we can trust the testimony of *The Prelude*, these visions
came to Wordsworth during his student days at Cambridge.

> Oft did I leave
> My Comrades, and the Crowd, Buildings and Groves,
> And walked along the fields, the level fields,
> With Heaven's blue concave rear'd above my head. . . .
> As if awaken'd, summon'd, rous'd, constrain'd,
> I look'd for universal things; perused
> The common countenance of earth and heaven;
> And, turning the mind in upon itself,
> Pored, watch'd, expected, listen'd; spread my thoughts
> And spread them with a wider creeping; felt
> Incumbences more awful, visitings
> Of the Upholder of the tranquil Soul,
> Which underneath all passion lives secure
> A steadfast life.[2]

Here the mind is not only regarded as able to turn in upon itself,
as in Locke's psychology, but Wordsworth goes far beyond Locke
in stating that it can thereby feel visitings from God. A few
lines later he speaks of God in the language of pantheism as 'the
one Presence, and the Life of the great whole'.

The conviction that sense arouses transcendental ideas is also

---

[1] *Poetical Works*, i, p. 9.   [2] *Prelude* (1805), III, 97–100, 109–18.

expressed in Wordsworth's account of crossing the Alps with Robert Jones. The two young vacationers from Cambridge were astonished when they discovered that they had actually passed over the summit of the mountains. In a Platonic spirit Wordsworth explains their feelings by suggesting that the mind approaches nature with ideal norms and standards to which outer things imperfectly correspond. Thus there is evidence in the workings of man's consciousness that

> Our destiny, our being's heart and home,
> Is with infinitude, and only there.[1]

The poet therefore feels that man's primary allegiance is with the unbounded, the eternal. This interpretation, it should be remarked, is from the later perspective of *The Prelude*, not from the account in the *Descriptive Sketches*, written shortly after the event.[2]

A passage in Book V of *The Prelude* indicates the co-working of the senses and the intuitive faculties. The child's imagination is represented as seizing with avidity upon the books of 'dreamers' and of 'forgers of lawless tales'. This hunger is caused by the 'dumb yearnings' and 'hidden appetites' that characterize childhood. The intensity of the inward urge is ground for profound hope:

> Our childhood sits,
> Our simple childhood, sits upon a throne
> That hath more power than all the elements.
> I guess not what this tells of Being past,
> Nor what it augurs of the life to come.[3]

This passage represents excellent Platonic doctrine. The soul, even of a child, has immortal longings and ideal standards. These hunger for the right sense stimulation to evoke them, but they tell 'of Being past' and 'of the life to come' because they so far transcend the world of experience. Pre-existence and immortality are inferred because the mind, thus inwardly pricked on, is 'unwilling to forego, confess, submit, Uneasy,

---

[1] *Prelude*, VI. 604–5.
[2] Cf. Geoffrey H. Hartman, *Wordsworth's Poetry 1784–1814* (Yale University Press, 1964), pp. 102–15. Hartman interprets the *Descriptive Sketches* as leading '*through* nature *beyond* it', and as foreshadowing *The Prelude*.
[3] *Prelude*, V. 507–11.

and unsettled', and hence appears to belong to an infinite and eternal order.

Writing of the benefits derived from mathematics Wordsworth again expresses himself after the Platonic mode. In a passage in which he renounces his early pantheism he considers the abstractions of 'geometric science' as the finite 'type' of the infinite thought:

> Yet from this source more frequently I drew
> A pleasure calm and deeper, a still sense
> Of permanent and universal sway
> And paramount endowment in the mind,
> An image not unworthy of the one
> Surpassing Life, which out of space and time,
> Nor touch'd by welterings of passion, is
> And hath the name of God.[1]

The Platonists have loved to rise in the same way from the thought of the pure forms of geometry, which resemble God's 'ideas', to the conception of an ideal and timeless existence.

In a section of the poem full of the language of transcendentalism Wordsworth writes of the 'higher minds' inspired by imagination:

> They need not extraordinary calls
> To rouze them, in a world of life they live,
> By sensible impressions not enthrall'd,
> But quicken'd, rouz'd, and made thereby more fit
> To hold communion with the invisible world.
> Such minds are truly from the Deity,
> For they are Powers; and hence the highest bliss
> That can be known is theirs, the consciousness
> Of whom they are habitually infused
> Through every image, and through every thought,
> And all impressions; hence religion, faith,
> And endless occupation for the soul
> Whether discursive or intuitive;
> Hence sovereignty within and peace at will
> Emotion which best foresight need not fear
> Most worthy then of trust when most intense.
> Hence chearfulness in every act of life
> Hence truth in moral judgements and delight
> That fails not in the external universe.[2]

[1] *Prelude* (1805), VI. 150–9.   [2] Ibid. XIII. 101–19.

This passage states that higher minds 'hold communion with the invisible world' by 'intuitive' insight: 'hence the highest bliss That can be known is theirs'. Wordsworth is making a very high claim, the highest of all claims, one that Hartley or Locke would never dream of making.

In the concluding lines of *The Prelude* Wordsworth announces that he will teach men the divinity of human faculties; he will

> Instruct them how the mind of man becomes
> A thousand times more beautiful than the earth
> On which he dwells, above this frame of things
> (Which, 'mid all revolution in the hopes
> And fears of men, doth still remain unchanged)
> In beauty exalted, as it is itself
> Of quality and fabric more divine.

If the mind is a 'thousand times' more beautiful and 'divine' than the earth, there must surely be some internal, supersensuous mode of receiving God into the soul.

In March and April 1800 Wordsworth wrote 'Home at Grasmere'—the one book of *The Recluse* that he managed to complete.[1] Here he likewise employed language that would be difficult to reconcile with a sensationist epistemology:

> To these emotions, whencesoe'er they come,
> Whether from breath of outward circumstance,
> Or from the Soul—an impulse to herself—
> I would give utterance in numerous verse.[2]

In another passage the poet speaks

> Of the individual Mind that keeps her own
> Inviolate retirement, subject there
> To Conscience only, and the law supreme
> Of that Intelligence which governs all.[3]

The meaning is clear. Only a far-fetched interpretation could wrench these passages into conformity with the Lockian tradition.

The sense of God's presence in the soul has never been expressed more tenderly than in the sonnet that Wordsworth

---

[1] As originally conceived, Wordsworth's entire philosophical *magnum opus* was to be called *The Recluse*. Later this title was reserved for the second part of the total work (of which *The Prelude* was to be the first and *The Excursion* the third part).

[2] *Recluse*, 763–6. [3] Ibid. 772–5.

composed on the shore at Calais in August 1802. As he walked along the beach with his ten-year-old daughter Caroline (Annette's child), the stillness of the evening blended with the quietness of his heart:

> It is a beauteous evening, calm and free,
> The holy time is quiet as a Nun
> Breathless with adoration; the broad sun
> Is sinking down in its tranquillity;
> The gentleness of heaven broods o'er the Sea:
> Listen! the mighty Being is awake,
> And doth with his eternal motion make
> A sound like thunder—everlastingly.
> Dear Child! dear Girl! that walkest with me here,
> If thou appear untouched by solemn thought,
> Thy nature is not therefore less divine:
> Thou liest in Abraham's bosom all the year;
> And worship'st at the Temple's inner shrine,
> God being with thee when we know it not.

As in the *Ode on the Intimations of Immortality*, the child is haunted by 'the eternal mind'.

In a little poem written in 1806 Wordsworth definitely and unambiguously states that we hear 'voices of two different natures', and that one kind of voice comes 'from beyond the grave' and is the voice of God:

> Yes, it was the mountain Echo,
>   Solitary, clear, profound,
> Answering to the shouting Cuckoo,
>   Giving to her sound for sound!
>
> Unsolicited reply
>   To a babbling wanderer sent;
> Like her ordinary cry,
>   Like—but oh, how different!
>
> Hears not also mortal Life?
>   Hear not we, unthinking Creatures!
> Slaves of folly, love, or strife—
>   Voices of two different natures?
>
> Have not *we* too?—yes, we have
>   Answers, and we know not whence;
> Echoes from beyond the grave,
>   Recognized intelligence!

> Such rebounds our inward ear
> Catches sometimes from afar—
> Listen, ponder, hold them dear;
> For of God,—of God they are.

In interpreting this little poem as transcendentalist in sentiment we surely pass beyond the realm of conjecture. These lines are proof that in 1806 Wordsworth did not accept the empiricist principle that all mental states originate solely in sensation or experience. Note that the two voices, although of 'different natures', are so closely related that the second is like an echo of the first. Wordsworth thus implies that the senses and the intuitive faculties work together harmoniously.

In 1807 Wordsworth published another transcendentalist poem, which was composed in the previous year:

> Nor will I praise a cloud, however bright,
> Disparaging Man's gifts, and proper food.
> Grove, isle, with every shape of sky-built dome,
> Though clad in colours beautiful and pure,
> Find in the heart of man no natural home:
> The immortal Mind craves objects that endure:
> These cleave to it; from these it cannot roam,
> Nor they from it: their fellowship is secure.[1]

In these words the poet announces that the mind is linked to eternal things, and that the transitory objects of sensation find in the heart of man no natural home. It was the voice from God to the inward ear that the Wordsworth of this period considered fundamentally important.

The Excursion was written piecemeal from 1795 until 1814 and in subsequent editions was subjected to further revision. As it finally took shape much of it reflects the more conservative thought of Wordsworth's later years. The transcendentalist tenor of some of the passages is unmistakable. For instance, the Wanderer, addressing himself to God, refers to the 'particle' that has been in his soul 'from childhood':

> By thy grace
> The particle divine remained unquenched;
> And, 'mid the wild weeds of a rugged soil,
> Thy bounty caused to flourish deathless flowers,
> From paradise transplanted. . . .[2]

[1] 'Those words were uttered as in pensive mood', *Poetical Works*, iii. 26.
[2] *Excursion*, IV. 50–54.

Here is an express statement of the doctrine of grace—the orthodox form of transcendentalism. In another passage the Wanderer asks:

> How shall man unite
> With self-forgetting tenderness of heart
> An earth-despising dignity of soul?
> Wise in that union, and without it blind![1]

'An earth-despising dignity of soul' would be a very odd possession for a devoted follower of Hartley or Locke. Wordsworth had travelled a long distance from *Tintern Abbey*, but not in the direction of naturalism.

A beautiful passage from *The Excursion* can be taken as representative of the transcendentalism of his later years:

> I have seen
> A curious child, who dwelt upon a tract
> Of inland ground, applying to his ear
> The convolutions of a smooth-lipped shell;
> To which, in silence hushed, his very soul
> Listened intensely; and his countenance soon
> Brightened with joy; for from within were heard
> Murmurings, whereby the monitor expressed
> Mysterious union with its native sea.
> Even such a shell the universe itself
> Is to the ear of Faith; and there are times,
> I doubt not, when to you it doth impart
> Authentic tidings of invisible things;
> Of ebb and flow, and ever-during power;
> And central peace, subsisting at the heart
> Of endless agitation.[2]

Since Wordsworth could no longer rely upon the immediacy of mystical experience, he had to fall back upon faith; but he still believed in the 'authentic tidings of invisible things'. This is a Christian version of transcendentalism.

4. *The 'Immortal Ode'*

The *Ode on the Intimations of Immortality* deserves special mention because of its intrinsic merit and its high place in Wordsworth's regard. In his edition of the *Poetical Works*

---

[1] *Excursion*, V. 576–9.   [2] Ibid. IV. 1132–47.

William Knight remarks of the *Ode*: 'Mr. Aubrey de Vere has urged me to take it out of its chronological place, and let it conclude the whole series of Wordsworth's poems, as the greatest, and that to which all others lead up. Mr. de Vere's wish is based on conversation which he had with the poet himself.'[1] The critics likewise have emphasized the importance of the poem while disagreeing as to its meaning.

Some Wordsworthian scholars think that the subject of the *Ode* is simply the universal experience of 'growing up' from childhood to maturity. H. W. Garrod, for example, finds the central idea in the lines from the Rainbow poem prefixed to the *Ode*:

> The Child is father of the Man;
> And I could wish my days to be
> Bound each to each by natural piety.[2]

Harper also quotes these lines, contending that the purpose of the *Ode* is to trace the gains as well as the losses in the process of attaining manhood.[3] Beatty finds in the poem 'the constant theme' of Wordsworth's poetry: 'the justification of hope and the triumph of life in the coming of maturity, with its . . . deepening of thought and emotion, and that profounder understanding of Man, the heart of Man, and human life'.[4] Lionel Trilling's interpretation can be stated in Biblical language: 'When I was a child, I spake as a child, I understood as a child, I thought as a child: but when I became a man, I put away childish things.' But the gospel that Trilling cites is Freud's *Civilization and its Discontents* and not Paul's First Epistle to the Corinthians. According to Trilling, what Wordsworth (the 'I' of the poem) finally put away was the childish illusion of 'the perfect union of the self and the universe'—an illusion like the 'oceanic sense' of the infinite dismissed by Freud.[5] All four critics—Garrod, Harper, Beatty, and Trilling—find little or nothing in the poem that could be called 'transcendentalist'.

It would be foolish to deny that there is much in the *Ode* that conforms to these interpretations. The poem depicts 'the

---

[1] Wordsworth, *Poetical Works*, ed. William Knight (London: Simpkin, 1882–9), viii, p. 199 fn.
[2] Cf. Garrod, *Wordsworth*, op. cit., pp. 112–24.
[3] Harper, *William Wordsworth*, op. cit. ii, p. 449.
[4] Beatty, *William Wordsworth*, op. cit., p. 84.
[5] Cf. Trilling, *The Liberal Imagination* (New York: Viking Press, 1950).

glory and the dream' of childhood, the fading of youthful vision with the advance of age, the natural piety that binds our days each to each, and the philosophical compensations of maturity. But it also expresses the idea of pre-existence and the hope of immortality—not as an illusion but as a 'master light'.

The title places the theme of immortality absolutely in the foreground. Originally the poem did not bear this title, being simply designated as *Ode*. Noting the uncertainty of some reviewers Henry Crabb Robinson suggested to Wordsworth that there should be a descriptive title for the work 'to guide the reader to a perception of its drift'.[1] Wordsworth then deliberately chose the title, *Ode: Intimations of Immortality from Recollections of Early Childhood*, to emphasize what he conceived to be the essential meaning.

This meaning is indicated by the recurring references to pre-existence and immortality. Over the child

> . . . Immortality
> Broods like the Day, a Master o'er a Slave,
> A presence which is not to be put by.

If we were to eliminate these lines, and the birth that 'is but a sleep and a forgetting', and the 'immortal sea which brought us hither', and 'the faith that looks through death', we should cut out the very heart of the poem. We should then have no correct basis for interpreting the 'splendour in the grass' and 'glory in the flower', or 'the obstinate questionings of sense and outward things'—since the recollections of these trance-like states and visionary experiences are the very 'intimations of immortality' of which Wordsworth speaks.

In the fifth stanza Wordsworth attributes the child's mystical intuitions to the presence of innate factors in knowledge. The soul does not come into the world in 'utter nakedness'; it 'cometh from afar' with its glory still trailing and never wholly to depart. It is possible to urge against this interpretation Wordsworth's comment that he never meant to inculcate a belief in a prior state of existence but employed the idea for its poetic effectiveness.[2] But does this note really dispose of the problem? The central meaning of the passage is not the idea of

[1] *The Correspondence of Henry Crabb Robinson with the Wordsworth Circle*, op. cit. ii, pp. 838–9.
[2] See the note which accompanies the *Ode* in most editions.

pre-existence but the thought that we come into the world with innate forms of thought which have been bestowed on us by God.

Nothing in the statement of Wordsworth would contradict this doctrine. Many men have believed in the doctrine of innate knowledge who have rejected the idea of pre-existence. We have no reason, therefore, to believe that the poet was indulging in a mere conceit when he wrote '. . . trailing clouds of glory do we come'. In Wordsworth's comment, moreover, the poet does not deny belief even in the Platonic theory of 'reminiscence'; he merely says that he did not mean 'to inculcate such a belief'. This comment, written in Wordsworth's old age, after ortho-doxy had gained control of his mind, contains the additional declaration: 'It [the theory of reminiscence] is far too shadowy a notion to be recommended to faith as more than an element in our instincts of immortality. But let us bear in mind that, though the idea is not advanced in Revelation, there is nothing there to contradict it, and the fall of man presents an analogy in its favour.' These words suggest that Wordsworth, even at this more pious period, was half-convinced of pre-existence. Perhaps no stronger belief should be attributed to Plato.

Even if we should decide that this portion of the *Ode* must be discounted because the poet did not believe in Platonic remini-scence, the meaning of what remains is proof enough for my contention. If a child in reading the 'eternal deep, haunted forever by the eternal mind' attains to truth that makes him the 'best' of philosophers, the truth must be, at least partially, intuitive; for older individuals have all the evidence of their wider experience and their much more advanced reason at their disposal, yet they are said to be more blind than the child. Upon the basis of a philosophy quite untranscendentalist one would expect increasing insight as the individual matures; yet Wordsworth announces that the contrary is too often the fact. This point of view is the exact reverse of the standpoint of Hartleian psychology, according to which our spirituality is the *end-product* of the long process of maturation.

It is sometimes argued that Wordsworth's characteriza-tion of childhood is inconsistent with other parts of the poem. Walter Garstang has written:

Not all the poet's skill and sustained beauty of language have been able to blend the two voices speaking in this famous Ode. In particular, as various critics have pointed out, the second group of four stanzas (v-viii), is, in effect, an interpolation, alien to the poet's whole philosophy of life, and inconsistent with both the opening and closing sections of the poem. By exaggerating the divinity of the child, he is compelled in those stanzas to treat the attainment of manhood in terms of loss instead of gain, whereas in the noble peroration of the Ode, as everywhere else, the 'years that bring the philosophic mind' are regarded as bringing with them an access of serenity and power and human sympathy which more than compensates for the dizzy raptures of youth.[1]

But it is only in a restricted sense that the child is said to be the best of philosophers: he perceives *intuitively* what the wise adult perceives *reflectively*.

In his letter of December 1814 to Mrs. Clarkson, Wordsworth points out the characteristics of childhood 'recollected' in the *Ode*: 'This poem rests entirely upon two recollections of childhood; one that of splendour in the objects of sense which is passed away; and the other an indisposition to bend to the law of death, as applying to our own particular case. A reader who has not a vivid recollection of these feelings having existed in his mind in childhood cannot understand that poem.'[2] One can recollect these feelings without disparaging the quite different gifts of manhood. There is both gain and loss in 'growing up': the vision lost is at once more intense and less profound than the insight gained.

Wordsworth is concerned about the *continuity* that binds together the two poles of his personal history, the visionary gleam and the mature philosophy. His outburst of joy at the beginning of stanza X, and the following tribute to the philosophic mind, are inspired by the deep harmony between his childish intuitions and his final convictions. Hence there is no great inconsistency between his reverence for the child and his appreciation of the thoughts too deep for tears.

Both Wordsworth and the Platonists emphasize recollection as a basis for believing in the dignity of man's soul. In Plato's *Phaedo*, for example, Socrates rebuts Simmias' epiphenomenalism by appealing to the doctrine of 'reminiscence'. The argu-

---

[1] Walter Garstang, 'Wordsworth's Interpretation of Nature', *Nature*, Supplement, vol. 117 (16 Jan. 1926), p. 6.

[2] *Letters: The Middle Years*, ii, p. 619.

ment in this dialogue (a favourite of Wordsworth) is related both to the refutation of materialism and to the hope of immortality. Likewise, in the *Phaedrus*, Socrates maintains that the young soul fresh in the world has the most visionary perceptions. It seems likely that Wordsworth, perhaps under the guidance of Coleridge, would have been attracted to the *Phaedrus*, because it contains much concerning immortality and reminiscence. Similarly Proclus, who probably influenced the *Ode*,[1] argued that the incorporeality of thought, that is, its independence of the perishable body, is shown by the mind's turning back upon itself in the act of memory. The very ability to remember, Proclus maintained, is inexplicable upon the basis of a materialistic philosophy.[2] Possibly Wordsworth had in mind this argument when he wrote:

> But for those first affections,
> Those shadowy recollections,
> Which, *be they what they may,*
> Are yet the fountain light of all our day,
> Are yet a master light of all our seeing.

Wordsworth evidently felt that his conclusions were valid even if the 'recollections' were not 'reminiscences' of pre-existence— for it is the mysterious power of memory, and not merely the reminiscence of a previous existence, that attests to the spiritual nature of man.[3]

The contrasting themes of memory and immortality and of time and eternity coalesce in the total meaning of the *Ode*. All through the poem there is the sense of the transitory.

> The Rainbow *comes and goes*,
> And lovely is the Rose.

The child is no sooner old enough to think than the 'celestial light' begins to fade, but there is always 'the eternal deep'. For the grown-up poet:

[1] Cf. John D. Rea, 'Coleridge's Intimations of Immortality from Proclus', *Modern Philology*, vol. 26 (Nov. 1928). Rea argues that Proclus influenced stanzas V–VIII of the *Ode*.

[2] Proclus, *Theological Elements*, in Thomas Whittaker, *The Neo-Platonists* (Cambridge University Press, 1901), p. 177.

[3] For further evidence of Platonic and neo-Platonic influences on the *Ode*, see the studies listed by James V. Logan, *Wordsworthian Criticism*, op. cit., pp. 119–21.

> The Pansy at my feet
> Doth the same tale repeat:
> Whither is fled the visionary gleam?
> Where is it now, the glory and the dream?

The adult's sense of mutability, poignant thought it be, is balanced by an equally profound sense of the eternal.

> Our Souls have sight of that immortal sea
> Which brought us hither,
> Can in a moment travel thither,
> And see the Children sport upon the shore,
> And hear the mighty waters rolling evermore.

The *Ode* concludes with 'the *faith* that looks through death'— not with proof or absolute assurance. Indeed, there is some reason to doubt that Wordsworth ever attained a secure conviction that there is an after-life. Henry Crabb Robinson once confessed to the elderly poet that he had *tried* to believe, and Wordsworth replied: 'That is pretty much my case.'[1] When his beloved daughter Dora, after a long illness, died, it was nearly a year before he could quiet his grief. James, the faithful servant, 'took the liberty' of saying to his master: 'But Sir, don't you think she is brighter now than she ever was?' Wordsworth's response was to burst into a flood of tears. 'Those', observed Crabb Robinson, 'were not tears of unmixed grief.'[2] It is not clear what Robinson meant, but perhaps he intended to say that Wordsworth's attitude was ambivalent.

Not only these incidents but some of the poems make one wonder about the firmness of his religious faith. For instance, he evidently felt that Lucy in her grave was wholly assimilated to inorganic things:

> No motion has she now, no force;
> She neither hears nor sees;
> Rolled round in earth's diurnal course,
> With rocks, and stones, and trees.[3]

Late in his life, Wordsworth spoke of the death of his friends, Coleridge, Lamb, Scott, and others, in similar words:

---

[1] *Henry Crabb Robinson on Books and Their Writers*, ed. Edith J. Morley (London: Dent, 1938), ii. 482.
[2] Ibid. iii. 855. See also ii. 628.
[3] 'A slumber did my spirit seal', *Poetical Works*, ii. 216.

> Like clouds that rake the mountain-summits,
> Or waves that own no curbing hand,
> How fast has brother followed brother
> From sunshine to the sunless land![1]

The 'sunless land' is hardly the right symbol to denote immortality. Again, in a poem addressed to his wife he confessed his occasional doubts:

> Trembling, through my unworthiness, with fear
> That friends, by death disjoined, may meet no more![2]

Deep in his subconscious mind there was no unshakeable belief in an after-life.

But *eternity*, as distinguished from immortality, seems to have commanded his absolute belief. As Whitehead points out, the eternal objects are always there for him, 'the light that never was, on sea or land'. The poet was gifted, so to speak, with binocular vision, time and eternity being the two lenses through which he scanned the abyss of things. No modern writer, unless it be Proust, was more concerned with memory and the passage of time; but no one, not even Spinoza, was more intent upon eternity.

> Our noisy years seem moments in the being
> Of the eternal Silence.

Throughout Wordsworth's poetry there is stillness amid the noise of change.

> A voice so thrilling ne'er was heard
> In spring-time from the Cuckoo-bird,
> Breaking the silence of the seas
> Among the farthest Hebrides.[3]

As a kind of nature-mystic, Wordsworth sought the enduring in the transient, the infinite in the finite, Being in being. All that he saw was

> Suspended in a stream as clear as sky,
> Where earth and heaven do make one imagery.[4]

Nowhere is this more evident than in the Immortality Ode; but

---

[1] *Extempore Effusion upon the Death of James Hogg* (1835). *Poetical Works*, iv. 276.
[2] 'O dearer far than light and life are dear,' *Poetical Works*, ii. 36.
[3] *The Solitary Reaper. Poetical Works*, iii. 77.
[4] *To H. C. Six Years Old* (1802). *Poetical Works*, i. 247.

the unity therein is not perfect: the sense of fading glory is more convincing than the recovery of faith: earth and heaven do not quite blend in one imagery. So far as there is a blend of the opposites—time and eternity, sense and vision, intuition and idea, recollection and foreshadowing—the *Ode* is the epitome of Wordsworth's total achievement. *Tintern Abbey* is more seamless in its unity; the *Ode* is grander in its design.

5. *The Transcendental Faculties*

Among the mental faculties of which Wordsworth speaks are the senses, the emotions, the fancy, the imagination, the reason, and the will. Which of these faculties can be called 'transcendental'?

The question is complicated by their interpenetration and multi-dimensional character. The spiritual faculties make use of the senses, the imagination draws upon the fancy, the higher reason does not exclude the lower, the moral will seeks support in emotion and reason and imagination. All the faculties operate together to provide meaning and insight, but we can speak of different levels of mental functioning. In their *deepest* level of operation, they express the unity of all existence. Hence the synthesizing power in the mind of a genius can simultaneously be labelled reason, imagination, moral will, and 'intellectual love'.

In the last book of *The Prelude* Wordsworth imbeds love, as well as imagination, within the 'mighty mind . . . that feeds upon infinity' and

> . . . is exalted by an underpresence,
> The sense of God, or whatsoe'er is dim
> Or vast in its own being.[1]

This deepest love is the essence and foundation of life: 'for here do we begin and end', from here 'all grandeur comes, all truth and beauty'. It is conceivable that the poet was speaking loosely when he celebrated a love which is more than human, a 'divine' love, which works within the brooding soul of man; but the safest interpretation is that he meant exactly what he said. He conceived of the profoundest love as welling up from the under-

[1] *Prelude* (1805), XIII. 71–73.

presence of God, from the 'soul divine which we participate'.[1]
The unity 'In which all beings live with God, themselves Are
God' no longer received full credence, but the most intense joy,
he was still convinced, might be felt through inmost participation in the divine life. At a considerably later time he abandoned this conviction in favour of the doctrine of grace.

There can be little question, in face of the complete evidence,
that Wordsworth believed morality to rest upon a transcendental
foundation. A passage in *The Convention of Cintra* indicates his
sympathy for Old England, when Richard Hooker, Jeremy Taylor,
John Milton, and the Cambridge Platonists were influential,
before the time of the empirical ethics of the eighteenth century
and the utilitarianism of his own day. The poet's open hostility
to the 'Experimental Philosophy' is recorded, and the 'dictates
of paramount and infallible Conscience' are contrasted with the
'calculations of presumptuous expediency'.[2] Surely we shall not
confuse 'infallible dictates' with the often fallible insight of experience.

The impression of some critics that the poet never held to
a transcendental theory of morality may arise from the tendency of all his thought to make the higher states include the
lower. These scholars rightly suppose that the poet harkened
to the voice of experience. But he would supplement this voice
by another; he believed that men would attain to the highest
morality through a co-working of experiential foresight and
transcendental wisdom.

If the moral will is a transcendental faculty, so must be
reason, which establishes the moral laws:

> Reason and her pure
> Reflective acts to fix the moral law
> Deep in the conscience.[3]

The phrase 'pure reflective acts' is suggestive of the non-
evidential character of the process. In another passage of *The
Prelude* Wordsworth identifies the profounder reason with the
very base of human life.[4]

---

[1] Cf. ibid. XIII. 149–65 and V. 16.
[2] *Prose Works*, ed. Grosart, i, pp. 153–4.
[3] *Prelude*, III. 83–85.
[4] Cf. *Prelude* (1805), X. 386–93. It does not contradict transcendentalism to
assert as Wordsworth does in his *Letter to 'Mathetes'*: 'Our eyes have not been
fixed upon virtue that lies apart from human nature, or transcends it. In fact, there

It is typical of his thought that he often does not clearly distinguish between reason and imagination; he refers to them as if they were two aspects of one faculty. The explanation is that he regarded both as an expression of the divine principle in man. When he spoke of either imagination or reason in its highest signification, he was touching upon the very root of life, which he identified with divine love:

> Thy love is human merely; this proceeds
> More from the brooding Soul, and is divine.[1]

> Imagination having been our theme,
> So also hath that intellectual love,
> For they are each in each, and cannot stand
> Dividually.[2]

This passage indicates that life is essentially one, so that love and reason and imagination are almost interchangeable terms.

Wordsworth is at a loss to describe this power, which perhaps may best be called imagination. Since it is the faculty by which we commune with infinity, it transcends all our efforts to define it:

> Imagination—here the Power so called
> Through sad incompetence of human speech,
> That awful Power arose from the mind's abyss
> Like an unfathered vapour that enwraps,
> At once, some lonely traveller. I was lost;
> Halted without an effort to break through;
> But to my conscious soul I now can say—
> 'I recognize thy glory': in such strength
> Of usurpation, when the light of sense
> Goes out, but with a flash that has revealed
> The invisible world, doth greatness make abode,
> There harbours; whether we be young or old,
> Our destiny, our being's heart and home,
> Is with infinitude, and only there.[3]

I believe we shall not read this passage aright unless we interpret the 'mind's abyss' as the centre of being, where we are in contact with God. This power, arising from its 'blind cavern',

is no such virtue.' At this time in his life (1809), Wordsworth's conception of human nature was so august that almost nothing seemed beyond it. Later he spoke of man as 'kindred to the worm'.

[1] Cf. *Prelude* (1805), XIII. 164–5.   [2] Ibid. XIII. 185–8.
[3] *Prelude*, VI. 592–605.

works in and through sensation, thus informing sense by the immortal mind.

We can now summarize in a few words the philosophy that dominates Wordsworth's thought. The base of the world is God, from 'whence our dignity originates'. The highest faculties, when pricked on by the senses, arise inwardly from this base. These powers or faculties not only give being to man, but also maintain an 'ennobling interchange' with the outer world, which rests upon the same foundation and which calls them into play. Since in Wordsworth's view the transcendental faculties seem thus always to implicate sensation or introspective experience, he appears to discard all 'innate ideas' in the *strict* sense of the term. He gives great weight to the sensory factors in knowledge, because he realizes 'how exquisitely . . . the external World is fitted to the Mind'. In *Tintern Abbey* he even goes so far as to state that nature and the language of the sense is the soul of all his moral being. By this he does not mean that there is nothing in the mind not derived from sensation; he simply affirms that the inward faculties must be aroused by the 'speaking face of nature'. The mightiest life is to be achieved by combining the empirical and transcendental factors into a most potent unity.

VI. THE LIFE OF THINGS

1. *The Poet and the Metaphysician*

A PAINTER or a nature-poet apprehends the sensible world in all its vivid qualities. Wordsworth, for instance, notices details that would escape the attention of the ordinary person. His description of the running hare is an example:

> The grass is bright with rain-drops;—on the moors
> The hare is running races in her mirth;
> And with her feet she from the plashy earth
> Raises a mist, that, glittering in the sun,
> Runs with her all the way, wherever she doth run.[1]

To cite another striking example, Wordsworth observed that, as birds swoop down upon the surface of a frozen lake, their reflections become more soft as they approach:

> They tempt . . . the gleaming ice
> To shew them a fair image,—'tis themselves,
> Their own fair forms, upon the glimmering plain
> Painted more soft and fair as they descend,
> Almost to touch.[2]

Similarly precise is Wordsworth's description of the Green Linnet:

> Amid yon tuft of hazel trees,
> That twinkle to the gusty breeze,
> Behold him perched in ecstasies,
>   Yet seeming still to hover;
> There! where the flutter of his wings
> Upon his back and body flings
> Shadows and sunny glimmerings,
>   That cover him all over.[3]

Most people notice inattentively, or notice not at all, such exquisite details as these.

---

[1] *Resolution and Independence. Poetical Works*, ii. 235.   [2] *Recluse*, 222–27.
[3] *The Green Linnet. Poetical Works*, ii. 189.

A nature-poet or a painter not only notices but *studies* the myriad qualities of the sensible world. These include the rich, variegated, fleeting immediacies of sensory appearance, and also the feeling-tones attached thereto. As Whitehead observes: 'We enjoy the sunset with an emotional pattern including among its elements the colours and the contrasts of the vision.'[1] The pattern, emotions, colours, and contrasts are inextricably blended. Natural objects as the artist perceives them exhibit not only 'secondary qualities', such as visual redness or tactual hardness, but also 'tertiary qualities', such as cheerfulness, serenity, or grace. In describing the Vale of Grasmere, Wordsworth, of course, employs sight and sound, but no less

> the sense
> Of majesty, and beauty, and repose,
> A blended holiness of earth and sky.[2]

So it is in all his poetry: there is a fusion of sensation with the nuances of emotion and desire. As in dreams, subjective thought and feeling are embodied in sensory imagery. This embodiment is characteristic not only of Wordsworth's poetry but of art as such.

Now one of the important questions of philosophy is the relation of the artist's world to things as they 'really are'. We might maintain that reality is best revealed in the depth and spiritual force of the artist's vision. Or we might consider the world of the physicist, a world of abstract mathematical properties and relations, as *real*, and dismiss the artist's world, a world of vivid perspectives and prospects, as *unreal*. Or we might regard both worlds as human constructions, each valuable in its own way, but neither representative of 'things in themselves'.

The answer that Wordsworth must have received as a student at Cambridge was unequivocal. It was believed by the educated men of that time that Newton had solved the riddle of existence once and for all. They supposed that the Newtonian universe was one vast harmonious order, created by God, and so arranged by Him that mathematical physics could very satisfactorily describe it. The contradictory notions of deity in the revealed

---

[1] Alfred North Whitehead, *Adventures of Ideas* (New York: Macmillan, 1923), p. 321.

[2] *Recluse*, 142–4.

religions had been replaced by a new idea, that of a Being known to us by his works and discoverable by science. The universal order, symbolized by the law of gravitation, had taken on a clear and positive meaning. This order is accessible to the human understanding; it is the most perspicuous of truths, the reality confirmed by proven methods of science. Just as Lucretius delineated the atomic 'science' of Democritus and Epicurus, so the modern philosophical poet can celebrate the wonders of the Newtonian universe—but he has no objective truth of his own to express. As I have pointed out in Chapter II, this mechanistic interpretation is contrary to Newton's own religious convictions, but it reflects the dominant notions at the University when Wordsworth was a student.

The only figure whose influence at Cambridge was comparable to that of Newton was the philosopher John Locke. The latter attributed objective reality to such abstract qualities as number, shape, and motion, relegating colour, odour, sound, taste, and tactile qualities to the subjective reactions of the sentient organism. The abstract character of the external world as he conceived it was accentuated by his doctrine of substance. Beneath both mind and body as known phenomenally, beneath even the abstract primary qualities, there is a 'substance' of which we can tell nothing. This 'supposed I-know-not-what' is the fundamental ground of mind and matter, but it is as unknown and unknowable as Kant's 'thing-in-itself'.

The aesthetic implications of this philosophy are strikingly expressed by Whitehead:

[According to Locke] the occurrences of nature are in some way apprehended by minds, which are in some way associated with living bodies. Primarily, the mental apprehension is aroused by the occurrences in certain parts of the correlated body, the occurrences in the brain, for instance. But the mind in apprehending also experiences sensations which, properly speaking, are qualities of the mind alone. These sensations are projected by the mind so as to clothe appropriate bodies in external nature. Thus the bodies are perceived as with qualities which in reality do not belong to them, qualities which in fact are purely the offspring of the mind. Thus nature gets credit which should in truth be reserved for ourselves: the rose for its scent: the nightingale for his song: and the sun for his radiance. The poets are entirely mistaken. They should address their lyrics to themselves, and should turn them into odes of self-congratulation on the excellency of the human mind. Nature is a dull affair, soundless, scentless, colorless: merely the hurrying of material, endlessly, meaninglessly.[1]

The external world of Lockian philosophy is undeniably abstract, and to that degree is unfavourable to poetic representation.

The philosophy of David Hartley was likewise uncongenial to poetic 'truth'. His tendency was to render the 'world-machine' even more machine-like, although his religiosity here and there broke forth in incongruous passages. He believed that the two great sources of truth are science and religion, while he looked upon art with suspicion. 'Most kinds of music, painting, and poetry', he remarked, 'have close connexions with vice', and 'the polite arts are scarce to be allowed, except when consecrated to religious purposes.'[2] With this puritanical conception of art, he never dreamt that it might rank with science and religion as a source of truth.

The scientific–philosophical synthesis of Locke and Hartley was bound to make the mystic and the poet uneasy. God, far from being the indwelling spirit loved by the mystic, appeared to be an external contriver; and the world as described by the scientist was remote from the poet's vision. The only function of art or poetry, according to this point of view, is either to entertain, or to serve as a handmaiden to morality, religion, or science. It has no autonomous role of its own in disclosing the nature of reality.

Wordsworth was far from content with this conception of poetry. In the Preface to the *Lyrical Ballads* he declared: '. . . The Poet, singing a song in which all human beings join with him, rejoices in the presence of truth as our visible friend and hourly companion. Poetry is the breath and finer spirit of all knowledge.' It is true that fifteen years later, in his 'Essay, Supplementary to the Preface', he appeared to reject the claim of poetry to know reality: 'The appropriate business of poetry . . . , her privilege and her *duty*, is to treat of things not as they *are*, but as they *seem* to exist to the *senses*, and to the *passions*.' The poet lives in a world of perspectives and prospects: his poetry is sensory and impassioned. It depicts not only con-

---

[1] Alfred North Whitehead, *Science and the Modern World*, op. cit., pp. 79–80.
[2] David Hartley, *Observations on Man*, sixth edition (1834), p. 481.

crete qualities, such as colour and sound, but also feeling-tones, such as urgency and grandeur. Wordsworth, in a passage that I have already quoted, speaks of 'the souls of lonely places', and 'the characters of danger or desire' impressed 'on caves and trees, upon the woods and hills'. Such tertiary qualities and vivid values are the characteristic stuff of poetry. This is what Wordsworth means, I believe, when he says that poetry depicts things 'not as they *are*', but as they *appear*.

He does not deny that appearances may be more or less veridical, or that art can have its own kind of truth. 'In the higher poetry', he goes on to say, 'an enlightened critic chiefly looks for a reflection of the wisdom of the heart. . . .'[1] This wisdom is not to be found in the high-order abstractions of science but in the rich, concrete, warm-hearted perceptions of art. Although the poet's visions are not literally true, they can express, in their own symbolical way, some of the deepest insights of the human mind. Wordsworth, I think, never abandoned the conviction, stated in the Preface to the *Lyrical Ballads*, that 'poetry is the first and last of all knowledge—it is as immortal as the heart of man'.

He also maintained in the Preface that poetry is 'in the countenance of all Science'. He was thus sympathetic to science so long as it was not distorted, but he thought that the advocates of minute scientific analysis had misconceived it. The 'inferior faculty' of reason—not 'the Grand and Simple Reason' but that 'false secondary power By which we multiply distinctions'—carries the analytic procedure to the point of stultification. It comes between us and reality, substituting lifeless abstractions in place of vital truths:

> Enquire of ancient Wisdom; go, demand
> Of mighty Nature, if 'twas ever meant
> That we should pry far off yet be unraised;
> That we should pore, and dwindle as we pore,
> Viewing all objects unremittingly
> In disconnexion dead and spiritless;
> And still dividing, and dividing still,
> Break down all grandeur, still unsatisfied
> With the perverse attempt, while littleness
> May yet become more little; waging thus

[1] Essay, Supplementary to the Preface (1815).

> An impious warfare with the very life
> Of our own souls![1]

Wordsworth reacted vehemently against a *merely* analytical approach because it neglects the configurations and inter-relations of things. But he did not deny that analysis, when kept within proper bounds, can enrich our appreciation and insight: 'Some are of the opinion that the habit of analysing, de-composing, and anatomizing is inevitably unfavourable to the perception of beauty. . . . The beauty in form of a plant or an animal is not made less but more apparent as a whole by more accurate insight into its constituent properties and powers.'[2] Thus Wordsworth did not condemn science or analysis as such, but its insensitive and obsessive use.

Locke and Hartley, carrying analysis too far, inadequately recognized the structural elements in nature and thought. Through Coleridge's report of Kant's doctrines Wordsworth must have learned something of the rigorous criticism that could be made of any such conception of knowledge. But Kant's theory may have struck him as just as unsatisfactory as Locke's. According to Kant, the stuff of sensation is non-relational and comes to us from the unknown world outside; this stuff is then organized in accordance with the universal and necessary laws of consciousness. This synthesizing process, which takes place before experience and renders experience possible, is effected by 'the productive imagination' operating subconsciously. Thus matter and form, sensation and synthesis, the original stuff of knowledge and the unity introduced into it, are distinguished and assigned to separate origins.[3] By making the formal elements subjective Kant was forced to regard ultimate being as unknowable.

This sceptical conclusion was bound to prove unsatisfactory to an idealistic poet such as Wordsworth. As I have said in Chapter IV, he agreed with Kant to the extent that he recognized in imagination a faculty that penetrates down into the

---

[1] *Excursion*, IV. 957–68.

[2] Wordsworth's note to 'This Lawn, a carpet all alive', in *Poetical Works*, iv. 425.

[3] Kant himself altered this position in the portions of *The Critique of Pure Reason* later in composition. This late theory, however, did not make a very deep impression on his contemporaries and its meaning remains obscure. Cf. Norman Kemp Smith, *A Commentary to Kant's 'Critique of Pure Reason'* (London: Macmillan, 1918), especially pp. 312–15.

subconscious and transcendental roots of being; but he departed
from Kant in his theory of outer reality. Instead of viewing
things in themselves as unknowable, he regarded external
reality as infected through and through with relations and
organic complexes and as exhibiting concrete characteristics
such as we find in immediate experience. In this way he gave a
deeper meaning to two of his fundamental convictions: first,
that the external world is exquisitely fitted to the mind, and
second, that there is a mighty unity in which all things inhere.
Reflecting the real nature of things, sense-impressions possess
a primary relational character which render them fit to be
incorporated into the patterns of thought. Yet neither the inner
processes that remould sensations nor the synthetic character
of the original stuff of experience can wholly account for the
universal and unconditional elements in consciousness. To
explain these Wordsworth, like Coleridge, fell back upon
transcendental factors.

It was not so much Kant or Plato but the transformation of
Platonism and Kantianism in the fertile mind of Coleridge that
impressed Wordsworth. From Kant's *Critique of Judgment*
Coleridge may have drawn his distinction between 'mechanic'
and 'organic' form: 'The form is mechanic when on any given
material we impress a pre-determined form, not necessarily
arising out of the properties of the material, as when to a mass
of wet clay we give whatever shape we wish it to retain when
hardened. The organic form, on the other hand, is innate; it
shapes as it develops itself from within, and the fullness of its
development is one and the same with the perfection of its
outward form.'[1] This distinction underlies Coleridge's contrast
between fancy and imagination. The form devised by fancy is
mechanic in the sense that it is artificially superinduced and
lacks genuine cohesion. The form created by imagination is
'organic'—in other words, it is no independent thing, imposed
as from the outside upon an alien content, but is the inner
structural harmony of the subject-matter brought to completion.
Hence the poetic genius, when 'his heart and intellect have been
intimately combined and unified with the great appearances of
nature', expresses the underlying unity of things. His poem is

[1] Coleridge, *Shakespearean Criticism*, edited by T. M. Raysor (Harvard University Press, 1930), i, p. 224.

'the shorthand hieroglyphic of Truth—the Mediator between Truth and Feeling, the Head and the Heart'.[1]

In thus insisting upon poetry's revelatory power Coleridge was going beyond Kant and was adopting a position more akin to Schelling. The ideas of God, the self, and the spiritual world, which for Kant are regulative only, or uncertain articles of faith, are for Coleridge constitutive and real. The poet, rather than the man of science, is in touch with these realities. The peculiar power of genius is to disclose them in poetic symbols. In Book XII of the *Biographia Literaria* Coleridge identified 'philosophic imagination' with 'the highest intuitive knowledge'.

We do not know just when he first formulated these ideas, but it seems likely that they were taking shape during his early friendship with Wordsworth. How much the latter derived from Coleridge and how much from his own thought and observation we shall never be able to judge with accuracy. It is possible that he influenced Coleridge quite as much as Coleridge influenced him. Of this we can be sure: his poetry represents a protest against the 'mechanical philosophy' and a passionate celebration of the human imagination. The world as he envisaged it is pervaded everywhere with life, organic relations, and vivid values. The poet, rising to the level of imaginative genius, is by very nature a kind of metaphysician, and his insight into the meaning of things is not one whit inferior to that of the scientist. In holding these convictions Wordsworth was more firm than Coleridge, for he could never have written, even in a mood of depression, the lines of the *Ode to Dejection*:

> . . . We receive but what we give
> And in our life alone does Nature live.

Wordsworth believed, and believed firmly, that perception is the confluence of mind and nature, revealing the spiritual forces common to both.

He thought of images, not as figments of the imagination, but as inhering in external objects.

> . . . I still
> At all times had a real solid world
> Of images about me.[2]

---

[1] Manuscript 'Semina Rerum', quoted by John H. Muirhead, *Coleridge as Philosopher* (London: George Allen & Unwin, 1930), p. 195.
[2] *Prelude* (1805), VIII. 602–4.

They belong to the mind, as all images do, and yet they are real and solid. Among other passages that might be cited are the following lines from *The Recluse*:

> Joy spreads, and sorrow spreads; and this whole Vale,
> Home of untutored Sheperds as it is,
> Swarms with sensation, as with gleams of sunshine,
> Shadows or breezes, scents or sounds.[1]

In quoting this passage, C. C. Clarke remarks: 'Again and again the poetry demonstrates that joy spreads, and sorrow spreads, because sensations have dimensions that are at once mental and spatial.'[2]

The same notion is expressed in *The Prelude*:

> Oh, then, the calm
> And dead still water lay upon my mind
> Even with a weight of pleasure, and the sky
> Never before so beautiful, sank down
> Into my heart, and held me like a dream![3]

As one studies these lines and similar passages, one sees that there is a double movement in Wordsworth's poetry. There is *the objectification of spirit*, the imagination imparting its own dreamlike vividness and splendour to the things of sense. On the other hand, there is *the subjectification of nature*, the sky sinking down into the heart, and the dead still water lying upon the mind even with a weight of pleasure. As Clarke remarks, things exist both outwardly and inwardly: objects become subjects and subjects objects.

This way of looking at nature fits in with a phenomenalistic idealism like that of Berkeley, or a perspectival realism like that of Whitehead. It does not fit Locke's abstract world of primary qualities and unknowable substances. It makes the perspectives of art metaphysically relevant.

2. *Freedom and Joy in Nature*

In reacting against the notion of the world-machine the poet formulated an account of existence in terms of freedom and

---

[1] *Recluse*, 445–8.
[2] C. C. Clarke, *Romantic Paradox: An Essay on the Poetry of Wordsworth* (London: Routledge & Kegan Paul, 1962), p. 65. (A brilliant discussion of Wordsworth's theory of perception.)   [3] *Prelude*, II. 170–4.

activity everywhere to be found in nature. He applied the idea of freedom to least and greatest:

> How does the Meadow-flower its bloom unfold?
> Because the lovely little flower is free
> Down to its root, and in that freedom, bold;
> And so the grandeur of the Forest-tree
> Comes not by casting in a formal mould,
> But from its *own* divine vitality.[1]

As a complement to this attribution of creativeness and liberty to flower or tree, *The Excursion* announces that there is a 'freedom of the universe'. An 'active principle' is assigned to every form of being, so that no spot is insulated, and the free 'soul of all the worlds' subsists in all things, in all natures.[2] Likewise in the first text of *The Prelude* Wordsworth indicates his belief in an '*active* universe'.[3]

If we now explore this inner life of nature as he conceives it, we find that one of its characteristics is its joy. Some of his remarks to this effect we may perhaps dismiss as metaphorical. The sonnet 'Brook! whose society the Poet seeks' announces that 'unwearied Joy' has been bestowed upon the stream. *To the Daisy* speaks of the 'cheerful Flower' as alert and gay. 'I wandered lonely as a cloud' depicts the jocund daffodils that outdo the sparkling waves in glee. In all three poems Wordsworth may be only figurative in expression. He may not be literal in 'Three years she grew in sun and shower', in which he represents nature as moulding Lucy and imparting to her its own 'vital feelings of delight'. We are not so much inclined, on the other hand, to dismiss as a mere play of fancy his statement in *The Prelude*: 'Oh! soul of Nature, . . . That didst rejoice with me, . . . that dost overflow With passion and with life.'[4] Nor can we regard the following assertion as other than literal:

> Yet, whate'er enjoyments dwell
> In the impenetrable cell

---

[1] '*A Poet!*—He hath put his heart to school,' *Poetical Works*, iii. 52.

[2] *Excursion*, IX. 1–18. This portion of *The Excursion* was written in 1798–9. (See *Poetical Works*, v, p. 471.)

[3] *Prelude* (1805), II. 266.

[4] Ibid. XI. 138–9, 146–7. Only line 139 is reproduced in the corresponding 1850 text, XII. 94.

Of the silent heart which Nature
Furnishes to every creature;
Whatsoe'er we feel and know
Too sedate for outward show,
Such a light of gladness breaks,
Pretty Kitten! from thy freaks.[1]

We have Wordsworth's own word that this section of the poem should be taken in all seriousness. Robinson recorded in his *Diary*, 10 September 1816, that Wordsworth 'quoted from *The Kitten and Falling Leaves*, to show that he had connected even the kitten with the great, awful, and mysterious powers of nature'. No other passage is relevant to the assertion. This record in the *Diary* should warn us that danger attends upon an interpretation of such declarations as mere examples of 'charming fancy'.[2]

The clearest statement to be found in Wordsworth of his belief in nature's joyous life occurs in *Lines Written in Early Spring*. Herein he states his 'faith that every flower Enjoys the air it breathes'. In the birds and the budding twigs there is also enjoyment:

And I must think, do all I can,
That there was pleasure there.

In *To My Sister* the poet recognizes 'a sense of joy' in nature and a 'blessed power' that rolls through all things about us. These poems deserve a more absolute acceptance as a record of Wordsworth's thought than some critics have been inclined to give to them.

His conception of an indwelling life and soul is expressed in passage after passage:

O! Soul of Nature! that dost overflow
With passion and with life.[3]

. . . the one interior life
That lives in all things.[4]

---

[1] *The Kitten and the Falling Leaves*, 95–103. *Poetical Works*, ii. 170.
[2] As in Lord Morley's Introduction to *The Complete Poetical Works of William Wordsworth* (New York: Crowell, 1907), p. lxv.
[3] *Prelude* (1805), XI. 146–7.
[4] *The Prelude*, ed. E. de Selincourt, first edition, p. 512.

There is an active principle alive
In all things, in all natures, in the flowers
And in the trees. . . .[1]

. . . the life
Of all things and the mighty unity
In all which we behold, and feel, and are.[2]

Even when sound and motion cease, Wordsworth finds in the
ensuing stillness not the silence of insensate things but the
hush of a living spirit.

The leaves stir not,
They all are steady as the cloudless sky;
How deep the Quiet: all is motionless,
As if the life of the vast world was hushed
Into a breathless dream.[3]

Life is everywhere, even in still and silent nature. As Charles
Lamb, who knew Wordsworth intimately, remarked: 'In his
poetry nothing in Nature is dead. Nature is synonymous with
life.'[4]

3. The Organic Interrelatedness of Things

The Old Cumberland Beggar introduces another aspect of
Wordsworth's conception of the natural world. It is 'Nature's
law', he says, that 'forms created the most vile and brute' should
not 'exist divorced from good'. The life of the whole imparts a
pulse of good to each fragment.[5] Value is not confined; it spreads
outward until it affects the entire circumambient region. As
Wordsworth declares in *The Excursion*:

Whate'er exists hath properties that spread
Beyond itself, communicating good,
A simple blessing, or with evil mixed;
Spirit that knows no insulated spot,
No chasm, no solitude.[6]

[1] Fragment in *Poetical Works*, v. 286.
[2] *Prelude* (1805), XIII. 253–5.
[3] Fragment, *Poetical Works*, v. 343.
[4] From Lamb's review of *The Excursion* in the *Quarterly Review*, October 1814.
Wordsworthiana, ed. William Knight (London: Macmillan, 1889), p. 246.
[5] *The Old Cumberland Beggar*, 73–79. *Poetical Works*, iv. 234.
[6] *Excursion*, IX. 10–14.

It is because the poet recognizes the organic emanation and collection of value that he protests vigorously against the false secondary power by which we multiply distinctions. It is because he feels that each small thing grasps together, within its inner being, the good that accumulates from the presence of surrounding things, that he maintains so deep a reverence for slight objects and that he affirms so often that 'we murder to dissect'.

Since every object impresses itself on others and each reflects its neighbours, the vice of ever 'dividing' falsifies reality.

> For all things in this little world of ours
> Are in one bosom of close neighbourhood.[1]

Wordsworth's disposition to regard natural objects as neighbourly, or even interpenetrative, appears in poem after poem. It constitutes much of the distinctiveness of 'I wandered lonely as a cloud'. The spiritual unity of nature enters into the design of *Nutting*, *Hart-Leap Well*, and *Lines Written in Early Spring*. A suggestion of life and interplay distinguishes many scattered lines:

> The Winds come to me from the fields of sleep,
> And all the earth is gay.[2]

> . . . 'mid all this mighty sum
> Of things for ever speaking.[3]

> Loud is the Vale! the Voice is up
> With which she speaks when storms are gone,
> A mighty unison of streams!
> Of all her Voices, One![4]

These passages reflect the mysterious bonds of unity behind the seeming disconnexion of things. The poet has a kind of primitive sense or intuition

> Of unknown modes of being which on earth,
> Or in the heavens, or in the heavens and earth
> Exist by mighty combinations, bound
> Together by a link, and with a soul
> Which makes all one.[5]

---

[1] *The Tuft of Primroses*, in *Poetical Works*, v. 351.
[2] *Ode: Intimations of Immortality. Poetical Works*, iv. 279.
[3] *Expostulation and Reply. Poetical Works*, iv. 56.
[4] '*Loud is the Vale!' Poetical Works*, iv. 266.
[5] Fragment, *Poetical Works*, v. 340–1. Wordsworth's theory of 'spots of time'

There is a life, a spirit, or a pervasive atmosphere that draws things together into a natural community.

The tendency to feel the life of nature as involved in each particular instance is illustrated by Wordsworth's *Guide* to the Lake Country—one of the first and best tourist manuals. There is a long discussion, for example, of the larch-tree, which Wordsworth condemns for its gross individualism. Imported into the Lake Country, the larch never fitted into its new habitat, the tens of thousands of 'separate individual trees, obstinately presenting themselves as such'.[1] They did not behave as members of the earth's ecological community ought to behave. Here and elsewhere the dominant idea is that of the interdependence and interrelatedness of all natural things.

Human beings fit into the midst of these interplaying forces. In 'Three years she grew in sun and shower' Lucy is taken up into the life of nature and incorporated with it. The same is true of Michael, the Leech Gatherer, the Solitary Reaper, the Highland Girl, the Danish Boy, and Louisa in the Shade: they seem made all of a piece with the world around them, so that they almost have their being in the elemental or beauteous forms that pervade their natural domain. Even the rebellious Toussaint L'Ouverture is a power among other powers in nature:

> Thou hast left behind
> Powers that will work for thee; air, earth, and skies;
> There's not a breathing of the common wind
> That will forget thee; thou hast great allies.[2]

He who cuts himself off from 'the filial bond of nature' has sundered the ties that unite him with the human community:

> Why is it we feel
> So little for each other, but for this,
> That we with nature have no sympathy,
> Or with such things as have no power to hold
> Articulate language?

indicates a similar knotting together of moments into organic complexes. See Book XIII. 208 ff.

[1] Cf. Wordsworth, *A Guide Through the District of the Lakes in the North of England* (London: Rupert Hart-Davis, 1951), p. 122. Original edition, 1835.

[2] *To Toussaint L'Ouverture. Poetical Works*, iii. 112.

> And never for each other shall we feel
> As we may feel, till we have sympathy
> With nature in her forms inanimate,
> With objects such as have no power to hold
> Articulate language. In all forms of things
> There is a mind.[1]

Thus instead of viewing the external world as an abstract flux of isolated particles, Wordsworth regarded reality as suffused throughout with relations and vital influences:

> All beings have their properties which spread
> Beyond themselves, a power by which they make
> Some other being conscious of their life.[2]

To find a parallel expression in philosophy we should have to go to the metaphysics of Whitehead. In this 'revolt against dualism' Wordsworth was anticipating some of the most significant intellectual developments of the twentieth century, but he was also going back to very primitive roots.

4. *Animism*

He was remarkably unaffected by the modifications in men's grasp of things brought about by our complex scientific civilization. It is as though he gazed at nature for the first time:

> You look round on your Mother Earth . . .
> As if you were her first-born birth,
> And none had lived before you![3]

One has to journey beyond the inhibitions and sophistications imposed by the modern intelligence to find a disposition of mind that is really similar to this. All poets in some degree brush away the frost of custom, but not to the same degree and in the same way. Perhaps only among uncivilized people can one find the almost *sensuous* animism that reappears in Wordsworth. The perceptions of nature, as represented in early folk religions or among savages, are commonly fused with a spontaneous spiritism. The world *appeared* to be alive to these people and was thought to be so.

---

[1] Fragment, *Poetical Works*, v. 340.
[2] Variant reading in Book IX of *The Excursion*, in ibid. v. 286. (From manuscript dated 1797–8.)
[3] *Expostulation and Reply. Poetical Works*, iv. 56.

Wordsworth's animistic bent may have been strengthened by books of history and travel, both of which he loved and read assiduously. In perusing these old travel books he came upon accounts of spirits that dwell in remote regions. Apparently he seized upon exactly this source in assisting Coleridge to plot *The Ancient Mariner*: 'Suppose', said I, 'you represent him as having killed one of these birds on entering the South Sea, and that the tutelary spirits of those regions take upon them to avenge the crime.'[1] In his report of the time when he first came to believe that there is a life in everything Wordsworth identified the conviction with the ideas current in the early cultural stages:

> . . . if things viewed
> By poets in old time, and higher up
> By the first men, earth's first inhabitants,
> May in these tutored days no more be seen
> With undisordered sight.[2]

In *The Excursion*, the poet recounted the mythological ideas of the ancient Persians and Chaldees and Greeks, and indicated his sympathy for their type of nature worship.[3] One suspects that if a similar passage had been introduced into the early text of *The Prelude*, it would have dealt with a period of more primitive thought and would have presented more completely animistic doctrine. At least the first version of *The Prelude* is far more spiritistic than *The Excursion*.

These animistic touches appear in the form of simple perceptions:

> The Moon doth with delight
> Look round her when the heavens are bare.[4]

More is demanded of the reader of these lines than the willing suspension of disbelief that we all bring to poetry anyway. The words so perfectly fit the visionary mood of the poem that they appear to be the report of something actually seen. Similarly the following lines carry us back to a pre-analytical mode of perception:

---

[1] Wordsworth's note to *We are Seven*. *Poetical Works*, i. 361.
[2] *Prelude*, III. 153–7.
[3] *Excursion*, IV. 663–762.
[4] *Ode: Intimations of Immortality*, 12–13.

Unruffled doth the blue lake lie,
The mountains looking on.[1]

Yon star upon the mountain-top
Is listening quietly.[2]

The river glideth at his own sweet will.[3]

The consciousness of life is undifferentiated from sense perception.

At times the animism becomes more absolute. Some of the early readings of *The Prelude* make use of the idea of 'tutelary powers' which dwell in nature and guard over men. In a description of a country fair held at the base of Helvellyn the author at first planned to introduce the following comment:

Immense
Is the Recess, the circumambient World
Magnificent, by which they are embraced.
They move about upon the soft green field:
How little They, they and their doings seem,
Their herds and flocks about them, they themselves,
And all that they can further or obstruct!
Through utter weakness pitiably dear
As tender Infants are: and yet how great!
For all things serve them, serve them for delight
Or profit from the moment when the dawn
Ah surely not without attendant gleams
Of heart illumination strikes the sense
With its first glistening on the silent rock
Whose evening shadows led them to repose
And doubt ye that these solitudes are paced
By tutelary Powers more safely versed
In weal and woe than aught that fabling Greece
Invented, Spirits gentle and benign
Who now perhaps from yon reposing cloud
Look down upon them or frequent the ridge
Of old Helvellyn listening to the stir
That with this ancient festival returns
To animate and chear their calm abode.[4]

---

[1] 'The sylvan slopes with corn-clad fields', *Poetical Works*, iv. 98.
[2] 'Loud is the Vale!' *Poetical Works*, iv. 266.
[3] *Composed upon Westminster Bridge. Poetical Works*, iii. 38.
[4] Corresponding to *Prelude* (1805), VIII. 44–61. The variant reading begins with line 55.

Another animistic portion of *The Prelude* in its earliest form occurs in a passage that was designed to introduce the famous boat-stealing episode of the first book:

I believe
That there are Spirits which, when they would form
A favoured being, from his very dawn
Of infancy do open out the clouds
As at the touch of lightning, seeking him
With gentle visitations, quiet Powers!
Retired and seldom recognized, yet kind
And to the very meanest not unknown.
With me though rarely in my boyish days
They communed; others too there are who use
Yet haply aiming at the self-same end
Severer interventions, ministry
More palpable, and of their school was I.
They guided me: one evening led by them
I went alone into a Shepherd's Boat,
A Skiff that to a willow tree was tied
Within a rocky Cave, its usual home.[1]

This first draft indicates how very animistic in inspiration certain now familiar passages may have been in their first conception.

We can only conjecture how the following statement might once have stood:

A gracious spirit o'er this earth presides,
And o'er the heart of man: invisibly
It comes, to works of unreproved delight,
And tendency benign, directing those
Who care not, know not, think not what they do.[2]

Even if this reading represents the first draft, such a conception of a spirit's ministrations seems to be merely a refinement of the early notion of tutelary powers. If we return to the passage in which the poet speaks of the 'Souls of lonely places', we find that the language here too is not far removed from a frank animism. We have a variant reading in this instance that makes the meaning indubitable:

Ye Powers of earth, ye genii of the Springs
And ye that have your voices in the clouds

[1] Corresponding to *Prelude* (1805), I. 352–75.
[2] *Prelude*, V. 491–5. Same in 1805 text.

And ye that are familiars of the Lakes
And standing pools, Ah, not for trivial ends
Through snow and sunshine, through the sparkling plains
Of moonlight frost and in the stormy day
Did ye with such assiduous love pursue
Your favourite and your joy.[1]

In the light of such unmitigated animism, we can attribute to some of Wordsworth's early poems a more literal signification than we have been wont to find in them. In *Nutting*, for example, the author may have meant quite unmetaphorically that there is 'a spirit in the woods'. In 'Three years she grew in sun and shower' the personification of nature and the conscious overseeing power attributed to her may not be fictitious from the point of view of the man who wrote the poem in 1799. Wordsworth might likewise have meant quite literally his explanation of the strange transformation around Hart-Leap Well:

The Being, that is in the clouds and air,
That is in the green leaves among the groves,
Maintains a deep and reverential care
For the unoffending creatures whom he loves.[2]

Perhaps, too, he intends to be more matter-of-fact than one would suppose in the engaging lines:

Listen! the mighty Being is awake,
And doth with his eternal motion make
A sound like thunder.[3]

Again, he may be expressing his animism in *Expostulation and Reply*:

Nor less I deem that there are Powers
Which of themselves our minds impress;
That we can feed this mind of ours
In a wise passiveness.

These powers, we are led to suppose from passages written for *The Prelude* at about the same time, are no other than the quiet tutelary powers, the powers of earth, that have voices in the clouds and are familiars of the Lakes.

---

[1] Variant reading for I. 490–2 in 1805 version.
[2] *Hart-Leap Well*, 165–8. *Poetical Works*, ii. 249.
[3] 'It is a beauteous evening, calm and free,' *Poetical Works*, iii. 17.

Even more light is thrown upon the puzzling *Peter Bell*. Some readers have had a rather hard time with this poem, because it seems to express the thought that nature exerts a conscious moral influence over men. Since many people are loath to recognize ideas of this kind, they have simply been puzzled and have passed on to other poems. We can now recognize in the work another application of the early animism of Wordsworth. Thus the poet invokes the help of 'Dread Spirits' for his wayward Peter:

> Your presence often have I felt
> In darkness and the stormy night;
> And with like force, if need there be,
> Ye can put forth your agency
> When earth is calm, and heaven is bright.
>
> Then coming from the wayward world,
> That powerful world in which ye dwell,
> Come, Spirits of the Mind! and try,
> To-night, beneath the moonlight sky,
> What may be done with Peter Bell![1]

So the spirits set to work on Peter:

> And now the Spirits of the Mind
> Are busy with poor Peter Bell;
> Upon the rights of visual sense
> Usurping, with a prevalence
> More terrible than magic spell.[2]

Thus was wrought the hallucination which had a large share in Peter's regeneration. The poem seems partly designed to celebrate the power over the mind of the animistic forces that dwell in nature.

If anyone feels that this interpretation does violence to a sober-minded poet, he can take comfort in the thought that Wordsworth might be presenting what he conceived to be possible, not what he knew to be true. But the reader should bear in mind that poets commonly have the eccentricity of believing in worlds that their imaginations have fashioned.

---

[1] Ll. 776–85. It is clear from these stanzas that the spirits dwell in nature, even though they are called 'Spirits of the Mind'.
[2] Ll. 916–20.

5. *The Immanence of God*

We have discriminated certain features of Wordsworth's theory of nature: that sense-qualities are objectively real; that freedom and activity are to be found everywhere in the world around us; that pleasure and other mental states reside in outer objects; that form, synthesis, and relation bind external things into close communities; and that nature exercises a moral influence over man through spirits and tutelary powers. All except the last conviction remained as an element in the poet's mature thought, and traces of a primitivistic animism may be found even in the later writings. As a final inclusive idea we must consider his pantheism, which bound together these various convictions during the earlier phase of Wordsworth's thought.

Despite his denial of pantheistic convictions in 1814, we are practically compelled to recognize his early belief that God was at one with man and nature. How else can we interpret the passage that I have quoted repeatedly, in which he refers to 'the one interior life'

> —In which all beings live with god, themselves
> Are god, Existing in the mighty whole,
> As indistinguishable as the cloudless East
> At noon is from the cloudless west, when all
> The hemisphere is one cerulean blue.

If any language is pantheistic, this surely is.

Such an outlook came to him at an early age. He definitely records that when his 'seventeenth year was come' he had attained the conviction that a unitary 'Being' is everywhere:

> . . . in all things now
> I saw one life, and felt that it was joy.[1]

The youth was still fanciful in the application of this new belief; he was too prone to 'see blessings spread around' him 'like a sea'. Yet he had discovered an idea that was to cling to him. As the years passed by, he modified his views, but a good many passages in the original version of *The Prelude* are still tinged with pantheistic convictions:

> Thus much for the one Presence, and the Life
> Of the great whole.[2]

[1] *Prelude* (1805), II. 429–30. [2] Ibid. III. 130–1.

Of Genius, Power
Creation and Divinity itself
I have been speaking, for my theme has been
What pass'd within me.[1]

A soul divine which we participate,
A deathless spirit.[2]

. . . God and nature's single sovereignty.[3]

. . . a sense,
Of treachery and desertion in the place
The holiest that I knew of, my own soul.[4]

Great God!
Who send'st thyself into this breathing world
Through Nature and through every kind of life,
And mak'st Man what he is, Creature divine.[5]

The feeling of life endless, the great thought
By which we live, Infinity and God.[6]

These lines, to a variable extent, state the pantheistic faith that
still appeared in traces.

Quite a number of Wordsworthian scholars have protested
against ascribing pantheism to *Tintern Abbey* or any other of
the poet's works. Willard L. Sperry, for example, has written:

. . . Whatever sort of believer Wordsworth was, he was not a
pantheist. Pantheism is amoral; it does not recognize the existence
of evil and therefore does not have to wrestle with the problem of evil.
Not so with Wordsworth. He was burdened with the mystery and the
heavy and the weary weight of all this unintelligible world. He felt the
general sorrow of mankind. He heard the still, sad music of humanity.
He saw the race moving in a mighty caravan of pain. In particular he
was aware of man's inhumanity to man. All this lies far apart from
pantheism.[7]

To a certain extent we can agree with this statement. Wordsworth was certainly aware of the pain and mystery of life, and

[1] Ibid. III. 171–4. [2] Ibid. V. 16–17.
[3] Ibid. IX. 237. [4] Ibid. X. 379–81.
[5] Ibid. X. 386–9. [6] Ibid. XIII. 183–4.
[7] Willard L. Sperry, 'Wordsworth's Religion', in Gilbert T. Dunklin (editor),
Wordsworth (Princeton University Press, 1951), p. 153.

he wrestled with the problem of evil more than he ever confessed. But, like most of us, he was not always consistent. His sense of the divine spirit in all the workings of nature may not have been logically compatible with his profound realization of suffering, but it is characteristic of his poetic vision.

So strong was his conviction of God's immanence that even dire events seemed to subserve the divine plan. In 1816 he thus addressed 'Almighty God':

> But thy most dreaded instrument
> For working out a pure intent
> Is Man—arrayed for mutual slaughter,
> Yea—Carnage is thy daughter![1]

The poet apparently believed, when he wrote these words, that even the harshest discords are ultimately resolved in harmony. The reader may be repelled by this doctrine, but he should not blink what Wordsworth says in this rather late period of his career.

Noting that the poet refers to the transcendence as well as the immanence of God, some scholars have spoken of his *panentheism* rather than his *pantheism*. Perhaps 'panentheism', which means that nature is *in* God rather than that *God* is in nature, is the more accurate term. Spinoza's philosophy is usually called 'pantheistic', but it might more truly be described as 'panentheistic'—since he believed that all that we ordinarily term 'nature', whether it be mind or matter, is included in the larger being of God, as the Infinite of infinites. So it may be with Wordsworth's theory during certain periods of his life. The important thing is not to cling to a word but correctly to interpret his ideas. As Walter Pater remarked, Wordsworth was possessed by 'the thought of a spirit of life in outward things, a single, all-pervading mind in them, of which man, and even the poet's imaginative energy, are but moments'.[2] Call this 'thought' what you will, it is the heart and core of the poet's faith during his most creative years. Gradually his emphasis changed from immanence to transcendence, but he never went so far as to believe in an absentee God.

---

[1] *Ode*, 'Imagination—ne'er before content,' 106–9, version of 1816. *Poetical Works*, iii. 151.

[2] Walter Pater, *Appreciations* (London: Macmillan, 1920), p. 56.

In contrast with changing points of view there were certain characteristic ideas that persisted until his late period. What we call physical matter, he thought, is the outer form of things, not the inner content, and the content eludes the purely analytical thinker. Mind and natural objects, since they manifest certain characteristics in common, such as freedom, activity, synthesis, and organic interrelation, may be considered similar in their inner being, although the inorganic world is far more rudimentary than man. As a consequence of this similarity, the inner order no longer seems so different from the mis-called 'mechanical' universe, for underlying all reality is a kind of mind-stuff, that in man quickens into a truly magnanimous existence. Since this 'under-presence' may be discovered within the interior life of each person, no one is wholly dependent upon sensation for the source of truth. It is this 'internal brightness' that makes man a 'Creature divine'. Hence a profound awe fell upon Wordsworth when he looked into the Mind of Man, his haunt and the main region of his song.

CONCLUSION

Wᴏʀᴅsᴡᴏʀᴛʜ defined the poet as a man who has more than usual organic sensibility and has also thought long and deeply. In his own poetry he was true to this definition, wakening 'a sort of thought in sense'.[1] He differed in this respect from Coleridge, who was more of a philosopher, but was almost incapable of turning philosophical ideas into poetry. Coleridge's meditative verse was rarely successful, and the ideas expressed were sadly limited. If we examine his 'poetic thought'—explicit in his more reflective poems and implicit in the *Ancient Mariner, Christabel,* and *Kubla Khan*—the range is confined mainly to ideas of guilt and conflict, escape and frustration. Although some successful poems, such as *Frost at Midnight,* are partial exceptions, these are few.

To illustrate the comparison let us turn to a typical poem of Coleridge:

> A sunny shaft did I behold,
>   From sky to earth it slanted;
> And poised therein a bird so bold—
>   Sweet bird, thou wert enchanted!
>
> He sank, he rose, he twinkled, he troll'd
>   Within that shaft of sunny mist;
> His eyes of fire, his beak of gold,
>   All else of amethyst!
>
> And thus he sang: 'Adieu! adieu!
> Love's dreams prove seldom true.
> The blossoms, they make no delay:
> The sparkling dew-drops will not stay.
>   Sweet month of May,
>   We must away;
>   Far, far away!
>   To-day! to-day!'[2]

---

[1] Cf. Wordsworth's Preface to the *Lyrical Ballads* and Shelley's comment in *Peter Bell the Third,* IV. x. 5.   [2] Song from *Zapolya* (1815).

This is the poetry of enchantment. The bird of the poem is not
real and actual but a bird of paradise. Despite the sparkling
imagery, the mood is escapist; and it is the mood of the song,
not the shopworn ideas of love's inconstancy and beauty's
transitoriness, that counts.

Coleridge's song-bird invites us to hie 'far, far away!' Very
different is the robin in Wordsworth's poem 'To My Sister':

> It is the first mild day of March:
> Each minute sweeter than before,
> The redbreast sings from the tall larch
> That stands beside our door.
>
> There is a blessing in the air,
> Which seems a sense of joy to yield
> To the bare trees, and mountains bare,
> And grass in the green field.

This too is the poetry of mood, but it is the real world of grass
and bare mountains and trees to which the robin summons us.
The remainder of the poem is not as weighty in ideas as some
examples that I might cite, but it is a bold celebration of the
holy passion of love and the unity of all things.

Even when Wordsworth turns away from 'the common
growth of mother-earth' to write of ancient legend, of Proteus
rising from the sea or old Triton blowing his wreathèd horn, it
is not without comment upon the goings-on of life. 'The world
is too much with us' is a good example of his meditative poetry.
Within its brief compass it implies a judgement upon the quality
of modern civilization—its poverty of imagination, the stuffiness
of its creeds, the rush and push of its public life. We are invited
to live in harmony with nature and to renounce 'the fretful stir
Unprofitable, and the fever of the world'.[1] In the richness of its
values and the range of its ideas this is a large poem, although
it numbers only fourteen lines. It is what Matthew Arnold called
'a criticism of life'.

Wordsworth is most successful when he is convinced that the
mind and the external world are 'exquisitely fitted' to one
another.

> And in this season of his second birth . . .
> He feels that, be his mind however great

[1] *Tintern Abbey*, 52–53.

                In aspiration, the universe in which
                He lives is equal to his mind, that each
                Is worthy of the other; if the one
                Be insatiate, the other is inexhaustible.[1]

Wordsworth is here stating prosaically what he expressed with
great poetic vigour in *Tintern Abbey*, *The Recluse*, and the
earlier parts of *The Prelude*.

The counterpoise between inner and outer things was too
precarious to be long sustained. In the concluding lines of the
1805 version of *The Prelude* Wordsworth abandoned his view
that the mind and external nature are equal to each other. The
human mind, he said, is a 'thousand times' more beautiful than
the earth. Two years later he declared that 'a cloud, however
bright' finds 'in the heart of man no natural home'. He could no
longer *feel* that 'the discerning intellect of Man' is 'wedded to
this goodly universe In love and holy passion', nor write 'the
spousal verse Of this great consummation'. Disparaging nature,
he was finally led to disparage the natural man, 'Born of dust
and kindred to the worm'.[2] The decline in his poetic power was
sealed by this loss of naturalistic faith.

But even in these later years he did not wholly cut himself off
from the sources of his strength. In the 'Essay Supplementary
to the Preface' (1815) he wrote that 'in nature everything is
distinct, yet nothing defined into absolute independent single-
ness'. In a letter to Landor, 21 January 1824, he spoke of his
liking for poetry 'where things are lost in each other, and limits
vanish, and aspirations are raised'.[3] These remarks define what
is most characteristic of his poetry.

The 'blending' of distinct things is nowhere better illustrated
than in the following passage:

                —How vast the compass of this theatre,
                Yet nothing to be seen but lovely pomp
                And silent majesty; the birch-tree woods
                Are hung with thousand thousand diamond drops
                Of melted hoar-frost, every tiny knot

---

[1] *The Prelude*, ed. Ernest de Selincourt and Helen Darbishire, revised edition
(Oxford University Press, 1959), pp. 575–6.
[2] *Prelude*, VIII. 487–8. Cf. revised edition, ibid., pp. lxviii–lxxiv, for similar
changes of idea in Wordsworth's late revision of *The Prelude*.
[3] *Letters: The Later Years*, i, p. 135.

In the bare twigs, each little budding-place
Cased with its several bead, what myriads there
Upon one tree, while all the distant grove
That rises to the summit of the steep,
Shows like a mountain built of silver light.
See yonder the same pageant, and again
Behold the universal imagery
Inverted, all its sun-bright features touched
As with the varnish, and the gloss of dreams;
Dreamlike the blending also of the whole
Harmonious landscape: all along the shore
The boundary lost, the line invisible
That parts the image from reality;
And the clear hills, as high as they ascend
Heavenward, so deep piercing the lake below.[1]

Each diamond drop of melted hoar-frost stands out as a separate bead; yet all the thousand thousand drops are touched and blended with the gloss of dreams. The boundary is lost that parts the image from reality; the clear hills pierce deep the lake.

No poet has been more struck by the beauty of solitary things:

> Fair as a star when only one
> Is shining in the sky.

But none has been more haunted by the sense of blending and relation. Not only do reality and image interpenetrate, but sense and soul, time and eternity, earth and sky, head and heart, order and spontaneity, emotion and tranquillity, memory and immediate intuition. Wordsworth's vision of things is dialectical, thesis and antithesis being reconciled in a wider construct. Those who have failed to grasp this unity of distinct and even contrary things have misinterpreted Wordsworth. They have seen him as only half the poet that he was—as either one-sidedly naturalistic or one-sidedly transcendentalist.

Some critics have denied that he ever could have been a mystic, wrongly supposing that all mysticism is radically monistic. William Blake, mystic though he was, insisted that distinctness is 'the great and golden rule of life'. His mysticism, as Wicksteed has described it, is very much like that of Wordsworth.[2] The difference is that the Lake poet found in the

---

[1] *Recluse*, 560–79.
[2] Cf. Joseph H. Wicksteed, *Blake's Vision of the Book of Job*, revised edition

206 *Conclusion*

meadows and the woods and mountains the spiritual stimulus that Blake sought in purely imaginary visions. In his copy of Wordsworth's *Poems* Blake wrote the comment: 'Natural Objects always did and now do weaken, deaden and obliterate Imagination in Me. Wordsworth must know that what he Writes Valuable is Not to be found in Nature.'[1] As the more comprehensive poet, Wordsworth wanted to go beyond but not away from nature. Nevertheless, the two poets were alike in their love of the minute and the determinate.

For a certain sort of analytical mind it makes little sense to say that things while remaining distinct are or should be united. 'I prefer sharp outlines and definite separations', remarked Bertrand Russell.[2] If we can believe Wordsworth, the dichotomy between unity and separation is not so ultimate as these analysts have supposed. The most moving kind of unity is the unity of difference.

Coleridge believed that the essence of Wordsworth's genius was the ability to combine opposites, such as lyricism and meditation, ideality and realism:

It was the union of deep feeling with profound thought; the fine balance of truth in observing, with the imaginative faculty in modifying the objects observed; and above all the original gift of spreading the tone, the *atmosphere*, and with it the depth and height of the ideal world around forms, incidents, and situations, of which, for the common view, custom had bedimmed all the lustre, had dried up the sparkle and the dew drops.[3]

Art is the great reconciler of opposites which, in our practical life, exclude each other. Wordsworth was, in this sense, a great artist.

His greatness has been questioned by a number of contemporary critics. They doubt the relevance of his values to our age of technology and science. Douglas Bush, for example, believes that 'he has meant very little to most modern poets',

(London: Dent, 1924), especially pp. 181–91, 223–6. Mark Schorer, in *William Blake* (New York: Holt, 1946), denies that Blake was a mystic, but his conception of mysticism is more negativistic than that of Wicksteed or the view stated in the present book.

[1] *Poetry and Prose of William Blake*, ed. Geoffrey Keynes (London: Nonesuch Press, 1927), pp. 1024–5.

[2] Bertrand Russell, *Portraits from Memory* (London: Allen & Unwin, 1956), p. 38.

[3] *Biographia Literaria*, i, p. 59.

and that the ordinary reader has lost spiritual touch with him. He 'dreamed of the humanizing of what was to grow more and more inhuman', but his 'rural romanticism' was inadequate as a remedy. His optimistic faith in man underestimated the depths of human depravity; his faith in nature evaded rather than answered the challenge of scientific rationalism. 'If Wordsworth is not an active force in our time (and the mainly negative evidence suggests that he is not)', the explanation is to be sought in 'the nebulous quality of his mysticism and of his sentimental ethics, and the really very limited range of experience that he explores'.[1]

I would challenge some of these judgements. When Wordsworth extols 'the grand elementary principle of pleasure', or 'joy in widest commonalty spread', his optimism may appear superficial; but actually he was moved profoundly by the 'sorrow barricadoed evermore Within the walls of cities', and listened intently when he heard 'Humanity in fields and groves Pipe solitary anguish'.[2] The spiritual strength exhibited by Michael beside the unfinished sheep-fold, or by the Leech Gatherer on the lonely moor, is not aptly described as 'sentimental'. It would be more accurate to see in these figures 'the native and naked dignity of man'. Wordsworth's determination to 'keep his eye on the object', and his minutely accurate characterizations of natural appearances, can scarcely be called a *'nebulous* mysticism'. To speak of the 'very limited range' of his experience is less than just. He felt more and knew more than most of us ever will, and *The Prelude* covers a pretty wide gamut of human experience.

I cannot judge to what extent Bush is correct in his estimate of Wordsworth's present influence. Most people now live in cities, and they may say to themselves

> A house is more to my taste than a tree
> And for groves, oh! a good grove of chimneys for me.[3]

---

[1] Douglas Bush, 'Wordsworth: A Minority Report', in *Wordsworth*, ed. Gilbert T. Dunklin (Princeton University Press, 1951), pp. 9, 20. For a similar criticism see Aldous Huxley, 'Wordsworth in the Tropics', *Do What You Will* (London: Chatto & Windus, 1929).

[2] *Recluse*, 829–33.

[3] Charles Morris, 'The Contrast'. Quoted by W. T. Jones, *The Romantic Syndrome* (The Hague: Martinus Nijhoff, 1961), p. 135.

They are not living the kind of life that fits them to appreciate Wordsworth. Most literature now is written by, and for, a metropolitan intelligentsia, and the poetry of nature is out of fashion.

But Wordsworth deserves a higher mark than Bush is prepared to give him. Let us admit that he ranks below Chaucer and Shakespeare and Milton; that he lacks Byron's wit and Burns's homely realism; that he is not so easy to like as Keats, and appeals less to contemporary taste than T. S. Eliot; and that he wrote little outside his supreme creative period (1797–1807) that satisfies us today. But I think John Crowe Ransom is right when he says, 'Our poet is one of the giants'.[1]

Whatever we may think of Wordsworth's poetry, we cannot deny his vital role in the history of ideas. As a major figure in the Romantic Movement he contributed a new keen sense of the values of childhood and rural life; of the importance of memory, of time, growth, and continuity; of the necessity to explore one's own past and to establish a personal sense of identity; of the need to probe the mysteries of life and the unconscious depths of the human soul. Dissatisfied with a dualistic metaphysics, he softened its traditional sharp distinctions between appearance and reality, mind and matter, body and soul, nature and supernature. He was convinced that analytical reason is inadequate to portray the integrality and flow of experience; reacted against industrial mechanization and the 'monstrous anthill' of the metropolis; recognized the supreme value of freedom, and shared in the widening sympathy for the poorer classes. He appreciated afresh the poetry of common life and the beauty of wild nature, and he realized that a work of art grows as a tree does, with an organic unity all its own. In most of these respects he agreed with other great romantics. Arthur O. Lovejoy has argued that 'the word "romantic" has come to mean so many things that, by itself, it means nothing'.[2] Perhaps. But the leaders of the Romantic Movement exhibited, as Wittgenstein would say, a 'family resemblance'. Wordsworth was a most important member of that family.

---

[1] John Crowe Ransom, 'William Wordsworth: Notes toward an Understanding of Poetry,' in Dunklin, op. cit., p. 91.

[2] Arthur O. Lovejoy, 'On the Discrimination of Romanticisms', *Essays in the History of Ideas* (Baltimore: The Johns Hopkins University Press, 1948), p. 232.

If we turn from his role in the Romantic period to his status in our own times, his place is less secure. The present climate of thought hardly works in his favour: British–American philosophy is predominantly analytical. As in the eighteenth century, there is a tendency to reduce the whole to the parts, the grand to the humdrum, the mysterious to the patent. An uneasy coalition of analysts and positivists has restored philosophy to the tradition of Hobbes, Locke, and Hume. Some of us think that this is not the last word in human wisdom. Although we find the older idealism and transcendentalism too fuzzy, and we rightly admire the intellectual rigour of the Anglo-American tradition, we think the interpretation of nature should be based upon the whole range of experience and not upon a desiccated version of it. For those who seek this integral vision Words-worth answers a need of the human spirit.

INDEX

PRINTED IN GREAT BRITAIN
AT THE UNIVERSITY PRESS, OXFORD
BY VIVIAN RIDLER
PRINTER TO THE UNIVERSITY